ABSOLUTE BEGINNER'S GUIDE

 TO

Microsoft®

Windows® XP Media Center

Steve Kovsky

800 East 96th Street
Indianapolis, Indiana 46240

Absolute Beginner's Guide to Microsoft Windows XP Media Center

Copyright © 2004 by Que Publishing

International Standard Book Number: 0-7897-3003-0

Library of Congress Catalog Card Number: 2003108694

Printed in the United States of America

First Printing: February 2004

07   06   05   04   4   3   2   1

Trademarks

All terms mentioned in this book that are known to be trademarks or service marks have been appropriately capitalized. Que Publishing cannot attest to the accuracy of this information. Use of a term in this book should not be regarded as affecting the validity of any trademark or service mark.

Warning and Disclaimer

Every effort has been made to make this book as complete and as accurate as possible, but no warranty or fitness is implied. The information provided is on an "as is" basis. The author and the publisher shall have neither liability nor responsibility to any person or entity with respect to any loss or damages arising from the information contained in this book.

Bulk Sales

Que Publishing offers excellent discounts on this book when ordered in quantity for bulk purchases or special sales. For more information, please contact

U.S. Corporate and Government Sales
1-800-382-3419
corpsales@pearsontechgroup.com

For sales outside of the U.S., please contact

International Sales
1-317-428-3341
international@pearsontechgroup.com

Associate Publisher
Greg Wiegand

Executive Editor
Rick Kughen

Development Editor
Kevin Howard

Technical Editor
Mark Reddin

Managing Editor
Charlotte Clapp

Project Editor
Dan Knott

Copy Editor
Cheri Clark

Indexer
Mandie Frank

Proofreader
Tracy Donhardt

Publishing Coordinator
Sharry Lee Gregory

Interior Designer
Anne Jones

Cover Designer
Dan Armstrong

Page Layout
Ron Wise
Michelle Mitchell
Susan Geiselman

Contents at a Glance

Table of Contents

Foreword

The Evolution of the Media Center PC

In the fall of 2000, HP and Microsoft had a vision for a new kind of personal computer and operating system. This vision would allow consumers to manipulate and store all their digital content and converge many of their digital devices. It had to be fresh and different, and reflect the changing dynamics of the digital world we live in. The vision went well beyond adding bells and whistles to traditional PCs; we needed to build the system from the ground up. It needed to be a system that consumers could use to enhance their digital entertainment experience, yet still use and interact with in a "traditional PC way" for everything from surfing the Web to sending email.

The result was the HP Media Center PC, a groundbreaking PC that combined HP's innovative design with the Microsoft Windows XP Media Center Edition operating system. The HP Media Center PC unlocked the door for an entirely new market of PCs with an additional suite of home entertainment features that could be enjoyed in the traditional two-foot experience, as well as by remote control from across the room like most consumer electronic devices. When it was released in October 2002, the excitement around this new PC category far exceeded everyone's expectations.

The New Digital Experience

There is no question that the influx of digital devices has truly changed the way we live. For instance, I know quite a few people who swear their personal video recorder is the best invention since sliced bread—they can't imagine life without it. And you can scarcely leave the house these days without seeing someone rocking to the music from an MP3 player or snapping pictures from a digital camera. Paper calendars are quickly being dismissed for electronic organizers, and DVD players continue to lead as one of the hottest-selling consumer electronics devices. The world is definitely going digital—and people like you are leading the way.

Since you've purchased this book, you must be one of the tech-savvy, early adopters who is very interested in purchasing a Media Center PC, or have already purchased one.

You will be thrilled to find that Media Center PCs are the first solutions that enable you to combine your digital content and devices—allowing you to control your pictures, music, videos, and television from one central location with one remote control. No doubt you'll be more than happy to cast away that pile of remotes on your coffee table.

You will be able to record all 162 of your favorite major-league baseball team's regular season games; set your child's last track-and-field meet to the music of *Chariots of Fire*; burn a CD of your favorite tunes for your next big road trip; email digital photos to your mother; and download and set your favorite music to your cell-phone ring. Remember, you can do it all from this one system, instead of separate ones. (Note: HP does not support the recording and playback of protected broadcasts. HP products should be used for lawful purposes only.)

The Media Center PC even makes your old subscription to *TV Guide* passé—because you can quickly retrieve broadcast information nearly two weeks ahead of time off the Internet. Just set your Media Center PC to record, and be on your way.

The Future of the Market

The Media Center PC should continue to evolve into a management hub of your home digital entertainment universe. Connecting through home networks and new classes of devices, such as digital media receivers, consumers can stream content from their PC to anywhere in the house where their electronic devices reside.

And one of the biggest limitations we can expect to see in this new class of entertainment PCs, oddly enough, may not even be technology-related. As the digital content market and devices continue to evolve, so does the very public discussion over Digital Rights Management. There is no doubt that this will be a long and challenging dialog that may ultimately change how and what consumers download.

You Be the Judge

We encourage you to push these machines to their limits and get the most out of the digital entertainment experience they provide. This book definitely equips you with all the tricks and tools to do so.

Be sure to contact your manufacturer to give feedback on how the product is working and say what improvements you would like to see in the future. As consumer users of this new class of PCs, you are the best and only sounding board that truly matters, and you have the greatest impact on where the future of these solutions will go.

But more important, have fun and be creative. Become your own personal DJ, or the "Steven Spielberg" of personal home videos.

The biggest limitation on these PCs is your imagination. So, let it run wild.

Duane Zitzner,
Executive Vice President, Personal Systems Group
Hewlett-Packard Company

About the Author

Journalist and author **Steve Kovsky** has covered every aspect of high technology in the past 19 years. His reports have appeared internationally in newspapers, magazines, television, radio, and on the Internet. Currently, he is a Contributing Editor for ZDNet AnchorDesk and a Technology Commentator on CBS Radio (KFWB AM 980, Los Angeles). In addition, Kovsky serves as Vice President and Editorial Director for Centric Events Group, an organizer of technical trade shows and conferences across North America. His first book, High-Tech Toys for Your TV: Secrets of TiVo, Xbox, ReplayTV, UltimateTV, and More, was published in March 2002 by Que Publishing.

Dedication

In memory of Brian Kovsky

1925–2003

Acknowledgments

My deepest thanks to Rick Kughen and the Que Publishing team, who love cool, new consumer-oriented technologies as much as I do.

I'd also like to express my appreciation to Tom Laemmle from Microsoft for answering endless questions, and sending me beta after beta as I tried to write knowledgeably about an operating system that seemed to be evolving on a daily basis.
Ed Rich, the Windows eHome program manager, also generously gave of his time to track down pesky details and troubleshoot undocumented procedures. He even performed a comprehensive technical edit of the book just days before its publication.
Special thanks also go to Kristen Reeves representing Hewlett-Packard, and the PR folks from Gateway, Toshiba, ABS Technologies, Sonic, Movielink, CinemaNow, and other companies who were so accommodating with their products and knowledge.

Above all, I'd like to thank my family—Julie, Nick, Aaron & Jenna—for their love, support, and forbearance. I couldn't have done it without them (and I wouldn't have wanted to, anyway).

We Want to Hear from You!

As the reader of this book, *you* are our most important critic and commentator. We value your opinion and want to know what we're doing right, what we could do better, what areas you'd like to see us publish in, and any other words of wisdom you're willing to pass our way.

As an associate publisher for Que Publishing, I welcome your comments. You can email or write me directly to let me know what you did or didn't like about this book—as well as what we can do to make our books better.

Please note that I cannot help you with technical problems related to the topic of this book. We do have a User Services group, however, where I will forward specific technical questions related to the book.

When you write, please be sure to include this book's title and author, as well as your name, email address, and phone number. I will carefully review your comments and share them with the author and editors who worked on the book.

Email: feedback@quepublishing.com

Mail: Greg Wiegand
          Associate Publisher
          Que Publishing
          800 East 96th Street
          Indianapolis, IN 46240 USA

For more information about this book or another Que Publishing title, visit our Web site at www.quepublishing.com. Type the ISBN (excluding hyphens) or the title of a book in the Search field to find the page you're looking for.

INTRODUCTION

If this book lies open in your hands, either you've heard of Windows XP Media Center Edition and its phenomenal capability to unite the worlds of computing and entertainment, or you're a close personal friend or relative of the author, wondering what those months of lost sleep and solitary scribbling were all about.

Either way, you're now officially in on the best-kept secret of the world's largest software company. Microsoft's Windows XP Media Center Edition blends the capabilities of a conventional PC with essentially every electronic entertainment device that is currently cluttering up your living room. It's a digital video recorder that lets you record and rewind live television; it's a digital jukebox that gives you unfettered access to your entire music collection; it's an intelligent DVD player (often a recorder as well); and it's even an FM radio with a replay button. It also offers new entertainment experiences as a sophisticated playback machine for your digital photos and home videos.

The Media Center software is designed to offer you the best of both worlds: a sophisticated, state-of-the-art computer operating system that can "get down to business" without any compromises in features or functionality—all delightfully hidden (if you so choose) behind a user-friendly interface that a child could control. It's the perfect balance of work and play.

Why This Book?

If Windows XP Media Center Edition is so darn easy to use, you might ask, why a book? Well, easy and simple are different things. Although it's extremely rare, it is possible for something to be easy while also being highly complex, and that is precisely the kind of delicate balance that Microsoft set out to achieve with this operating system.

If you can operate a television set, you can get the same results out of Windows XP Media Center: changing channels, adjusting volume, and so on. If you're content to leave it at that, put the book back on the shelf and walk on. But before you do, ask yourself whether you want more. What if you crave the ability to filter out the "noise" in our multimedia society and create an entertainment experience that is perfectly and precisely tailored to your tastes and temperament?

When you turn on your Media Center PC and pick up the remote control, you'll suddenly find yourself in the driver's seat of what is arguably the most powerful all-purpose entertainment device ever devised. As you come to discover the power you now wield over the world of personal entertainment, you'll probably reach the conclusion that a few friendly tips would not be out of line.

Media Center changes more than channels—it changes *everything*.

How We Got Here

Call it sibling rivalry. Ever since the personal computer arrived on the scene, it has displayed an irrational jealousy of its less intelligent predecessor, the television set.

To some degree, it's understandable. While one member of the cathode ray tube family was clearly the more gifted one, having played a pivotal role in nearly every significant human endeavor of the 20th century, its bumbling older brother—the "Boob Tube"—managed to steal the limelight every time.

Maybe this is why the PC industry has so cherished the dream of uniting these two devices: style and substance, together at last. Yet every attempt to add PC sophistication to television's mass appeal has left us yawning. With WebTV as the most recent example of a keyboard-equipped television experience, hybrid PC-TV devices have consistently failed to fire our imaginations or convince us to part with our hard-earned cash.

That's one of the reasons that the runaway success of the Microsoft Windows Media Center Edition PCs has been so surprising. As it turns out, we never really wanted a computer in our television set. We wanted a TV in our PC.

It seems like a subtle distinction, but it isn't. At least not for Microsoft, Hewlett-Packard, Gateway, and a growing list of PC makers. HP was the first computer company to sign on with what many in the PC industry dismissed as a harebrained idea—just another hopeless attempt to marry the PC and the TV into a single "infotainment" device.

Although they'd never admit it now, I'm sure that industry observers were surprised, if not outright shocked, when people actually started buying these media-centric computers as fast as the manufacturers could build them. Perhaps the most surprising part is what they paid for them. Just at a time when every economic indicator was in the gutter, and computer sales forecasters were sounding more like weather forecasters who had just witnessed a groundhog see its shadow and dive for cover, people started opening their wallets in response to the new Media Center PCs. Few industry pundits guessed that consumers would keep pushing their shopping carts right past those $399 bargain PC specials and instead load up with a fully loaded Media Center machine costing $2,000 and up.

HP smiled all the way to the bank, as its Personal Systems Division turned, in one quarter, from an operating loss of $68 million to a profit of $33 million. Microsoft sent its OS designers scurrying back to their workstations to cook up a new and improved version of the Media Center operating system. Meanwhile, a slew of new hardware companies jumped on the Media Center bandwagon to try their luck at selling high-priced, high-performance media PCs. With the added injection of volume, prices actually began to drop, fueling even more demand.

But what of the consumers? How about those intrepid early adopters who have already taken a Media Center PC into their home and made it a member of their family? Have they achieved the "infotainment" nirvana they hoped for?

Although overall satisfaction with the Media Center systems appears pretty high, many consumers have been faced with the stark reality that these systems are quite complicated compared to a typical TV—or PC, for that matter. In fact, there's little doubt that if televisions had been anywhere near as complex to set up and operate as a Media Center PC, most of us would still be gathered around our radios, warming ourselves by the glow of the vacuum tubes while we laughed along with some modern-day Fibber McGee & Molly.

Luckily, with this book you hold in your hands—*The Absolute Beginner's Guide to Microsoft Windows XP Media Center*—help has arrived.

How to Use This Book

To the greatest extent possible, this book has been written to correspond to your initial experience with an XP Media Center machine:

- Part I, "Getting Started," takes you from opening the carton through the complete setup of your Media Center system. You'll go on a tour of the basic features, and find out how to get around using your remote control, mouse, and keyboard.

- Part II, "My TV," goes straight to the coolest and most impressive capabilities of your Media Center system. You'll learn how to manipulate video like a pro, rewinding live television, skipping past commercials, and recording an entire TV series with the press of a button. You'll also learn how to use Media Center's free electronic program guide, how to set up parental controls, and more.

- Part III, "My Videos," focuses on how to capture, create, and organize your digital home movies using the system's impressive media-handling capabilities. Prepare to unleash your inner cinematographer!

- Part IV, "Playing and Recording DVDs," covers one of the trickier and ultimately most rewarding features of the Media Center architecture: the capability to build and burn your own DVD discs directly from your favorite TV shows. You'll also find tips on how to customize DVD playback features to make the most of Media Center's home theater experience.

- Part V, "My Music," delves into Media Center's audio arsenal, including the capability to rewind live FM radio (if your system comes equipped with a radio tuner). By blending your personal music collection with live radio and audio streamed and downloaded from the Internet, Media Center's My Music offers you access to an awesome audio apparatus.

- Part VI, "My Pictures," takes you through the digital photography display and processing features built into Media Center, and shows you how to use add-on software to get professional darkroom results. Kiss your red-eye goodbye.

- Part VII, "Advanced Media Center Settings and Options," provides additional tips and tools for the power user you've become, allowing you to get maximum performance and satisfaction from your Media Center system. In the final chapter, you'll find a complete guide to Media Center hardware, including the pros and cons of many different PC styles and designs of Media Center systems.

On a Personal Note

As a professional broadcast journalist, I've used studio equipment worth hundreds of thousands of dollars that was capable of doing only a tenth of what a $1,200 Media Center PC can accomplish. This fact may say more about my advancing age than about the advancement of desktop technology, but it was nevertheless a powerful motivator in my deciding to write this book.

If you already enjoy using computers, your cup truly runneth over. Each Media Center machine is a full-fledged XP Professional PC, with all the cool multimedia capabilities you could wish for thrown in as a bonus. On the other hand, if you think of PCs as a work tool better left at the office, you're in for a pleasant surprise as you get acquainted with Media Center's fun-loving side. Either way, I hope you'll agree that Media Center represents one of the most interesting and exciting new technologies on the PC landscape.

If you have any questions, comments, or suggestions about the book, please don't hesitate to email me at steve@tvtechtoys.com, or visit my Web site at www.tvtechtoys.com.

PART i

Getting Started

1

Preparing for XP Media Center

Unless you're a media fiend who already went to the trouble and expense of building a TV-capable PC from scratch, your new Windows XP Media Center Edition PC will be unlike any personal computer you've ever experienced. We're going to get you into the right mindset by telling you up front what your Media PC will and won't do, and help you get prepared mentally and physically for the Herculean task ahead: setting up your Media PC.

Getting Prepared Mentally

Welcome to the world of Windows XP Media Center Edition. Unless this is your first experience with a personal computer, you're going to find many things that are familiar to you. In fact, if you've ever used any version of Microsoft Windows before—and particularly if you've been previously exposed to Windows XP—most of the operations of your new Media Center PC will seem completely normal and natural. For that reason, we'll dispense with all the ordinary Windows-related matters and get right to the meaty stuff: what's new and cool about your Windows XP Media Center Edition PC and how you can get the most out of it.

Let's assume that your new Media Center PC is still in the box. Your fingers are already twitching in anticipation of the glorious experience that awaits you. But before you cut into that carton, let's get mentally prepared for what lies ahead. I've always found that I'm happiest with my purchase—whether it's a new gadget or a used car—when I know exactly what I'm getting into.

Setting Your Expectations: Knowing What Your Media Center PC Does and Doesn't Do

For starters, there are some very unique aspects of your new Media Center PC:

- It is the first Windows PC desktop operating system for consumers that cannot be purchased separately. As of this writing, the only legal way to lay your hands on it is to buy it as part of a bundled system.
- It is the first major version of the Windows PC operating system to ship with a remote control as standard equipment.

These two attributes tell you a lot about what Microsoft had in mind when it created Windows XP Media Center Edition. By making this an OEM-only product, meaning that you can get the OS only if it's running on a PC made by an Original Equipment Manufacturer who has adhered to Microsoft's strict guidelines for constructing a media PC, Microsoft deliberately stole a page from the Apple Computer playbook.

One of the reasons Apple machines have always been great at handling "media" (complex video, audio, and graphical data files) is that not just anybody is allowed to build a Macintosh computer. Apple may not build the machines itself, but the contractors it uses are stringently controlled by Apple engineers so that every machine the company places its operating system on works the way it was designed. It's a much more controlled manufacturing environment than simply slapping together a hodge-podge of off-the-shelf computer parts. However, that is exactly how Windows PCs have always been made: a come-one-come-all manufacturing free-for-all that allowed anyone anywhere to build a Windows-compatible PC. Naturally, some are built to exacting standards, and cost a pretty penny. Others aren't, and don't.

When you think about it, it's quite an amazing achievement to create a software platform that operates seamlessly (well, almost) on literally millions of hardware variations. When you add the variables of different peripherals and device drivers into the constantly moving target of hardware that Microsoft has had to design for in the past, it becomes a lot easier to forgive the occasional system crash. However, when it comes to watching or recording your favorite show or Bowl Game on television, or making your own music and movies on your PC, you need the stability and precision that can be achieved only through a meticulous and tightly-integrated design. That's why Microsoft has released the Media Center Edition software only to qualified OEMs (Original Equipment Manufacturers) who agree to build their Media Center systems from approved parts, according to a strict reference design. This limits the ability of each OEM to truly differentiate its Media Center products, but it goes a long way toward ensuring that your Media Center machine provides you with seamless, stable operation.

Although the OEM-only part of Microsoft's plan is a bit subtle, the other unique aspect—the remote control—is quite blatant. The message: This PC is about entertainment. It's about kicking back on the couch and enjoying the same audio and video experience you've become accustomed to in your living room—only better.

What Your Media Center PC Does

In a nutshell, your Media Center PC allows you to do all the following, and more:

- Record, pause, and rewind live television programming, just like a TiVo or ReplayTV set-top box.
- Find shows to watch and record, using a free, interactive electronic program guide.
- Pause and rewind live FM radio. Isn't it about time somebody finally married the radio to a hard-drive recorder?
- Watch commercially released DVD movies, and create your own DVD-quality videos. If you have the right third-party software, you can burn your own recordable DVDs, as well.
- Conveniently store, organize, and browse your digital video, photo, and audio collections, all with the click of a mouse or the press of a button on your Media Center remote control.
- Listen to, rip, and burn your own audio CDs.
- Do anything you can do on a conventional personal computer running Windows XP. After all, it *is* a Windows XP Professional machine—just with a few added entertainment-related extras to make it a star in the living room as well as the home office.

What Your Media Center PC Doesn't Do

What can't you do with a Media Center PC? The primary thing you can't do is make major modifications to your PC—at least not with impunity.

As pointed out in the preceding list, you can essentially do anything on an XP Media Center Edition–based machine that you can on any Windows XP–based personal computer, and more. However, making major changes to your hardware and software configuration may carry some consequences, particularly if you want to keep all the audio and video functions working precisely as they did when your Media Center PC was factory fresh. Although you might not think twice about swapping out the components of your typical Windows desktop machine, you'll want to give careful consideration before making the same types of changes to your tightly integrated Media Center system. Remember that page from the Apple playbook: Controlling what's inside the box is what allows the Media Center to do all its fancy tricks with audio and video files.

Does a Media Center PC Do Everything a TiVo or ReplayTV Can Do?

It's a reasonable question; you just paid a heck of a lot more for your Windows XP Media Center machine than you would have for a dedicated DVR (digital video recorder), such as a typical TiVo or a ReplayTV, so you'd like to know whether your XP Media Center can do everything a DVR can. Well, no. It can't.

For instance, at the time of this writing, Windows XP Media Center Edition supports only a single TV tuner. So although a dual-tuner DVR such as many TiVo models (or one of Microsoft's own UltimateTV devices) would allow you to record two shows at once—all while you watch a third, already-recorded show, if you want to get fancy— you can't do that on your Media Center PC. Yes, you can record one show while watching some other prerecorded show, but that's as far as it goes. And, of course, you can work on a spreadsheet or fire up your word processor or browser while you're at it—try *that* on a TiVo!

caution

What about gamers who want the freedom to constantly upgrade their video cards to get bleeding-edge performance as new games and hardware are released? It's possible that you may one day find yourself upgrading right out of compliance with the Media Center "spec." If you're a serial upgrader, you probably know how to make comprehensive backups before you tweak your system—so if your next upgrade "breaks" any of Media Center's capabilities, at least you'll have a choice whether to press ahead or fall back to your previous configuration.

Another thing you can't do with your Media Center PC (that you can with most other DVRs) is use the remote control to operate other entertainment devices, such as your TV, VCR, or standalone DVD player.

Getting Prepared Physically

The idea of this section is not that you need to start lifting weights before setting up your Windows Media Center PC (although, if you opted to buy a Gateway machine with an optional 42-inch plasma display, as shown in Figure 1.1, remember that baby weighs in at approximately 115 pounds—so if you plan to move it by yourself, you *had* better start pumping up!). Getting ready physically means making plans for the physical requirements of your new system. You need to make some decisions and lay some groundwork before you can break ground on your new digital entertainment experience.

FIGURE 1.1

Gateway's Media Center PC can be combined with an optional 42-inch plasma display. Just make sure you've got a buddy to help you lift it into place.

Gathering Your Wits and Materials

Bringing home a new Media PC is a little like bringing home a new puppy; a little planning is required. If you want it to meet your expectations of being a loving, faithful, and (ideally) well-behaved friend, you first have to meet its expectations. You're going to have to find a place for it to stay and make sure it has all the things it requires to be happy and healthy.

It's true, you don't have to feed your Media Center PC, and there's no danger of it messing on the carpet. But to enjoy the full benefit of this powerful device, you're going to have to provide it with a few basics: electricity, of course; a source of TV programming (cable, satellite, and so on); and a way to reach the Internet so that it can download current program-guide information. That's the minimum. You may also want to connect your Media PC to your home network.

That covers just the inputs you need to get ready before installing your new Media PC. What about outputs? Do you want to connect to an existing home entertainment system? That would typically include a TV, a VCR, a standalone DVD player (although you don't really need one—it's included in your PC), and a sound system.

You're probably getting the idea by now; this is much more than your typical desktop PC installation. In fact, your Media PC probably isn't a "desktop" machine at all. It's very likely to be a tower design, made to sit on the floor. The HP machine shown in Figure 1.2 is typical of the tower design.

note

Even if you have some kind of broadband connection to the Internet—that is, something other than a dial-up connection, such as a DSL or cable modem—you may want to connect your Media PC to a phone line as well. For instance, you need phone-line access to take advantage of the built-in fax features that come with Windows XP.

FIGURE 1.2

Hewlett-Packard's Media Center PC is the original— the first Windows XP Media Center Edition system to ship, and probably the best-selling model to date. Its classic tower design is still the most prevalent among Media PC makers.

Depending on the manufacturer, it could even be a laptop machine, or a new compact shape designed to tuck away into your entertainment center, like the one in Figure 1.3.

FIGURE 1.3

ZT Group is among those smaller PC makers that took the plunge into manufacturing a compact Media PC design. The Model Z2062 shown here is roughly the size of a 7-inch-tall stack of copy paper.

Whatever the Media Center PC's shape or size, the addition of audio and video inputs and outputs adds quite a bit to the complexity of the setup process. But don't worry, your eyes and ears will thank you for your extra efforts.

Choosing Where to Put Your Media Center, and Developing an Installation Plan

The toughest decision of all may be where to put your new Media PC. Here are some things you'll want to consider:

- Are you planning to use it primarily as a PC, or as an entertainment device? In other words, will you spend more time sitting in a chair next to the monitor, controlling it with your mouse (the so-called "2-foot experience"), or will you prefer kicking back on the sofa, controlling it with your remote (the "10-foot experience")? The answer will give you a lot of information about where in your home you'll feel most comfortable using the device. Think about lighting—will there be adequate light for working around your Media PC? Is there a bright window facing the screen that could make viewing difficult from the sofa?

- Are you the only user for this machine, or will you be sharing it with other members of your household? If there are going to be multiple users, think about their preferences, and how they'll be using the system.

- Is there more than one area of your home where you can conceivably connect your Media PC to all the types of wires it needs (electrical, TV, phone, and network)?

- Will you be using your Media PC as a standalone device, or do you need it to be snuggled up against your other computing or entertainment devices—or both?

After you've decided where to place your system, you may want to grab a sheet of paper and sketch an installation plan. Nothing too elaborate, but it may help you recognize which steps need to occur—and in what order—before you can get your Media PC completely up and running.

A Few Words About Your TV Programming Source

Quite a few types of TV programming sources are available these days, depending on where you live:

- *Over-the-air antenna*—This is the most ubiquitous, cheapest (how does "free" grab you?), and generally lowest quality signal available. If you've still got one of those aluminum dinosaurs up on your roof (and why not; did we mention that it's free?), it should work fine with your Media Center machine. You will need to get a transformer to connect the bare wires from your antenna line to the coaxial barrel connector on your Media PC—but don't worry, it'll only set you back about $1.25.

- *Standard cable*—This cable comes up from the ground or down from a utility pole, and it can be distributed to multiple points in your home via standard coaxial wires. It may or may not require a set-top receiver/descrambler box in each room, depending on your cable provider, but because you're not really buying the equipment, there should be only a nominal fee for multiple receivers. Picture quality can be pretty good. It is more expensive than over-the-air programming (but then, most things are).

caution

If you do opt to use your Media Center with only an antenna for your TV reception, you may find that you're missing out on more than just a digital-quality signal. It will be very difficult for Media Center's program guide to match precisely the channel lineup you are able to receive. Plan on spending some time finding the closest guide match that provides specifics on the local channels you can receive; then edit the channel lineup as necessary to list only the channels you actually receive, and delete the ones you don't. With some time and patience, you should be able to eventually get all the program-guide benefits available to cable or satellite TV subscribers.

- *Digital cable*—You'll pay more for digital cable, but don't expect shockingly better picture quality. In fact, digital cable's quality is pretty comparable with standard analog (that is, *not* digital) cable in most cases—because most of the channels you receive will still be broadcast in analog anyway, and even the ones that *are* digital get translated to analog, unless you have a digital TV. The bigger difference between digital cable and analog cable is probably the addition of an interactive program guide, digital music channels, and some of those types of features that used to be available only from the digital satellite services. Of course, you'll be using the free interactive programming guide that comes with Windows XP Media Center Edition, so is it really worth the extra money?

- *Satellite*—Now you're talking! Picture quality can be very good with satellite—except during a storm—and you'll never need another cable guy to come over to your house. The dish generally goes on your roof and provides one to four video outputs, which can be multiplied further using a signal booster called (strangely enough) a "multiplexer." Satellite TV can be pretty pricey, though, especially because you'll probably need a separate satellite receiver in each room where you want to watch TV.

- *HDTV*—This was not supported in the final release of Windows XP Media Center Edition 2004, but there are some positive indications that Microsoft will address that issue in a future version of the operating system.

A Few Words About Your Internet Connection

While you're still in the early planning stages of setting up your Media PC, it's a good time to think about how you're going to download your free program guide on a regular basis. Windows XP Media Center Edition requires an Internet connection to get the program guide information, even if you happen to subscribe to a digital television system that encodes the guide information directly into the TV signal.

Of course, there are lots of other good reasons to connect to the Internet, as well. This is, after all, a fully functional PC, and having one of those that doesn't connect to the Internet in some fashion is practically unthinkable these days. Fortunately, there are many ways to merge onto the old Information Superhighway. As with TV programming sources, there are trade-offs, and you may or may not have access to all types of Internet connections, depending on where you live.

Here are the most common types of Internet service connections available to bring Web access into your home:

- *Modem/dial-up connection*—This is the most common way of connecting to the Internet, and usually the simplest and least expensive. All you need is a phone line—and some patience, because dial-up can be excruciatingly s-l-o-w. You're probably looking at a maximum of 56Kbps for downloading data, and only 33.6Kbps when you're uploading (these are best-case scenarios; your actual mileage will vary, and will probably be less). For updating your program guide, this is probably just fine. For anything else you want to do on the Internet—especially anything involving audio and video (and hey, isn't that what you bought the Media Center for?)—it's going to seem pretty sluggish.

- *Cable modem*—This connects to the Internet through your cable TV line. Many cable providers now offer the service. Unlike connecting your PC via your phone line, using one device doesn't cancel out the other. In other words, you can still watch TV while you surf the Web. The speed can be worth writing home about: up to 1000Kbps for downloads, 128–500Kbps for uploads. At peak speeds (and let's face it, you may experience less than peak performance for various reasons), Web pages will load quickly, and large audio and video files can be transferred almost effortlessly. You're also connected all the time that you have your PC and modem switched on—so there's no clunky connection sequence every time you get the urge to surf. Naturally, it costs more—way more—than a dial-up connection. At an average of $40 to $50 per month, cable modem connections are at least twice the cost of a typical dial-up service.

- *DSL*—DSL shares many of the same attributes as cable modems. It's as fast as cable, as long as you're located a reasonable distance from the nearest phone company facility. Like cable, it's always on, and although DSL (digital

> **note**
>
> In addition to considering how the Internet access comes into your home, you will need to figure out how it connects to your Media PC. These two sources of connection can be very different. For instance, you may have a dial-up, DSL, or cable modem connection coming into your home, but you might use another type of connection, such as Ethernet, wireless (Wi-Fi), or even phone-line or power-line networking, to share that connection among multiple PCs inside the home. We'll discuss home networking options in greater detail in Chapter 22, "XP Media Center and Your Home Network."

subscriber line) service comes through your existing phone line, it doesn't interfere with your voice service. The price is also usually pretty competitive with that of cable modems.

- *Satellite broadband*—Satellite broadband service is a relatively new way to get online, via a dish antenna located at your house. With one-way satellite, you still need a conventional modem and telephone line to send, or upload, data. However, newer two-way satellite systems actually let you download and upload through your satellite dish. If you're out in the sticks, beyond the service area of local cable and DSL providers, this may be the best way to get a fast Internet connection. All you need is an unobstructed line-of-sight to the south for your broadband dish—and a wad of cash. Satellite broadband can cost $70 per month and up, and that's after you buy the costly dish and related equipment, which will set you back hundreds. And even with its out-of-this-world price, satellite connectivity can leave a lot to be desired in the download department. A significant amount of latency is caused by sending every one of your Internet page requests into geostationary orbit, back down to Earth at the satellite provider's "head end" operation center, and then back up to the satellite for a return trip to your PC. Sometimes it's amazing what people way out in the sticks will put up with in order to avoid dependence on a dial-up connection.

- *ISDN and T-line*—Usually reserved for business users because of its price and complexity, ISDN and T-line (T1, T3, and so on) will require spending some quality time with your phone-company representative—and some serious cash. ISDN (Integrated Services Digital Network) generally runs up to four times faster than a dial-up modem. A single ISDN line can also handle up to eight devices, including PC, telephone, fax, and video, and you can have any two devices operating simultaneously. Speeds are in the neighborhood of 128Kbps, and costs include access, equipment, and installation. T-lines are generally quite expensive and are normally used by Internet service providers (ISPs) themselves to provide Internet access to subscribers like us.

- *Wireless*—Also known as Wi-Fi, networks using the 802.11 wireless standard are becoming common in both homes and businesses. Unless you plan to install your Media PC at a Starbucks (one of the national retail chains that has committed to offering Wi-Fi "hot spots" on its premises), this technology is going to make more sense as a way to share an existing Internet connection between computers on a home network, than as a means of connecting to an ISP. However, a few telecom companies do offer so-called fixed wireless connections, which involve a small dish antenna aimed at the ISP's transmitter. Availability is limited, but if you can get it, you may find that costs and connection speeds are comparable to those of DSL or cable modem.

THE ABSOLUTE MINIMUM

In this chapter, you read what Media Center is, and why it's unique, and you've had a chance to adjust your attitude and expectations. Most important, you now have a checklist for the basic essentials you're going to need to get your Media PC up and running. To recap, you will need the following:

- A spot to put your Media PC where you, your family, and your friends will be most comfortable while making use of your system's "2-foot" features as well as its "10-foot" features

- A connection to the source of television programming in your home, whether it comes in via antenna, cable, or satellite dish

- A connection to the Internet for updating the Media PC's electronic program guide

- An electrical outlet nearby

If you've assembled all the above, you're now ready to open the box and start setting up your new Media Center machine. Enjoy!

In This Chapter

- Taking inventory of your new Media PC
- Considering additional materials you may need for your installation
- Connecting your PC equipment (monitor, mouse, keyboard, and so on)
- Connecting your entertainment-oriented components (remote control and sensor, IR emitter, television, speakers, and so on)

2

Basic Setup Of An XP Media Center System

First of all, remember to breathe! You're about to unpack and set up your cool, new, expensive toy. This should be fun, but it can also be a little nerve-wracking—and it may even get downright frustrating at times. Setting up a Media PC is a bigger undertaking than simply plugging in your average desktop, but with a little patience, some common sense, and this book in your hands, we'll have you up and running in no time.

Taking Inventory

Every PC manufacturer in the world does things a little differently. Most of the good ones pay a lot of attention to the "out of box" (OOB) experience, which means making sure that from the first moment when you slice open the packing tape, it's absolutely clear what you need to do next. In fact, many manufacturers take great pains to ensure that the first thing you see when you open the box is an oversized instruction sheet that makes your next step patently obvious (see Figure 2.1).

FIGURE 2.1

Your first view inside the packing crate of a Media PC should be of a large set of instructions, leaving no guesswork as to your next step.

Well, at least that's the ideal scenario. But no matter what product you're assembling, a good first step is to stop and take inventory. The last thing you want is to spend two hours hooking everything up just right, only to find out that you're missing the one final piece needed to complete the project.

What's in the Box?

First off, you should find all the things you'd normally find as part of a new PC:

- A mouse
- A keyboard
- A monitor (if you bought one)

- The computer itself (also known as the CPU)
- A set of speakers (possibly a microphone as well)
- Assorted cables and wires
- Documents and software

Now here are a few extra, less-familiar items that typically come with Media PCs:

- A remote control (or as many as three of them, depending on which make and model you buy)
- An infrared (IR) receiver (for sensing instructions from the remote control)
- An infrared emitter (to relay instructions to a set-top box)
- Even more assorted cables and wires, some of which bear connectors you may not be used to seeing around a PC

If your Media PC's manufacturer has done its homework in creating an ideal OOB experience for you, you will have located everything you need to get started—right on down to a couple of AA batteries for the remote control. However, there's no way for the manufacturer to know or plan for every possible contingency that may occur in the user environment. In other words, they can't anticipate exactly how you want your Media PC hooked up, or what you may want to hook it up to. Don't be surprised if you find yourself making a fast trip to the local hardware or electronics store for a few last-minute items.

What You May Need to Supply for Yourself

Your Media PC probably came with everything you need for a very basic installation. If you're just connecting your modem to a telephone jack for a dial-up Internet connection and planning to watch everything on your computer monitor with no optional external inputs and outputs, it should be a simple matter of connecting a coaxial cable from your TV-signal source to the back of your Media PC, then connecting all the other parts supplied by the PC manufacturer.

However, if you already have a home network with a broadband connection, or some existing entertainment appliances you want to integrate with your Media PC, you will quickly find that you have veered off into the uncharted waters of a "custom installation." Here are a few things you may want to consider having on hand:

- *Some extra video cabling*—There are several types, and in some cases, you may need all of them to get your system put together just the way you want it. A Media PC is usually configured to accept various video inputs. These can come in the form of a coaxial cable (coax, for short), an S-Video cable, or composite video (see Figure 2.2). The composite video typically arrives via a yellow-tipped cable with an RCA-type connector, and is frequently paired with right-channel (red) and left-channel (white) audio cables. If you use either of the last two options—S-Video or composite—you're going to need a separate audio connection, because these are video-only connectors. Extra S-Video and component video cabling usually comes in 6-foot, 12-foot, and 25-foot lengths. If you're going to use common black coax cable instead, or if you just need some extra coax to complete a cable run to the area where your new Media PC will be located, something heavy-duty like RG6 cable is recommended.

FIGURE 2.2

An example of a standard coax, a three-way composite audio/video cable with RCA-type connectors, and an S-Video cable with its five-pin connector. They provide a range of picture quality options, with S-Video providing the best, and coax the worst.

Standard coax

Three-way composite cable

S-video cable

■ *Extra audio cabling*—This may come in handy if your set-top cable or satellite receiver box has the choice of S-Video or composite video outputs. Either of these will provide better picture quality than standard coax connections. Unlike coax, however, S-Video and composite video don't carry audio signals, so you'll need to connect some additional RCA-type cables (the connector looks just like the composite video connector shown in Figure 2.2). The Media PC reference design also supports digital audio, at least on the output side, so if you have a digital audio-capable output device (a high-end home theater-type surround sound speaker system, for instance), you may want to have some extra digital audio cabling on hand. Most media PCs don't include it, even if they do include a digital audio output jack.

DIGITAL AUDIO: CAN YOU SAY "SPDIF"?

SPDIF (Sony/Philips Digital Interface) is the most common digital audio interchange format found in today's high-end audio components. Connecting the SPDIF audio jacks from an input device (your Media PC) to an output device such as a home stereo or home theater system allows you to transfer the audio without first converting it from digital to analog format, which reduces the signal quality.

The most frequently used connector for SPDIF audio is actually a basic RCA connector (see Figure 2.2), the same one used for consumer audio and component video patch cables. An optical connector is also sometimes used.

Whether or not your media PC offers a SPDIF output jack will vary depending on the vendor, as will the use of an RCA-type or an optical cable connector.

■ *Connectors and adapters*—An S-Video-to-composite-video adapter (see Figure 2.3) is another handy thing to have when you're making your final connections, particularly if you're planning to watch the Media Center PC's video output on a television set that doesn't accept S-Video input. Your Media Center machine may or may not come with such an adapter. Note that if you have an older television that does not accept composite video input, you will still need an additional video signal converter, which will cost you approximately $20 or more.

FIGURE 2.3

The S-Video-to-composite-video adapter is included with some manufacturers' Media Center PCs.

FIGURE 2.4

Although Gateway recommends using a 1/8-inch stereo audio cable with a stereo 1/8-inch-to-RCA Y-patch cable, you might find it just as easy to use an all-in-one cable designed to connect a PC's stereo 1/8-inch audio output jack to a standard pair of left- and right-channel RCA connectors, like the one shown.

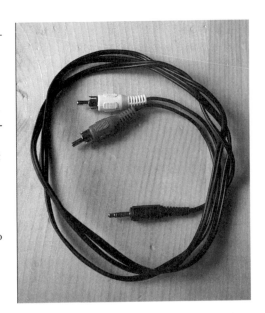

tip

The Gateway Media Center PC does supply a useful S-Video-to-composite-video adapter, but if you decide to use it to connect to a television set, this cable only gets you half the way there. You'll still need a separate audio cable to get your sound out of the PC and into the TV. For that, Gateway recommends using a 1/8-inch stereo audio cable with a 1/8-inch-to-RCA Y-patch cable (see Figure 2.4). These items are listed in the manual as "not supplied."

- *A power strip*—There are several good reasons to employ a decent power strip in hooking up your new PC. For one thing, you're going to fill up a lot of receptacles with the various plugs for your PC, your monitor, and your powered speakers (many or most Media PCs come with a set of them). If you're also plugging in a nearby cable or satellite receiver and a TV...well, you get the picture. If you really want to protect your investment, go the extra mile and get yourself an uninterruptible power supply (UPS). Not only will it protect your equipment in the event of an outage or a power surge, but its battery backup will buy you a little extra time to save an important document or two when the lights go out. Read the packaging carefully when choosing a UPS to make sure you're getting protection from power spikes, and not just a fancy extension cord with multiple outlets.

- *Network connections*—If you have an existing broadband connection in your home, you'll need to think about how to share it with your Media PC. This may be as simple as plugging in an extra Ethernet cable (which probably won't come with your Media PC, either), or as complex as setting up a new wireless or HPNA (Home Phoneline Networking Alliance) network. However you decide to do it, you can rest assured that the extra cabling and equipment is likely to be considered "optional and extra," as far as your Media PC maker is concerned.

More Optional Extras

Think you're done shopping for your new Media PC now? You may be right, but then again, there are a few other items you might want to think about, depending on where and how you plan to use your Media PC. Some of these items are included as standard equipment with some Media PC models. Others are definitely going to be coming out of your pocket, but they could make a world of difference in your enjoyment of the new system. These are some of the extras to consider:

- *Wireless keyboard and mouse*—Use these to extend that "2-foot experience" all the way back to your sofa. Of course, the farther you are from the screen, the harder it may be to make use of the Media PC's computer "personality." Some Media PCs include these wireless peripherals as standard equipment. Another option might be to purchase mouse and keyboard extension cables.

- *A USB extension cable*—This can be used to extend the connection from your PC to your USB keyboard and mouse so you can really control the action from your Barcalounger, without going wireless. It can also be used to extend the USB-based remote sensor, which is required to pick up the signals from your remote control. This can come in handy if you've decided to stash your Media PC in an out-of-the-way spot, such as behind furniture or inside a closed entertainment center.

caution

Being able to view typical desktop PC screen data from across the room can require a pretty big monitor, and those generally don't come cheap. A large-screen TV may do the job, but it can be difficult to achieve adequate visual quality on a television set. For more on this topic, see the section "A Few Words on Picture Quality," later in this chapter.

Of course, another way to handle this scenario is to invest in an IR remote sensor, such as the one shown in Figure 2.5. This pyramid-shaped sensor has to be located where it can pick up direct line-of-sight IR commands from the remote control. Then the sensor transmits those commands wirelessly to a complementary unit, which attaches to an IR emitter that can be aimed directly at the device being controlled. This setup can also be used to control your Media Center PC from another room of the house.

■ *An SVGA extension cable*—This comes in handy for people who want their Media Center PC across the living room next to their TV, but want to get up close and personal with a PC monitor. You may find that this kind of setup gives you the best of both worlds, by allowing your Media Center PC to provide entertainment via a TV placed across the room, while keeping a conventional CRT or flat-panel monitor up close for your personal computing tasks.

■ *An optical mouse*—This eliminates the need for a mouse pad. Again, that might be pretty useful if you want to mouse around and control things from the comfort of your couch. Check whether your Media PC already includes one of these before you go shopping.

Getting Connected

By now you're on a first-name basis with the counter guy at the electronics store, but that's okay; he's a friend and a kindred spirit. If anyone appreciates what you're doing—nothing less than dragging your entertainment experience kicking and screaming into the twenty-first century—it's him.

And you may need all the moral support you can get. Yes, everything seems pretty straightforward when you're looking over that beautifully organized, color-coded instruction sheet. But be forewarned: Things may look very different when you're crouched and cramped in the darkness under some heavy piece of furniture, sorting out a veritable rat's nest of assorted wires and peering hopelessly in the bad light at your Media PC's rear panel, which seems to have more holes in it than the surface of the moon.

Still, there's nothing for it but to forge ahead and get this thing connected. Assuming that you have paid attention up to this point, and have at least decided where you want your Media Center PC to be situated, it's time to get started by hooking up your PC components.

Hooking Up Your PC Components

This is the most straightforward part of putting your Media Center–based system together. Every manufacturer's hardware is a little different, but here's the basic routine:

1. Connect your mouse and keyboard to the PC. (If you have a wireless mouse and keyboard, install the batteries they require, and then plug the wireless receiver into a USB port on the PC's rear panel.)

2. Connect the monitor to the Media PC using the SVGA cable.

3. Connect the modem to a phone jack, if you plan to use the media PC with a dial-up Internet connection, or if you plan to use the built-in fax features of Windows XP Professional Edition (which provides the underlying OS for Windows XP Media Center Edition). If desired, you can go ahead and plug a phone into the pass-though phone jack on your modem. Alternatively, if you plan to use a broadband connection, plug one end of an Ethernet cable into the broadband (cable, DSL, and so on) modem, and the other into your Media PC's Ethernet jack. (For additional home-networking options and procedures, see Chapter 22, "XP Media Center and Your Home Network.")

4. Plug the monitor and PC into your power strip or UPS. Don't turn it on yet, though.

tip

When you're doing a relatively complex installation project, it's a good idea to hook things up in stages. Of course, it's tempting to get caught up in the moment and connect everything all at once, and then simply switch it on. But it's heartbreaking when you've followed every instruction to the letter, only to reach for the power button and get nothing, or in the case of Windows XP Media Center, to click on My TV and get No TV signal detected.

The best way to avoid that is to check every new device and connection as you add it to the system, constantly verifying the last step before you go on to the next. The downside is that this approach could add hours to your setup time. Instead, try a balanced approach, stopping every so often to see whether what you have connected is working. Even if you plan to use your PC display for watching TV, you may want to have a television set handy to check that your TV signal is actually working *before* you connect it to your Media PC.

The guiding principle is that the more often you stop and verify that everything is working, the less time you'll spend troubleshooting in the end.

Hooking Up Your Entertainment Components

Here's where the standard PC installation procedures give way and you start wading into the undocumented part of configuring your Media PC.

So let's get started:

1. Find your Media Center remote control (if you have more than one remote, find the one with the prominent green button), the IR receiver, and the IR emitter (see Figure 2.6).

2. Install the batteries in your remote control, and plug your IR receiver into a USB port in the rear of your Media PC. Place the receiver where it will have a direct line-of-sight connection to the remote control.

caution

The procedure described here is for a "typical" Media PC. However, there are already more than 50 manufacturers around the world building Media PCs as this book goes to press, and many dozens of models to choose from, all with a slightly different look on the outside, and a slightly different set of hardware features and components on the inside. It's a good idea to use this guide *in conjunction with* instructions you received from your Media PC's manufacturer.

FIGURE 2.6

Your IR receiver and IR emitter—also known as an IR "blaster"—may look a little different from the ones shown here. Connecting them correctly is critical to getting your Media PC to control your video source.

3. If you are using a set-top cable box or satellite receiver, plug the connector on your IR emitter (also known as an IR "blaster") into the back of the IR receiver (see Figure 2.7). The other end of the cable—the IR blaster itself—should be positioned directly in front of the IR sensor on the set-top box or receiver.

4. Now you'll need to connect the TV output of your set-top box to your Media Center. In many cases, you'll have a choice of using S-Video, composite video, or coax (for a more detailed discussion, see the section "What You May Need to Supply for Yourself," earlier in this chapter). Using the best-quality connection you have available, attach the audio/video output from your set-top box to the appropriate input port on the rear of your Media PC.

tip

You can locate your IR receiver just about anywhere in the vicinity of your Media PC, but somewhere on or near the PC monitor and/or the TV you plan to use for watching video is a good choice. That's where people are used to aiming the remote control to change channels, control audio volume, and so on.

caution

Depending on the design of your set-top box, locating the IR sensor can be a bit tricky. If you're looking at a lot of smoked black plastic in the front, for instance, it might be difficult to ascertain exactly where the right spot is to affix your IR blaster—and without it, your Media PC will not be able to successfully issue commands to change channels, and so on. If the location of the round sensor isn't obvious, try shining a flashlight into the area where you think the sensor is located and look for a 1/2- to 3/8-inch metallic rectangle with a 1/8-inch darker circle in the middle of it. That's where you want to place your IR blaster.

FIGURE 2.7

Chances are your Media PC's IR receiver will have two identical ports for plugging in your IR blaster. You can use either one.

Connecting Your Speakers

You've reached the point in the setup process of connecting your speakers, but first, a few considerations.

Your basic choices for connecting speakers include the following:

■ Connect a set of PC speakers, which very likely came with your Media PC

■ Connect your audio output to a television set, and use its built-in speaker

■ Connect your Media PC to an existing speaker system, such as speakers belonging to your stereo receiver or home theater system

Each of these options has merits, and the one you choose will depend heavily on what you want from your Media Center PC.

If you want the simplest setup procedure and good quality (possibly even great quality, such as if you bought an HP Media Center with Klipsch ProMedia THX 2.1 speakers, or even a Gateway model with Boston Acoustics BA745 speakers and a beefy subwoofer, and so on), hook up the speakers that came with your Media PC system.

If your Media Center system didn't come with speakers and/or you're planning to watch the video output on a television set, you can use a coax cable to output audio and video simultaneously on your TV, or connect S-Video or composite video to the television along with a separate audio cable.

Finally, if you plan to locate your Media PC in close proximity to a decent sound system you have already purchased for listening to your music collection or home theater audio, you'll probably want to connect your Media PC there to get the biggest bang—literally—for your buck.

A Few Words on Dolby 5.1 and Surround Sound

Surround sound is an audio technology that has the capability to simulate directional qualities of sound. When it works correctly, it allows you to hear directional sound effects, such as some incoming X-Wing fighters as they fly in from your right and zoom off to your left. One of the most popular formats for surround sound—and there are several—is Dolby Labs 5.1. Dolby 5.1 is designed for a six-speaker system, generally configured as

> **note**
>
> If you have a Dolby 5.1–compatible audio card in your Windows XP Media Center machine, you'll need to set up the audio software in your system to make use of the Surround Sound features. That procedure is outlined in Chapter 3, "Getting Started and Taking the Tour."

right and left speakers at both the front and the rear of the listener, and a center speaker that is usually placed near the screen. The ".1" in "5.1" refers to the sixth speaker: a subwoofer.

When you're positioning your speakers, the general concept is to place the left and right speakers (both front and rear) at about equal distances from where the listeners will be seated. Position the center channel speaker near the screen. Subwoofers are designed not to be directional, so, theoretically, you can place them anywhere in the room. After you've positioned all the speakers in the correct vicinity, try moving them around a bit to get the sound just the way you like it. See Figure 2.8 for a typical Dolby 5.1 speaker arrangement.

> **caution**
>
> You configured everything perfectly for Dolby 5.1, but it still doesn't work for live or recorded television programming in My TV? That's because TV stations don't broadcast programming in 5.1. Stereo audio is the best you'll get with this type of video content.

FIGURE 2.8

The exact position of each speaker can vary according to your personal preference. For instance, you may like having the rear right and left channel speakers a bit behind you, or you may prefer them more to the side.

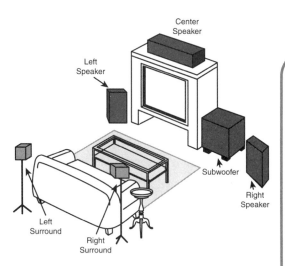

A Few Words on Picture Quality

Because the release of Windows XP Media Center Edition 2004 does not support HDTV, the best video quality most viewers will be capable of achieving will be by using an S-Video connection. If your TV doesn't have an S-Video input port, use an adapter such as the one shown earlier in Figure 2.3.

> **caution**
>
> When it comes to using the TV to view computer applications, once again, you may be in for a bit of disappointment. As one unofficial Microsoft source said in the company's Media Center Home Theater bulletin board, "Unfortunately, blurry is the best you can get on a regular TV." To get the display to be at least usable, you can try reducing your PC's resolution to 800×600 or 640×480 resolutions and enabling large fonts, but be prepared for fonts and other graphics to look much "softer" than you're used to seeing them on your PC monitor.

You should be aware that many people have been critical of the television quality available in the first version of Windows XP Media Center Edition. The second version of Media Center, shipped in the Fall of 2003, showed much improved video performance. However, it's important to let your own eyes be the judge, and decide for yourself whether the enhancements Microsoft is making to improve the video quality of Media Center are adequate to meet your needs and expectations.

A general word about video resolution when viewing the output of your Media Center PC on a television set: Bigger is better, but only up to a point. If you don't like the picture quality on a small-size TV, blowing it up to a larger size is not necessarily going to improve your opinion. However, you need a screen big enough to comfortably watch your movies without straining your eyes.

THE ABSOLUTE MINIMUM

In this chapter, we covered the basic concepts and procedures for setting up your Media Center hardware. Remember to do the following:

- Take inventory to make sure that you've gotten everything you were supposed to with your system, and get familiar with the equipment you're about to connect together.

- Find out what you still need—including extra audio or video cables, connectors, and a trusty power strip—so you can get your system up and running just the way you want it.

- Connect your standard PC components together, and then add the specialized entertainment components of your Media Center PC.

- Plug in and place your speakers for optimum audio performance.

- Connect a TV set to use as your primary or secondary display.

Now you're ready to turn on, boot up, and get in on some amazing graphics, audio, and video capabilities.

IN THIS CHAPTER

- Configure your Internet, TV signal, and program guide with the First Run Wizard
- Tour the highlights of Media Center
- Watch an introductory video or take a "walkthrough" tutorial
- Check for software updates

3

GETTING STARTED AND TAKING THE TOUR

Now that you've unpacked your hardware and gotten it all connected, it's time to configure your Windows XP Media Center Edition software and start getting acquainted with the system that's about to take center stage in your home entertainment activities.

In this chapter, we'll configure Media Center by running the First Run Wizard, which will set up several important aspects of the user interface and hardware features of your Media PC. After we've confirmed that everything is operating as it should be, we'll take a tour and point out some of the highlights.

Running the Setup Wizard

Among the first things you'll encounter when you turn on your Media PC the first time is an interactive setup module, appropriately called the First Run Wizard. As you step through the wizard, you'll encounter the following activities:

- Testing your Media Center remote control
- Configuring your Internet connection
- Configuring your television signal
- Setting up your electronic program guide (EPG)

To launch the First Run Wizard, complete the Windows XP Professional setup routine that runs after you boot up the Media Center PC the first time. After that initial Windows setup is completed, press the Media Center button (see Figure 3.1) on your remote control.

FIGURE 3.1

The prominent green button with the multi-colored Windows logo (circled) is the Media Center button, which launches the Media Center menu. On the first use, it will launch the First Run Wizard to configure your Media Center applications.

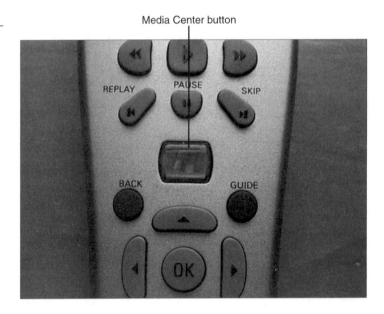

Media Center button

This action brings up the initial First Run Wizard screen, welcoming you to the Media Center setup wizard. Press the OK button on your remote control to proceed to the Getting Started screen (see Figure 3.2).

FIGURE 3.2

This primary screen shows you the First Run Wizard's agenda for getting your Media Center PC ready for active duty.

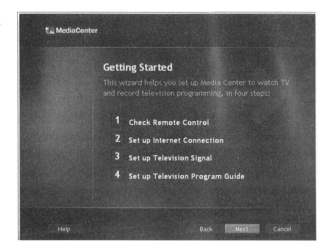

The primary order of business for the First Run Wizard is to check that your remote control is properly set up.

To respond to the wizard's instructions, do the following:

1. Use the directional (arrow) buttons on your remote control.
2. Make sure that the Next button is highlighted at the bottom of your screen.
3. Press OK on the remote control.

For the Media Center remote control to work properly, you must have already successfully installed the USB-based remote control sensor (see Chapter 2, "Basic Setup of an XP Media Center System") and made sure that you correctly inserted the batteries into the remote control. The wizard will display a numeric keypad onscreen and instruct you to press numbers on the remote control (see Figure 3.3). If everything is working correctly, you'll see the numbers light up onscreen, corresponding to the ones you pressed on the remote. If everything looks okay, select the option that says My Remote Control Is Working Properly.

tip

If, in fact, the First Run Wizard was initialized when you pressed the green button on your remote, it's a pretty good bet that your remote control is already set up correctly, so just follow the onscreen prompts.

FIGURE 3.3

This screen checks the operation of your remote control. If it isn't working properly, select the option I'm Having Problems with My Remote Control, and the wizard will launch a troubleshooting routine.

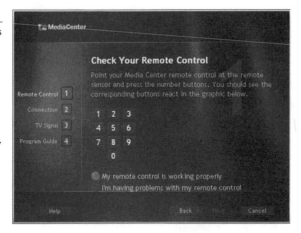

It's interesting to note at this point that you are already doing something that up until now has been very foreign to the mainstream Windows operating system experience: You are driving the whole user interface solely by using the remote control. There should be no reason to use the keyboard or mouse at all during this initial setup procedure. Get used to it, because this is standard operating procedure for Windows XP Media Center Edition–based PCs.

Setting Up Your Internet Connection

Now it's time to get your Internet connection up and running. This will allow you to take advantage of Media Center's capability to connect and receive TV guide data, and CD and DVD metadata, which we'll discuss in later chapters. It's also critical to email, chat, instant messaging, and other forms of PC-based communication, as well as browsing the World Wide Web.

The Internet connection setup screen of the First Run Wizard (see Figure 3.4) gives you a choice between two types of Internet access: high-speed broadband (cable modem, DSL, and so on), or via a LAN connection. You can also choose None, I Will Connect Manually, which is the correct response if you will be using a dial-up connection via an analog modem. At that point, the wizard will display additional screens to step you through the connection process you have chosen.

note

If you need more information on the types of Internet connections that are available, see the section "A Few Words About Your Internet Connection," in Chapter 1.

FIGURE 3.4

This screen is the first step in setting up your Internet connection, which Media Center needs to access its free program-guide data.

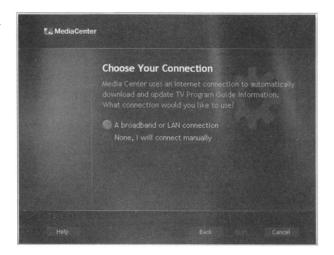

Setting Up Your TV Signal

Next, you'll tell Media Center how TV programming comes into your home. You'll be prompted for information about the source of your TV signal (antenna, cable, digital cable, or satellite), as well as details about the operation of your set-top box. Choose the appropriate TV services you receive, and then select Next.

Depending on your choice of TV programming source, you'll be asked which brand of service you subscribe to, and other questions that will help Media Center determine whether and how to configure your set-top box. (If you don't have a set-top box, the wizard will just move on to the next setup task.) You'll be prompted to confirm that your set-top box is turned on, that it is attached to your Media PC, and that your IR blaster is correctly positioned in front of the set-top box's IR sensor. Now you're ready to start the TV signal setup sequence, which includes the following steps:

note

There is also an option to select No TV Service at This Time. Choosing this will allow you to go back and configure your TV signal connection later.

1. Choose your TV signal. Pick whether your Media PC should look for the TV on channel 2, 3, 4, or S-Video (see Figure 3.5).

2. Choose the number of digits. You'll need to select how many digits there are in the highest channel numbers you receive on your system (that is, 2, 3, or 4 digits).

FIGURE 3.5

You should see a live TV signal display in a small window on the wizard screen, confirming that Media Center has located your video feed. If you don't see live video displaying as it does here, try verifying that your video feed is working by hooking it up to a regular television. After ensuring that you are getting a good signal feed, you can go back to configuring—and if necessary, troubleshooting—your Media Center setup.

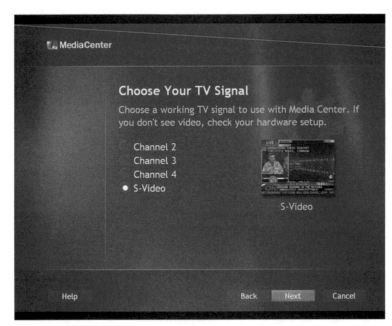

3. Specify how you change channels. The wizard needs to know whether you normally change channels by selecting the channel number only, or whether you typically have to press an Enter or OK button after selecting the channel number.

4. Choose your set-top box brand. Pick from dozens of brands to tell Media Center which set-top box you have.

5. Choose an RC code. If your set-top maker offers multiple models that use different code sets, Media Center will prompt you to try different ones until your set-top box responds.

6. Try changing channels using the number keys. You'll be asked to test the RC code set you selected by using your number buttons to choose a channel, and confirming that it worked as expected.

7. Try changing channels using the CH+ and CH- buttons. You'll be asked to try pressing your remote control's Channel Up and Channel Down keys to confirm that they are changing channels properly.

tip

If you think you made the wrong selection at any point, you can either select the Back option onscreen or use your remote control's Back button, located just to the lower left of the green Start button.

8. Choose a remote control speed. Here you'll have an opportunity to fine-tune the channel-changing speed, in some cases, so you can select "slow," "medium," or "fast," depending on which mode of operation is the most reliable.

Setting Up Your Program Guide

After you've finished setting up your TV signal, you'll be prompted to configure your program guide. This portion of the setup process is crucial to load your Media PC with correct data on the channels and programs available to watch and record.

Here's how to configure your program guide:

1. You must agree to the Media Center's Terms of Service by using the down-arrow button on the remote and scrolling through all 44 pages. When you reach the last page, you'll be able to select I Agree and continue.

2. Use the number buttons on your remote to enter your five-digit ZIP or postal code.

3. Select Next and Media Center will automatically begin downloading your program-guide information.

4. You'll be asked to select from various programming services that match the information you provided during the TV signal setup routine. When you select Next, Media Center will continue downloading program-guide information specific to your geographic area and TV programming service. A status bar will show your progress toward completing the program-guide update (see Figure 3.6).

5. Select Finish to complete the process and be taken to the Media Center startup screen.

note

If at any point you want to go back and reconfigure your program guide, you can restart that portion of the setup wizard by choosing Settings from the Media Center main menu. Then select TV/DVD and choose Guide Setup. The wizard starts when you pick Change Lineup.

caution

If you realize you made a mistake—such as entering an incorrect ZIP code—after you have already started downloading guide data, it's better to let Media Center finish downloading, and then go back and reconfigure the channel lineup. If you cancel the program-guide download while it is in progress, you may find yourself unable to reload the program-guide data without rebooting the system. An error indicating you cancelled the program-guide download will come up every time you try to reload the data until you reboot.

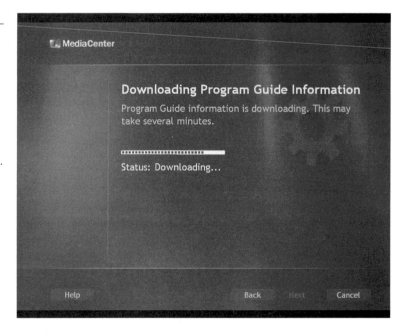

Taking In the Sights

You can now finally begin to enjoy some of the fruits of your labor. In this section, we'll start you off with a brief tour of the major menu choices available from the Media Center interface: My TV, My Music, My Pictures, My Videos, Play DVD, and Settings.

My TV

Most people will want to go straight for the Big Payoff: watching live TV on your PC. To do this, just click on My TV, and you'll be taken to the Media Center Television screen (see Figure 3.7). Media Center may take a few seconds to initialize your TV input signal, and then you should be rewarded with a view of your favorite TV station playing in a window at the right center of the screen. This TV home page will also display the local date and time, as well as the channel number and several TV-related menu choices. (For more information on using My TV, see Part II of this book.)

FIGURE 3.7
Media Center's
My TV main
screen is the
control center for
accessing guide
information, TV
recording, and
search features,
as well as access-
ing TV-related
settings.

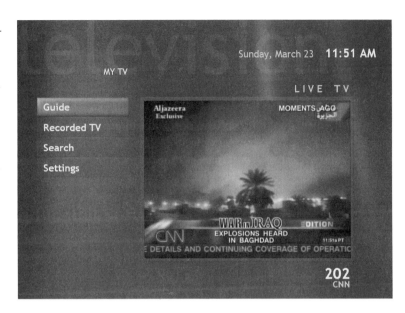

My Music

The My Music tab opens your portal to Media Center's audio control center (see
Figure 3.8). From here you can view and manage your digital music collection.
Menu choices include viewing your collection by album, artist, playlist, song, or
genre, or you can search your collection for a specific set of terms.

FIGURE 3.8
The first time
you open My
Music, it will
typically display
a message say-
ing that no
music has been
loaded into your
media library,
and instructing
you to first use
Windows Media
Player to popu-
late your media
library.

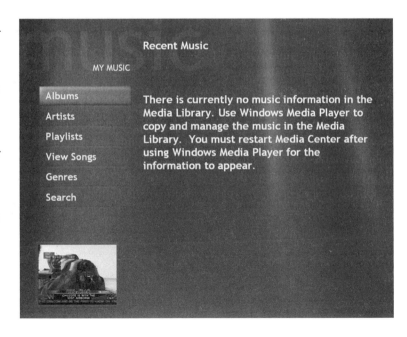

My Pictures

The My Pictures tab displays thumbnails of your stored images. Main menu choices from within My Pictures (see Figure 3.9) include Play Slide Show, Settings, Sort by Name, Sort by Date, My Pictures, and Shared Pictures. (More information on using My Pictures is located in Part VI of this book.)

Note that if you were watching TV before switching to My Pictures or one of the other main Media Center screens, your live TV view screen will continue to appear in a small window at the lower left of the display.

note

You may need to restart Media Center after using Windows Media Player to import and organize your music collection the first time. Detailed information on configuring and using your Media PC's My Music features can be found in Part V of this book.

FIGURE 3.9

The My Pictures screen is the launch point for viewing still images, including slide shows that display multiple images along with a music background, if desired.

My Videos

This section of the Media Center interface is designed primarily for sharing and enjoying your personal digital video files. The Shared Video folder is a place specifically designated for storing video files that are accessible to other computers on your network. Choices from the My Videos screen (see Figure 3.10) include Sort by Name, Sort by Date, My Videos, and Shared Video. (For more information on using My Videos, turn to Part III of this book.)

FIGURE 3.10
My Videos displays thumbnails of video files stored on your hard drive, allowing you to choose which videos to display on your Media PC computer screen or on an attached TV.

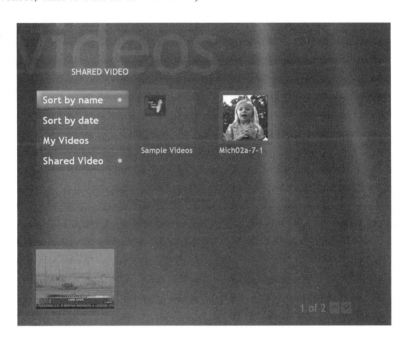

Play DVD

Selecting the Play DVD tab on the Media Center interface will immediately launch the DVD loaded in the PC's optical drive. If no DVD is currently loaded, you will see a pop-up message asking you to insert a disk (see Figure 3.11). Note that this style of pop-up message is specific to the Media Center interface. It's nice and large, with a big green button—perfect for viewing and responding to it from the comfort of your couch. (Additional information on playing DVDs is contained in Part IV of this book.)

FIGURE 3.11

If you inadvertently select Play DVD from the Media Center interface without first loading a DVD, you'll get a pop-up error message asking you to insert a DVD.

Radio

Choosing the Radio tab gives you access to a significant feature that was added in the second version of Windows XP Media Center Edition: the ability to listen to and control an FM radio built in to the TV tuner card of many new Media Center machines. Not only can you tune to or seek FM radio stations and assign up to nine presets (see Figure 3.12), but you can also use the remote control's transport control buttons to pause and rewind live radio.

FIGURE 3.12

This screen shot shows how you create a station preset. If you don't see a Radio tab when you open the Media Center interface, it means your tuner card does not include FM radio capabilities.

Online Spotlight

Media Center's Online Spotlight section was introduced in the 2004 edition to high-light Media Center–related offerings from Microsoft's partner companies. Content in the form of music, movies, software, and more is available here, usually as an additional purchase or for a subscription price.

Settings

The Media Center Settings screen provides access to the following menu choices: General, TV/DVD, Pictures, Data Credits, Privacy, and Terms of Use. The uses of these settings are discussed in various places throughout the book.

Watch the Introduction Video

Like a typical tourist, you've cruised past some of the major attractions of your new system. One good way to experience an overview of your Media Center's capabilities is to watch the 3-minute introduction video that comes loaded on your hard drive (see Figure 3.13).

FIGURE 3.13
The introduction video is designed to get you charged up about all the interesting things your Media PC will allow you to do. (Warning: Brightly decorated apartment and attractive friends are not included with your Media Center purchase. Sorry!)

If you have one of the earlier Media Center machines, you should be able to launch the video by selecting My Videos from the Media Center main menu. Use your directional buttons to scroll down to Shared Video, then select the Sample Videos folder and choose the thumbnail for the file "mcintro." If the file isn't there, try the following:

1. Close Media Center and select My Computer from the Windows XP Start menu.

2. Click on the Search button and select the "All files and folders" option under the heading "What do you want to search for?"

3. Type the word mcintro, and click on search.

4. Right click on the listing for mcintro.wmv, and choose Extract. Browse to the My Videos folder and select Extract.

5. Launch Media Center and return to the My Videos menu.

6. Select the video from the My Videos folder, and enjoy!

> **tip**
>
> As a general rule, wherever you see a button on the Media Center menu, you can activate it by highlighting it with the remote control or mouse so that the button turns green, and then you can either press OK on the remote or click once with your mouse.

More Orientation Tools and Options

Now you've gotten a brief look at what's in store for you with your Media Center entertainment features. If you're also new to the core Windows XP Professional operating system that Media Center is based on, you may want to take advantage of some of the other informative orientation materials Microsoft has included on your system.

Take the Windows XP Guided Tour

The Windows XP guided tour includes audio and animations to graphically present the major features of the operating system. The tour is broken down into the following sections:

- Best for Business
- Safe and Easy Personal Computing
- Unlock the World of Digital Media
- The Connected Home and Office
- Windows XP Basics

The easiest way to reach the animated slideshow (which uses Macromedia Flash technology) is by clicking on Start and then Help and Support, using your mouse, or by pressing the F1 key on your keyboard (make sure that you are on the Windows XP desktop when you do it—not in an application such as Media Center).

Either method will launch the Windows Help and Support Center, aka HelpSpot. Select the listing What's New in Windows XP under the Pick a Help Topic heading, and then click on Taking a Tour or Tutorial. You can also just type the word tutorials in the Search box and press Enter on your keyboard. Find the phrase in your search results and select it.

Take a "Walkthrough"

To "drill down" and learn more about specific topics in Windows XP operations, try taking an interactive "walkthrough." Among the walkthrough topics available are digital photos, personalizing your PC, making music, sharing your PC, and home networking.

To choose a walkthrough, click first on Start and then Help and Support, or press F1 from the desktop. From the HelpSpot page, type walkthroughs in the search box. Choose the topic you want from the search results box, and away you go on your voyage of XP discovery.

Check For and Install Software Updates

One last thing you may want to attend to before we jump in and really start using Windows XP Media Center Edition is to make sure you have all the latest features and versions of the software. To this end, Microsoft has provided a feature called the Automatic Updates Setup Wizard (see Figure 3.14). It can be activated by clicking on an icon in your system tray (located at the extreme lower right of your display). After you click on it, you will be allowed to select options such as Keep My Computer Up to Date, and Download the Updates Automatically and Notify Me When They Are Ready to Be Installed.

If you don't see the icon in your system tray, here's how to add it: From the Windows XP Start menu, right-click on My Computer, and then select Properties. Select the Automatic Update tab, and choose the option Download the Updates Automatically and Notify Me When They Are Ready to Be Installed. Click on OK, and you're all set.

Another place you can check to see whether additional software updates and add-ons are available is the Windows XP Media Center Edition home page at www.microsoft.com/windowsxp/mediacenter. You'll also find a link to this online resource from Media Center support. You can reach this by pressing the F1 key on your keyboard while you are within the Media Center interface, or by moving the mouse within Media Center, which will make a set of mouse support controls appear, and then clicking on the blue circled question-mark symbol. After the Media Center support window appears, choose the Help topic Media Center Technical Support. A link to the Media Center support page will appear in blue type on the left. Click on Downloads in the left column to display the page shown in Figure 3.15.

FIGURE 3.14

The Automatic Updates Setup Wizard keeps your XP operating system up-to-date, with minimal effort on your part. It is particularly useful for staying abreast of the frequent security updates called for by Windows systems.

FIGURE 3.15

A typical selection of the Windows XP Media Center Edition Downloads Web page reveals new performance updates, additional set-top box support files, and other media-centric utilities. Microsoft also posts a number of files "Just for Fun."

THE ABSOLUTE MINIMUM

After you complete your Media Center's software setup using the steps outlined in this chapter, you'll have created a solid platform for building your personalized entertainment experience. Here's all you need to do to finish setting up a centralized, single point of control for all your audio, video, and photographic media:

- Turn on your Media PC and use your remote control to activate the First Run Wizard.

- Follow the wizard's prompts to set up your Internet connection, TV signal, and electronic program guide.

- After you get your Internet, video, and data feeds configured, Media Center is ready to run. This is a good time to take a tour and view the highlights of your Media Center user interface.

- To get some ideas and inspiration about what you can accomplish with your Media PC, watch the introduction video Microsoft provides.

- If you're new to Windows XP, or just in need of a short refresher course, take advantage of one of the interactive tutorials on your hard drive.

- Make sure that your operating system and Media Center software are entirely up-to-date—and that they stay that way—by running the Automatic Updates Setup Wizard and visiting the Media Center Support Page.

4

NAVIGATING XP MEDIA CENTER'S "10-FOOT" INTERFACE

What makes the Media Center interface different from the typical desktop PC experience? It stems from the "eHome" development team at Microsoft going back to the drawing board and deciding what computing would be like if we did it 10 feet away from the computer screen, as opposed to the usual 2 feet. The result was Media Center's so-called "10-foot experience," which allows you to trade in your conventional PC input devices—the mouse and keyboard—for a remote control. Even if you've been using Windows-based personal computers for years, you'll find that the Media Center interface is distinctly different from any off-the-shelf computer you've ever used before.

This 10-foot user interface—essentially a shell running on top of the Microsoft XP Professional operating system—gets rid of all the extraneous folders and files and provides you with a clean, well-lighted place to kick back and enjoy the lighter side of computing, namely, digital entertainment.

But although this PC may seem like it just wants to have fun, its serious side (the "2-foot experience") is only a click away. In this chapter we'll get familiar with your Media PC's multiple personalities, and how to control them using keyboard, mouse, and remote control.

Getting to Know the Media Center Remote Control

The remote control that shipped with your Media PC may have some cosmetic differences from the one shown in Figure 4.1, but it should be functionally identical. Even if your Media PC came with more than one remote control (at least one manufacturer's model—ABS Systems' Media Center PC 8400—actually ships with three remote controls: one for the speaker system, one for the 30-inch LCD display, and the Media Center remote control), you'll have no problem recognizing the Media Center control by its prominent green button. Think of this button as "home base" because it always brings you back to the Media Center home interface, allowing you to gain immediate access to the core Media Center applications: My TV, My Music, My Pictures, My Videos, Play DVD, and Settings.

FIGURE 4.1

The remote control shown here is the classic hyperbolic-shaped model that comes with most Windows XP Media Center Edition–based PCs.

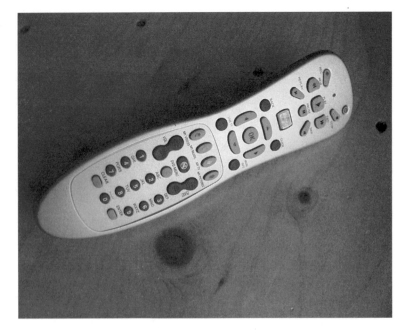

Before we dig into all the buttons on your remote control, it's important to have a general understanding of what your Media Center remote control can and can't do.

What the Media Center Remote Control Can Do

The Media Center remote control can do all the following:

- Navigate and control all primary Media Center features
- Control the video or live TV display, allowing you to change channels, adjust volume, pause, fast-forward and rewind, and so on
- Control DVD playback, allowing you to pause, fast-forward, and rewind, as well as navigate DVD menus to change settings for audio or captions, select scenes, and so on
- Enter numbers and characters to perform media searches, and so on
- Place the computer in standby mode, and revive it

What the Media Center Remote Control Cannot Do

The Media Center remote control cannot do any of the following:

- Allow you to navigate the Windows XP desktop or control other applications outside of Media Center
- Allow you to control an external DVD player, VCR, stereo, or the like
- Turn the Media PC on, or shut it down
- Control a TV that is connected to your Media PC (such as turn it on or off, or adjust its speaker volume)

The Media Center remote control contains four major functional areas, organized from top to bottom of the control: the power and transport section, the navigation section, the audio/video control section, and the data entry section.

tip

Although you may not be able to actually turn off your Media Center PC with the remote control, it does offer a "power" button that will put the machine into a suspended state. The machine is designed to operate in this fashion, rarely needing to be completely powered down.

By the same token, the remote control won't let you fully navigate and control Windows XP applications, but it may allow you to do some limited text entry and related functions.

Power and Transport

At the very top right of the remote control (closest to the end that you point at the Media Center PC), you'll find the power button. As noted previously, this button triggers a stand-by mode. To actually shut down the machine, you'll need to use the mouse.

Directly below the power button you'll find the transport buttons, used to control video and audio media, whether it's stored on the hard drive or a CD or DVD disc (see Figure 4.2). Specific buttons include Rec, Stop, Rew, Play, Fwd, Replay, Pause, and Skip.

FIGURE 4.2

The power and transport controls are where you'll go to play DVDs and to enjoy the wonders of time-shifted television, which allows you to pause and rewind live TV programming.

Table 4.1 details usage of the Media Center remote control's power and transport features.

TABLE 4.1 Remote Control Power and Transport Features

To	Press
Play the selected media (video, song, album, playlist, and so on)	Play ▶
Skip to the next track or scene	Skip Forward ▶❙
Skip to the previous track or scene	Skip Back ❙◀
Fast forward the selected media	▶▶
Rewind the selected media	◀◀
Stop the track completely (press Play to start playing again from the beginning)	Stop ■
Pause the audio or video (press Pause again to resume)	Pause ❙❙
Record the current live program or set record for a program guide item	Rec ●
Place the PC in standby mode (press again to revive the PC)	Pwr ⏻

Navigation

In addition to the green Media Center Start button, the remote is equipped with directional buttons (←, ↑, ↓, and →), an OK button to choose and activate selections, and a Back button. Various shortcut buttons are also found on the remote's midsection, including Guide, Live TV, and More Info buttons (see Figure 4.3). Below these, you'll find an additional row of shortcut buttons that allow you to go directly to the following Media Center applications:

■ My TV

■ My Music

■ My Pictures

■ My Videos

FIGURE 4.3

The navigation portion of the Media Center remote control is a crucial tool for getting around inside the Media Center interface.

This layout differs a bit on HP's version of the Media Center remote control, but the functions are essentially the same. The word "My" is missing on the shortcut buttons, and you'll find them located closer to the top of the remote, just below the power button. Also, the More Info button is labeled Details on the HP version, and is located directly below the green Start button.

Table 4.2 details the major navigation features of the Media Center remote control.

TABLE 4.2 Remote Control Navigation Features

To	Press
Start Media Center (or go to the Start menu if Media Center is already running)	Start (embossed green button with Windows logo)
Move to the selection above	Up (↑)
Move to the selection below	Down (↓)
Move to the selection on the left, or move to the menu	Left (←)
Move to the selection on the right, or move from the menu to the folder items	Right (→)
Select the active item	OK
Go to the previous screen	Back
Show information about the selected item	More Info
Go to the Electronic Programming Guide	Guide
Go to Live TV	Live TV

> **tip**
>
> If some of the onscreen buttons for My TV, My Music, or My Videos are missing from the Start page of Media Center, you can restore them by using the following steps (warning— you're going to need your mouse for this):
>
> 1. From the Start menu, choose Control Panel.
> 2. Click Add or Remove Programs.
> 3. Click Set Program Access and Defaults.
> 4. Double-click Custom.
> 5. Check the Enable Access to This Program box for the programs that you want to restore access to in Media Center.
> 6. Click OK.

Audio/Video Control

This section, shown in Figure 4.4, contains the remote control's Vol+ and Vol- buttons, as well as the corresponding Ch+ and Ch- buttons. You'll also find the Mute control here, as well as the DVD Menu button, which will give you access to DVD-specific options, such as onscreen controls for chapter and subtitle selections.

Table 4.3 describes the A/V functions available from the Media Center's remote control.

TABLE 4.3 Remote Control A/V Features

To	Press
Turn up or turn down the volume	Vol+/Vol-
Mute the sound without stopping playback	⊗(Mute)
Change the channel	Ch/Pg+ / Ch/Pg-
Access the DVD menu when a disc is inserted	DVD Menu

FIGURE 4.4

The Media
Center remote's
A/V controls
allow you to
change channels
(and page up or
down when
viewing the
program guide),
adjust the vol-
ume, and access
a DVD menu.

Data Entry

This section of the remote control (shown in Figure 4.5) is where you'll find number
buttons to input numerals 0–9, an Enter button, and a Clear button. Also note that,
just as on a telephone keypad, the number buttons have alphabetical values as well.
For instance, the 1 button can be used to input the letter A, B, and C (press once for
A, twice for B, three times for C). These buttons can be used to fill in onscreen fields
and forms, to input keywords for searching through the program guide or your
media collections, and so on (see Figure 4.6 for an example).

FIGURE 4.5

The data-entry
portion of your
Media Center
remote control
allows you to
input alphanu-
meric characters
without reaching
for the keyboard,
but for the most
part it will work
only within
Media Center
applications.

FIGURE 4.6

When you are presented with a data-entry screen inside the Media Center interface, such as when searching for programming, Media Center will display a graphic representation of the keypad for easy reference.

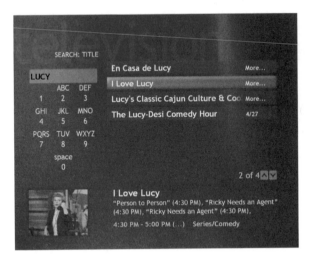

To input text with the Media Center remote, follow these steps:

1. Press a number to scroll through the choices available for that button. With each repeated press of the button, a different character will appear.

2. When you have entered the character you want to use, press Enter, or pause for a second. The cursor will advance to the next character position.

3. To backspace, press Clear.

4. Continue until the complete search term is entered, or until the search function has narrowed your choices sufficiently to select the item you are looking for.

5. To select an item from the search list, press the right arrow to access the list and use the up/down arrows to highlight your choice. Then press OK.

tip

Most functions of your remote control are limited to applications within Media Center, but there are some exceptions. For instance, you can use your remote to log on to Windows. When you turn on the computer and see the log-in window, press the arrow buttons on the remote to select your username, and then press OK. Microsoft Windows will start. You can even use the remote to enter your password when you log in—but your password must use only numeric characters. If you have a mixed-character password, you'll need to use the keyboard to enter it. (Note that mixed-character passwords are significantly more secure than passwords that use only numeric characters.)

Exploring the Media Center Interface

The sole reason for the existence of the Media Center remote control, which was developed jointly by Microsoft and Dutch electronics maker Philips, is to provide you with easy, across-the-room access to the Media Center interface (see Figure 4.7). Created as a sleek, highly visual "one-stop" destination for all your entertainment activities, Media Center's animated transitions and simple menu structure seem vaguely familiar, yet totally unlike any Windows desktop scheme that has come before it.

FIGURE 4.7

When you press the green Start button on the remote control, it will launch the Media Center interface; however, an inset window (lower left) always displays the current media selection.

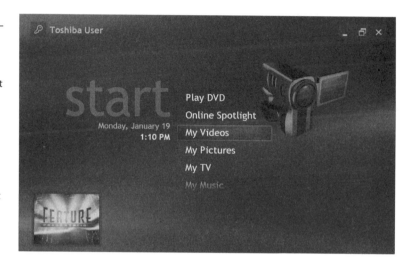

Switching from Media Center to the Windows XP Desktop

You can switch from the Media Center interface to the Microsoft Windows XP desktop at any time. Simply press the green Start button on the remote control, and then use the right-arrow key to select Minimize (see Figure 4.8), and press OK. Media Center will continue to run in the background. You can also use your remote control to maximize the Media Center screen, or to close the Media Center interface altogether.

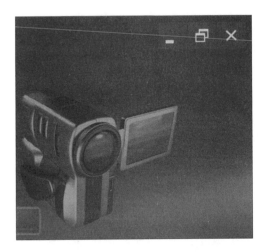

Customizing Your "10-Foot" Look and Feel

One of the cool things you can do to really customize your Media Center experience is add menu items. This allows you to select an application using the remote control, and have the link to that application appear in the Media Center menu stack right below the existing Media Center applications.

Adding Applications to the Start Menu

Here's how to add items to the Media Center Start menu. Essentially, you're going to add a new application link to the Media Center Programs folder in the Windows Start menu.

- Create a shortcut to the desired application by placing the cursor over the icon for the program you want to add, clicking the right mouse, and then selecting Send To, Desktop (Create Shortcut).

- Move or Copy the shortcut into the following folder: C:\Documents and Settings\All Users\Start Menu\Programs\Accessories\Media Center\Media Center Programs. (Instead of All Users in the pathname, you can specify a particular user folder. In this way, different users will see different menu items when they launch Media Center.)

- When you launch Media Center, your new application link will appear in the More Programs menu. When you select your application, the Media Center user interface will be replaced by your application. The next time you launch

Media Center, the link will appear at the bottom of the main menu list, before Settings. Make sure that the shortcut name is the same as the name of the application, with no "shortcut_to_" prefix or filename extension.

If you want your custom menu to look really slick, you can add an associated icon. It works like this: When you select an item from the Start menu item, an image (or icon) appears at the upper right of the screen (see Figure 4.9). You can assign one of your own images to any new menu item you add by doing the following:

- Find or create a graphic image. It must be in Portable Network Graphics (PNG) format, and it can't exceed 300×300 pixels. (There are already hundreds of PNG files on your system; you can run a search using Windows Explorer.)

- Give the file exactly the same name as the application you are launching (with a PNG extension instead of an EXE extension, of course), and place it in the same directory as that application—or "executable" file—on your hard drive. For example, if you added a link for the mspaint.exe program to your Media Center menu, you need to place a graphic file called mspaint.png in the same directory as the .exe file (which happens to be C:\WINNT\ system32, in this case).

FIGURE 4.9

Following the steps listed earlier, a link called Paint was created. A graphics file called mspaint.png— a pair of green handprints—was placed in the same directory. When the Paint item is selected, the green hands icon is displayed. When you select the Paint item, it automatically launches the MS Paint drawing program.

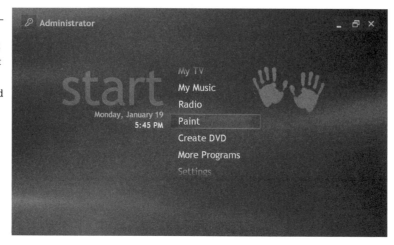

Turning Transition Animations On or Off

In the preceding text, we discussed how to set up your own graphics and animations, which occur when you change screens in Media Center. You can also turn the animations off if you like. To do so, follow these steps:

1. Press the green Start button on the remote.

2. Select Settings.

3. Select General.

4. Select Appearance.

5. Place a check mark in the Transition Animations check box.

If you want to turn the animations back on, follow the same procedure to uncheck Transition Animations.

Turning Notifications On or Off

Media Center is designed to keep you in-the-know when it comes to the status of your system, but you may reach a point where you become annoyed by its constant nudging about things such as whether you are low on disk space, when your TV signal goes out, or when there is an interruption in the availability of your Electronic Programming Guide data.

If you feel yourself getting fed up with information overload, here's how to turn off Media center's friendly reminders:

1. Follow the procedure given previously for turning off animation transitions.

2. When you reach the Appearance control menu, clear the check mark in the Notifications check box.

THE ABSOLUTE MINIMUM

Arguably, one of the most important pieces of new equipment included with your Media Center PC is the remote control. Because you've purchased one of the first personal computers that was designed to be used from across the room, it's important to get completely comfortable with controlling your Media PC remotely—and tailoring your PC's across-the-room interface to suit your needs and tastes. In this chapter, we detailed the following:

- How to get around your Media Center using the remote control, including what you can and cannot accomplish with the remote alone.

- Specific features and uses for your remote control's power and transport, navigation, audio/video, and data entry buttons.

- How to personalize your Media Center menu by creating new menu items. These can even include your own customized, animated icons to give them the "factory installed" look and feel.

- How to adjust your Media Center interface using the Settings menu, including specific steps for turning animations and notifications off and on.

5

NAVIGATING XP MEDIA CENTER'S "2-FOOT" INTERFACE

You've negotiated the "10-foot" experience and customized it to your taste. Now it's time to get up close and personal with your Media Center PC. So sit down at the screen, get comfortable with your mouse and keyboard at the ready, and we'll begin.

The first thing to understand is what we mean when it comes to your "2-foot" experience with the Media PC.

Every previous version of the Windows operating system—even the Windows CE/PocketPC variety that runs on handheld computers—was designed to be controlled from about 2 feet away from the device. (The only possible exceptions would be "embedded" versions of the operating system, which aren't designed for a personal computer at all, but which might be used to run anything from a set-top box to a dedicated command and control system in an airplane.) Thus, the whole modus operandi of Microsoft software to date has been built around the concept of "point and click." You select objects with a pointing device—usually a mouse, sometimes a stylus, or even your finger—and perform operations on that object.

Your Media Center remote control broke that mold, by allowing you to move away from your PC and retain control via a device that doesn't point at objects, but lets you select them by scrolling from one to the next, or by punching a predefined button. The fundamental difference is rooted in the way these devices work. With a mouse, you are actually selecting a particular pixel on the screen, and the PC translates that selection into the action it represents. For example, the PC displays a box that says Yes. When you click on any pixel point within that graphical box, Windows translates that action into an affirmative response to a query, and executes the corresponding command. The remote control, however, doesn't typically work with pixels. Instead, it transmits a code to the machine using the infrared spectrum. That IR code corresponds to a particular action, say, a channel change or a volume selection.

> **caution**
>
> We may call it a "2-foot interface," but that doesn't mean we actually advocate that you sit only 2 feet from your computer screen. In fact, unless you have very short arms, you should be sitting a bit further back from your monitor. In its "Healthy Computing Guide" to PC ergonomics (available online at www.microsoft.com/hardware/ergo), the software company advocates keeping your monitor at a distance of about arm's length when you're sitting down.

However handy the remote control is, there are still many features and functions of your Media PC that are not practical to access with a remote. In fact, just about all the traditional things we use PCs for fall into this category—everything from word processing to surfing the Web. (As for the latter example, just ask anyone who owns a WebTV device, the precursor to the Windows XP Media Center design for TV-centric computing—most will admit that browsing the Internet with a remote control is generally a pretty clumsy experience.)

In most respects, using the mouse and keyboard to get around on your Media PC is no different from your typical Windows PC experience. For that reason, we're going to bypass all that mundane stuff and get right to the meat of the matter: how to control a Media Center PC's specialized audio and video features *without* the remote control in your hand.

Your Windows XP Desktop

Up to this point, you've had no real need to use your mouse at all, because the remote control has been doing all the work interfacing with your Media Center PC during the setup process. When you finally do move your mouse—whether you give it a shove along the desktop, click a button, or give the scroll wheel a spin—the first thing you'll notice is the appearance of the toolbar view, which adds a menu bar and onscreen transport controls to the Media Center display (see Figure 5.1).

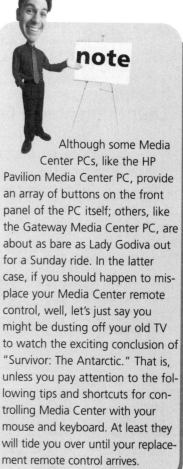

Although some Media Center PCs, like the HP Pavilion Media Center PC, provide an array of buttons on the front panel of the PC itself; others, like the Gateway Media Center PC, are about as bare as Lady Godiva out for a Sunday ride. In the latter case, if you should happen to misplace your Media Center remote control, well, let's just say you might be dusting off your old TV to watch the exciting conclusion of "Survivor: The Antarctic." That is, unless you pay attention to the following tips and shortcuts for controlling Media Center with your mouse and keyboard. At least they will tide you over until your replacement remote control arrives.

FIGURE 5.1

This illustration shows the transformation that takes place on your Media Center interface screen before (top) and after (bottom) you move your mouse.

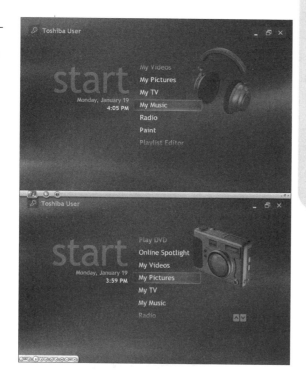

Controlling Media Center with Your Mouse

Maybe it's just a mouse to you, but to your Windows XP Media Center Edition machine, it's actually a "human interface device." Of course, one of the first things you'll want to do with your human interface device is start interfacing with your Media Center's audio and video content.

Launching Media Center

Unlike with your remote control, there is no single dedicated mouse button designed to launch Media Center (XP will create one after you use Media Center, however, as shown in Figure 5.2). So if you're ready to boot up Media Center for the first time using your mouse instead of your remote control, here's how:

1. Click on Start.
2. Click on the green Media Center logo.

If you don't find Media Center already listed in your Start menu, use this procedure:

1. Click Start.
2. Click All Programs.
3. Select Accessories.
4. Click on the Media Center folder.
5. Click Media Center.

FIGURE 5.2

Launching Media Center from the Startup menu gets easier, because Windows XP automatically puts shortcuts to recently used applications right in the start menu.

The Menu Bar

At the top of your Media Center interface screen, you'll now see the menu bar and its six control options (some of these are shown in the close-up in Figure 5.3). From left to right, you'll find the following:

- The green Media Center Start button. It takes you back to the main Media Center interface from wherever you may have wandered within Media Center.

- The green Back arrow button. It returns you to the screen you were viewing immediately before the one you are viewing now.

- The blue Help button. This opens a Media Center Help window to find answers to common questions.

- Minimize. A Windows standby, it will reduce your Media Center session to an icon on the taskbar. Although this gets Media Center out of your way in a hurry, your Media Center session remains active. Thus, if you are playing a show or a tune, you'll continue to hear it on your speakers after you minimize Media Center.

Notice that when you resize the Media Center window, it retains its original dimensions. You can make it bigger or smaller, but you can't stretch it into a different shape. In techie terms, we say that it maintains a "constant aspect ratio."

- Restore. This switches Media Center into "Windowed mode," meaning that it shrinks Media Center down from full-screen view to a smaller window, allowing you to access your other desktop applications while continuing to enjoy your Media Center content in a compact size. It also automatically places a resize handle in the lower-right corner of the Media Center screen (see the close-up in Figure 5.4). You can drag that handle to make the Media Center screen as large or as small as you like. When you want to return Media Center to its full-screen appearance, just click on the Restore button again.

- Close. This shuts down Media Center completely—but don't worry, it will continue recording any scheduled shows in the background. (You need not be present to win!) For more information on recording TV, turn to the Chapter 7 section called "Using the Program Guide."

FIGURE 5.3

The Media Center menu bar gives you six shortcuts, including the green Media Center button shown in this detail of the upper-left corner of the Media Center screen.

FIGURE 5.4

This detail of the lower-right corner of the Media Center screen running in Windowed mode shows the series of 10 small dots that denote a resize handle.

The Transport Control Bar

The other toolbar that appears when you move your mouse within the Media Center interface is the Transport Controls toolbar (see Figure 5.5) that stretches along the bottom of the Media Center window.

FIGURE 5.5

The Transport Controls toolbar (shown here in detail) will disappear after a few seconds of inactivity, or if you use your remote control or keyboard.

The Transport Controls work just like they do on the remote control (see the "Power and Transport" subsection of the "Getting to Know the Media Center Remote Control" section, in Chapter 4). To the far left are the Ch+ and Ch– buttons to change channels. Moving to the right, you'll find the Play, Stop, Record, Skip Back, Skip Forward, Mute, Vol+ and Vol– buttons.

Controlling Media Center with Your Keyboard

Navigating your Media Center interface with your keyboard is a snap, and it can also turn you into a "power user," giving you access to many more powerful commands than are available from your remote control alone.

These commands are issued by means of "hard-wired" buttons mounted on your keyboard in addition to the traditional "QWERTY" keyboard layout, as well as keyboard shortcuts, which are combinations of keystrokes that execute a particular action. Either method can be much faster than mousing your way through menu after menu, trying to find the right command to click on. They are also popular with people who suffer from repetitive strain injuries and experience wrist pain from using their mouse.

Using Hard-Wired Keyboard Buttons for Media Center

Making use of dedicated keyboard buttons that control media-related features is as simple as pressing the button on your remote control. Unfortunately, the degree to which your Media PC maker has included such buttons varies from "extensively" to "not at all." Even more unfortunately, currently available Media PCs have mostly failed to integrate their dedicated keyboard controls with the Media Center's TV and video playback interface. The transport controls used on the Gateway Media Center system, for example, are integrated with Media Center's audio CD playback features, but trying to use them to start, stop, fast-forward, and rewind a DVD movie playing within Media Center just doesn't work—at least not yet.

Figures 5.6 through 5.8 show three examples of keyboards shipped with Media Center PCs, demonstrating the range of hard-wired media-centric controls built into the designs.

FIGURE 5.6

This wireless keyboard supplied by Gateway features a row of CD transport control buttons across the top, as well as Mute and Vol+ and Vol– buttons (see inset).

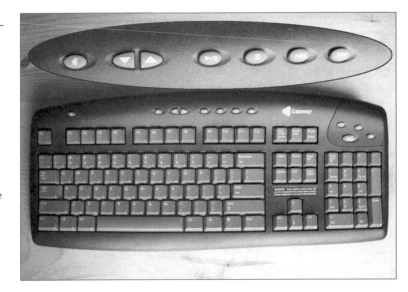

FIGURE 5.7

This wired version of the Gateway keyboard adds another row of dedicated buttons (see inset), for Web browsing, getting help, online shopping and browsing your My Documents folder.

FIGURE 5.8

This HP Pavilion keyboard has loads of extra buttons and even a volume knob (see inset), but it won't control Media Center's video applications.

Getting these hard-wired buttons to work seamlessly with the Media Center interface should be just a software fix away, so don't be surprised if someday your Automatic Update Wizard suddenly downloads something that repairs the problem. In the meantime, use the dedicated buttons for launching browsers and other applications outside of Media Center. Within Media Center, they won't do much more than allow you to listen to a CD and adjust the volume.

Using Keyboard Shortcuts for Media Center

Although the hard-wired keyboard buttons won't do much to enhance your Media Center enjoyment, using keyboard shortcuts is another story altogether. They're called shortcuts because of the time they save by eliminating mouse clicks. But although using the keyboard instead of the mouse may reduce the strain on your wrists, it may lead to increased strain on your brain: recalling all the correct key combinations can be difficult. The best way to remember particular keyboard shortcuts is to use them frequently, keeping them fresh in your mind. Otherwise, a "cheat sheet," along the lines of the following tables, can come in handy.

On the following pages, you'll find a collection of reference tables with shortcuts to some of the most useful keyboard time-savers available for Windows XP Media Center Edition.

Keyboard Shortcuts for Media Center Navigation

Table 5.1 lists several navigation-related keyboard shortcuts for getting around Media Center's screens and menus, including the TV program guide.

Table 5.1 Keyboard Shortcuts for Navigating Within Media Center

To	Press
Start Media Center	Windows logo key+Alt+Enter
Jump back one page at a time	Page Up
Jump ahead one page at a time	Page Down
Go back to the previous screen or backspace a single character in Search	Backspace
Move up	Up arrow
Move down	Down arrow
Move left	Left arrow
Move right	Right arrow
Select	Enter or spacebar

Changing Channels with the Keyboard

It may not be very intuitive at first, but changing TV channels with your keyboard is a simple matter, when you know the right keys to use. Table 5.2 shows you.

Table 5.2 Keyboard Shortcuts for Changing Channels

To	Press
Change to a specific channel	The number for the channel you want
Move up one channel	Equal (=) or Ctrl+equal
Move down one channel	Minus (–) or Ctrl+minus

Keyboard Shortcuts to Media Center Menus

Reaching the major menu features of Media Center from your keyboard is equally simple. The shortcuts listed in Table 5.3 will take you directly to the main Media Center menu areas.

TABLE 5.3 Keyboard Shortcuts for Accessing Media Center Menus

To Go to Top-Level Menus For	Press
My TV	Ctrl+Shift+T
My Music	Ctrl+M
My Videos	Ctrl+E
My Pictures	Ctrl+I

Keyboard Shortcuts for TV and DVD Menus

Table 5.4 shows the keystrokes you'll need in order to access the submenus available for watching TV and DVDs.

Table 5.4   Keyboard Shortcuts for Accessing TV and DVD Menus

To Go to TV and DVD Menus For	Press
Guide	Ctrl+G
Record	Ctrl+R
Details	Ctrl+D
DVD menu	Ctrl+Shift+M
Recorded TV	Ctrl+O
DVD audio	Ctrl+Shift+A
DVD subtitles	Ctrl+U

Keyboard Shortcuts for Audio and Video Transport Controls

Multitasking by getting some work done while watching a favorite show or video? No problem—and no need to reach for the remote just to rewind to that scene you want to see again. Table 5.5 shows you how to control the playback of your media without ever removing your fingers from the keyboard.

Table 5.5   Keyboard Shortcuts for Controlling Media Playback

To	Press
Pause	Ctrl+P
Play	Ctrl+Shift+P
Stop	Ctrl+Shift+S
Replay	Ctrl+B
Skip	Ctrl+F
Rewind	Ctrl+Shift+B
Fast-forward	Ctrl+Shift+F
Mute	F8
Volume down	F9
Volume up	F10

Customizing Your 2-Foot Look and Feel

Clearly, one of the big payoffs for plugging in a Media PC is the capability to work and watch TV—all on the same box, all at the same time. To achieve this marvel of multimedia multitasking, simply start Media Center and select Restore Down (the center icon in the upper right that looks like two windows, one on top of the other). This places Media Center in a movable, resizable window.

Now all you have to do to multitask is start the program you want to use; for example, surf the Web by using Internet Explorer, or check your email by using Outlook Express. Resize the window of the program you are using so that you can see both it and whatever you're watching with Media Center.

Keeping Media Center "Always on Top"

Of course, as you begin multitasking in earnest, you'll soon discover that other windows keep covering up your video window. This may provide a temporary boon to your productivity, but eventually, you'll get pretty tired of constantly needing to unbury your video. Here's how to change your settings so that the active video window is always on top of the desktop heap:

1. Open up the Media Center Start menu.

2. Select Settings.

3. Select General.

4. Select Appearance.

5. Click to place a check mark in the box for Window Always on Top. (See Figure 5.9.)

FIGURE 5.9

Changing this setting to Window Always on Top ensures that you'll never miss the big scene or the big play.

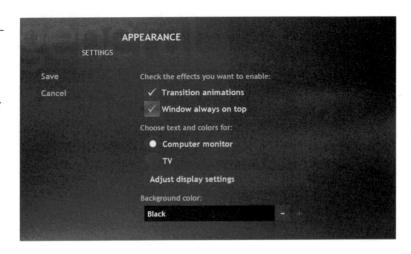

Capturing a New Background from Video

Now that you've got your 2-foot experience practically perfect, it's time to add some finishing touches and spruce the place up a bit. Here's a great way to do it, using your keyboard and mouse, and the unique properties of Media Center.

The next time you're enjoying a TV show—or video of any kind—on your Media Center, stay on the lookout for an eye-catching scene that would look good plastered all over your desktop. Then follow these steps:

tip

To find the perfect shot in your video, you can rewind or fast-forward to the approximate spot, then view it frame by frame. First pause the video, then press the Skip Forward button to view the next frame, or Skip Back for the previous frame.

1. Use your rewind control to get back to the perfect spot on the video screen, and press Pause to keep it right there.

2. If the video is not already being displayed in full–screen mode, select the inset window and press OK to make it full-screen.

3. Press the Print Screen key on your keyboard.

4. Open your Paint program. (You can launch it from the Windows XP desktop by clicking on Start, All Programs, Accessories, Paint.)

5. Press Ctrl+V, or select Edit, Paste.

6. Select File and Save As Background (Centered). (See Figure 5.10).

FIGURE 5.10

The Paint application allows you to save any image as a background for your Windows XP desktop.

THE ABSOLUTE MINIMUM

Your Media Center PC is a "split personality" machine: It was designed for use in remote-control mode (the "10-foot experience") and mouse-and-keyboard mode (the "2-foot experience"). In this chapter, we discussed getting around in—and getting the most out of—that 2-foot, face-to-face experience with your Media Center machine. These were some of the key points:

- The 2-foot interface was designed to allow you to experience all the entertainment features of the Media Center, while simultaneously making use of the powerful computing capabilities of your Media PC.

- The Media Center interface can sense when you want to use the mouse, and automatically places various mouse-operated media controls at your disposal.

- Although your Media Center keyboard may have come with several hard-wired buttons that resemble the transport controls on your Media Center remote, they mostly won't work with Media Center's video and DVD features. For more control over your Media PC, you'll find a slew of keyboard shortcuts that can streamline your media experience.

- You can improve your multitasking experience by changing the Media Center settings so that your video window is never covered up by other applications, and you can customize your PC's look and feel by plucking a scene from any video and turning it into wallpaper for your desktop.

PART

My TV

6

WATCHING THE SHOW

There are a lot of good reasons to buy a Media Center PC, but for most people, the feature that really sets it apart from the crowded field of PC competitors is the ability to watch, control, and record live television directly on the computer.

The integration of TV capture capability in a PC isn't brand-new, but to have the features built-in at the factory, and controlled as part of the PC's basic Windows operating system, *is* new. And by most accounts, it's been worth the wait.

Why Watching TV on Your Media Center Changes Everything

If you have no previous experience with a digital video recorder, or DVR, you should be forewarned that you're about to experience a level of freedom, convenience, and control over your television that is very likely to exceed your wildest expectations. The first such appliances to bring VCR-like control to live TV watching were called TiVo and ReplayTV, and they have elicited fierce customer loyalty in the few short years since they appeared on the market.

Through the crafty design of new hardware and software systems that were able to record and store, or "buffer," video in real-time, these new devices were able to give consumers capabilities that only TV studios could have afforded as late as the early 1990s—namely, the capability to treat live broadcast video as if it were a videotape. It no longer costs tens or hundreds of thousands of dollars for a machine that allows you to pause a live video feed, back it up, fast-forward it, or delay it—that is, to watch video that was broadcast a few moments ago and continue to view it while you simultaneously record it.

For more details on how DVRs and related devices work—and how to make them do what you want them to do—check out *High Tech Toys For Your TV: Secrets of TiVo, Xbox, ReplayTV, UltimateTV and More*, by Steve Kovsky, also published by Que (ISBN: 0-7897-2668-8).

A Few Words on Time-Shifting

How this wonder of video manipulation was extracted from TV production studios and implanted into our living rooms is not as important as what it allows us to do. Using the time-delay features, also known as time-shifting, in a very real sense actually gives us back time.

Consider that in a typical hour of primetime network TV programming, almost one-third of the time is devoted to commercials. What if your television could give you back 20 minutes on the hour, allowing you to condense your favorite one-hour TV drama into 40 minutes?

Ironically, a surprising number of people who don't own a DVR say they don't want one, either—because they believe it would cause them to spend more time watching TV. In fact, however, most people who own one will attest that a DVR is a great time-saving device. It allows you to watch what you want, when you want, without sitting through commercials if you don't want to. The TV networks may not like the idea, but DVRs such as TiVo, ReplayTV, UltimateTV, or XP Media Center Edition place the viewers in charge of their television viewing experience, allowing them to see more of what they want to see, and none of what they don't want to see. The final result is less time spent watching unwanted, uninteresting material. For many of us, that means less time watching TV in general, and a more satisfying TV-watching experience overall.

How much time could watching digitally recorded TV—and flipping past commercials—save you in a year? According to Table 6.1, if you watch only 3 hours of TV each week, commercials consume up to 3.6 days of your life every year. If you watch an average of 3 hours per day, more than 2 weeks out of every 52 are spent watching commercials! What are 2 weeks of your life worth to you?

Table 6.1   Skip the Ads, Reclaim Your Life

Total TV Watching Time	5 Hours per Week	10 Hours per Week	15 Hours per Week	20 Hours per Week
Time Spent Watching Program Content Each Week	3.3 Hours	6.7 Hours	10.0 Hours	13.3 Hours
Time Spent Watching Ads Each Week	1.7 Hours	3.3 Hours	5.0 Hours	6.7 Hours
Time Spent Watching Ads Each Year	3.7 Days	7.2 Days	10.8 Days	14.5 Days

Watching TV and Time-Shifting with Your Remote Control

Just as with watching on your conventional TV, the most natural way to enjoy video programming on your Media Center PC is with the remote control in one hand and a refreshing beverage in the other.

Watching Full-Screen TV

Watching television in full-screen mode on your Media PC is as easy as 1-2-3:

1. Press the green button on the remote, and select My TV.
2. Press the right-arrow button to navigate to and highlight the Live TV window (see Figure 6.1).
3. Press OK/Enter to maximize the TV viewing window to full-screen mode.

FIGURE 6.1

Make sure that the Live TV window is highlighted—with a green border around it—before selecting OK/Enter to watch full-screen.

To return to the My TV menu, just press Back.

Viewing TV Show Details

Although some of the TV-watching features of Media Center are pretty standard stuff—such as using the Ch+ and Ch- buttons to change channels, or pressing Mute or Vol+ and Vol- to adjust the audio—other buttons on your Media Center remote may be less familiar.

For instance, pressing the More Info button while the video window is selected, or while watching TV in full-screen mode (see Figure 6.2), brings up the Information Bar, which shows the following:

- Current time
- Channel
- TV show title
- Show start and end times
- Show genre/category
- Short description

Select the highlighted More Info onscreen button in the lower-right corner to view full details about the show (see Figure 6.3). Select Play on the screen or highlight the video window and press Select on the remote to return to full-screen viewing.

FIGURE 6.2

The Information Bar displays details about the show you're watching.

FIGURE 6.3

To get the real lowdown on the current program displayed on your screen, highlight and select the onscreen More Info.

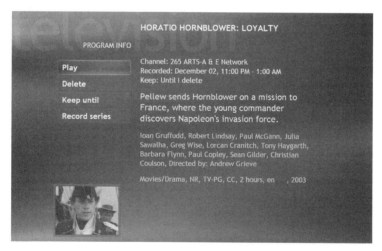

Pausing Live TV

This is definitely one of the "wow" features of your new Media PC: the ability to stop your live TV program in its tracks. When life suddenly begins to "happen"—the phone rings, or someone calls timeout for a snack or bathroom break—it no longer means missing part of your favorite program. Just press the Pause button once to freeze the live TV image.

Fast-Forwarding, Rewinding, Going Live, and Stopping

Here are a few more time-shifting tricks you can perform with your remote control:

- **Fwd**—Press this button to choose between three fast-forward speeds. To watch at 3x normal speed, press Fwd once. Press it a second time to speed it up, and a third time for maximum speed (see Figure 6.4).

- **Rew**—Press this button to make the show run backward. As with Fwd, there are three speed levels. Pressing the button a fourth time returns you to normal playback.

- **Live TV**—Press this button and, as advertised, you will be catapulted directly to the live TV signal on the channel that My TV is currently tuned to.

- **Stop**—Press this button to halt live TV. If you press Play again within 30 minutes, My TV will pick up right where you left off.

FIGURE 6.4

The three speeds of fast-forward motion are indicated by the number of arrows above the progress bar: two, three, or four.

Replaying and Skipping Ahead

Some of the most powerful features of your Media Center PC are contained in the tiny Replay and Skip buttons, located just to the right and left of the Pause button on your remote control.

The Replay, or "skip back," button instantly rewinds your program 7 seconds and shows you what *just* happened, allowing you to watch that amazing play one more time. It's also perfect for those "Did he/she really say that?" moments on your favorite soap or talk show. Press Replay repeatedly to keep moving back in 7-second increments, or to keep replaying the same classic moment of video, over and over again.

The Skip button is even more useful. This is the feature that will free you from the tyranny of TV advertising, as discussed previously. Every time you press it, you will be magically transported 29 seconds into the future of your recorded TV show. A few short presses and that annoying commercial break has come and gone without so much as interrupting the dialog of your favorite show. Remember, using the Skip button regularly can give you back days or even weeks of your life, over the course of a year (for details, see Table 6.1).

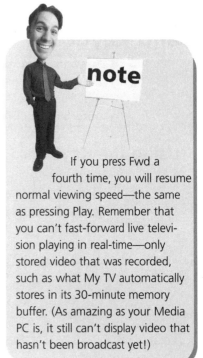

note

If you press Fwd a fourth time, you will resume normal viewing speed—the same as pressing Play. Remember that you can't fast-forward live television playing in real-time—only stored video that was recorded, such as what My TV automatically stores in its 30-minute memory buffer. (As amazing as your Media PC is, it still can't display video that hasn't been broadcast yet!)

tip

If your show is paused when you press the Skip button, the video will advance but remain paused. Press Play on the remote and the action will resume. The Replay button works in the same way. To quickly rewind or fast-forward to the beginning or end of the recorded buffer, press and hold Replay or Skip, and then press Play.

Watching TV and Time-Shifting with Your Mouse and Keyboard

Managing your My TV experience with keyboard and mouse is nearly as fun as using your remote control. The following shortcuts will also come in handy the next time your remote control mysteriously disappears without a trace (that is, until it miraculously turns up a few days later in the sofa cushions).

Using the Keyboard

As discussed in the preceding chapter, your keyboard may come equipped with a few multimedia controls built-in, but other than adjusting the audio, they won't do much in the way of helping you operate your My TV video features. For that, you'll need to remember a few keystroke combinations that invoke the same commands we discussed in the remote-control sections earlier in this chapter.

Table 6.2 offers a list of the major keyboard shortcuts for use with Media Center's My TV mode.

Table 6.2   My TV Keyboard Shortcuts

To	Press
Activate the My TV menu	Ctrl+Shift+T
Play	Ctrl+Shift+P
Stop	Ctrl+Shift+S
Skip back	Ctrl+B
Skip forward	Ctrl+F
Mute	F8
Volume down	F9
Volume up	F10

Using the Mouse

Controlling the basic TV-watching experience with your mouse is quite straightforward. Just move the mouse, and as discussed in the last chapter (see "Controlling Media Center with Your Mouse"), all the onscreen controls you need will automatically appear. You'll easily be able to

tip

Here's a little trick you can perform with your keyboard—one that you can't do with your remote control. Use Ctrl+Shift+C to toggle closed captioning on and off. The way to turn captions on with your remote is to press Mute, but there's no one-click way to activate closed captions while keeping the sound turned on—and you may want to do that if, for example, a hearing-impaired person is watching alongside other viewers who can hear. (Even if you're not hearing impaired, leaving captions turned on and the sound off can be a great way to watch TV unobtrusively, such as when you want to at least *look* as though you're working.)

change channels, adjust volume, pause, stop, record, rewind, and fast-forward. However, there are a few other idiosyncrasies related to using your mouse in My TV mode that can help you get the most out of your TV watching.

For starters, when you open My TV, it will typically be playing the currently selected TV channel in a window embedded within the My TV main menu screen. To quickly maximize the TV window to fill the screen, just place your cursor over the TV video window and click your left or right mouse button. This little trick works with any minimized TV video window, including the Media Center start page, guide, and so on.

Although you can perform most of the same feats using your mouse that you can with your remote control or keyboard, there are a few things you can't do with a simple mouse click, including these:

- Skip or Replay—Only basic fast-forward and rewind are available when you're using the mouse only.

- Live TV—You'll have to fast-forward to reach the end of the recorded video and see what's happening "live." You can click on fast-forward (or rewind) up to three times to increase the speed.

- More Info—This feature isn't accessible with the mouse.

Watching Out for the Kids: Using Parental Controls

If you have children in your home or workplace— wherever your Media Center PC resides—it's a good idea to think about using the parental controls that Microsoft has placed at your disposal. It might save you and the children that come in contact with your PC a great deal of embarrassment, or worse.

To set up parental controls, follow these steps:

1. Open the Media Center Start page.

2. Select Settings, and then General.

3. Scroll down to Parental Control, and select it.

4. Enter a four-digit PIN (personal identification number), and confirm it (see Figure 6.5).

caution

No parental control mechanism is foolproof. Remember that the best way to protect children from inappropriate content on TV or the Internet is to help them become "street smart." Tell them what you think is inappropriate for them, and make sure they know that anytime they see or hear something that makes them feel uncomfortable, they should immediately turn the machine off and/or tell a trusted adult. (For more resources on how to raise "street smart" kids in the Internet Age, check out the National Center for Missing and Exploited Children (NCMEC) Web site at www.netsmartz.org.)

FIGURE 6.5

If you forget your password for Parental Controls, you can reset it using the procedure described in the next section.

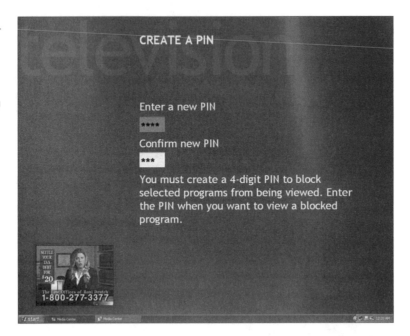

5. Select TV Ratings and Movie/DVD Ratings to set values for each content category.

6. Within each category, first place a check in the top box to turn on blocking for that category, and then place a check mark in the other box if you want to block all unrated content.

7. Finally, click on the – or + signs to view information on various rating levels, and select your choice for the maximum allowed rating (see Figure 6.6).

After your parental control levels are set, you can still watch shows that exceed the rating levels you have selected, but you'll first have to enter your PIN code.

note

If you change channels while watching a blocked show, and then return to that show, you'll have to reenter your password to unblock it again.

FIGURE 6.6

Using this screen, you'll be able to choose from seven levels of content ratings.

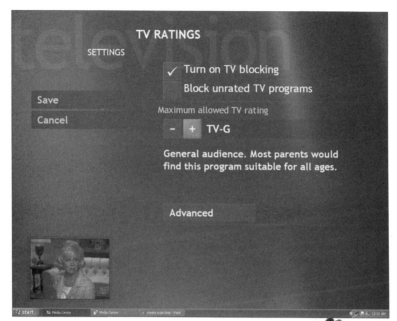

Resetting Parental Control Passwords

If you find that you can't remember your four-digit PIN for parental controls, you'll need to perform a reset of the code. First, you must be logged on to your Media Center PC as the administrator. Then you can follow these steps to reset the PIN:

1. Press Start on the remote, and then select My TV.

2. Select Settings.

3. Hold down Ctrl+Alt while you select Parental Control with the remote control.

Media Center will purge the existing 4-digit PIN. Follow the onscreen directions to enter a new parental control code.

> Can this note be edited to fit? It's too long to be placed on this page and cannot really flow to the next.

note

If you haven't considered setting up different user accounts on your Media Center machine, now's the time to start. If everyone who uses your machine is logging on as "administrator," they all have the authority to set and reset passwords and PIN codes, and so on. To add a new user account to your system, launch Control Panel from the Windows XP Start menu and select User Accounts. Click on Create a New Account, and follow the onscreen instructions.

THE ABSOLUTE MINIMUM

Your Media Center PC provides a powerful new way to enjoy television entertainment. Coupled with the recording features we'll discuss in Chapter 7, "Finding Shows to Record," the time-shifting features built into the Media Center My TV interface finally put you in control of your entertainment experience. You are literally running the show this time—not the TV networks. For example, in this chapter we covered the following:

- The simple act of using the Skip button on your remote control to zip past commercials can save you hours of watching content you don't care about. If you watch a lot of TV, the time you save can really add up.

- Time-shifting is one of the central benefits of the Media Center system. After you start pausing, rewinding, replaying, skipping, and fast-forwarding through your favorite TV shows, you'll soon wonder how you ever managed without it.

- Media Center was created with the remote control in mind. Knowing the use of every button on the remote—and combinations such as using Pause along with Skip or Replay to view action frame-by-frame—will help you get full enjoyment from your computerized entertainment system.

- When you're multitasking, such as watching TV and working on your PC at the same time, you may want to use your mouse and keyboard to control TV-related functions. Memorizing keystroke combinations will give you instant access to all the features available from your remote control—and more.

- Now that you've mastered Media Center's basic My TV features, take a moment to consider whether you have young people using your Media Center machine, and whether they might benefit from adult supervision of their viewing habits, via Media Center's built-in parental controls.

7

FINDING SHOWS TO RECORD

Have you ever traveled to a foreign country, or gone on an expedition in search of rare flora or fauna in some remote wilderness? Although it's theoretically possible to muddle through on your own, people often hire a guide in these situations. The guide's job is to help you locate the stuff you're looking for without a lot of wasted effort. Well, that's exactly what the electronic program guide does for you in Media Center: It lets you go straight to the good stuff on TV, without wasting a minute on the stuff you don't want to see.

About the Program Guide

One of the most powerful software components of your Media Center is the electronic program guide (EPG), which serves as your conduit to live television programming. If you have ever subscribed to a service such as TiVo or ReplayTV, or a digital cable offering, you may already have some experience with an interactive EPG. If not, you're in for a treat—especially because Microsoft is treating you to a free EPG. Although standalone digital video recorders such as those previously mentioned charge a subscription fee to use their EPG offering, Microsoft is giving away the service to users of its Windows XP Media Center Edition operating system.

The guide lets you check what's currently playing on TV and provides more details on each show, but that's just the beginning. You can also browse for TV shows, searching by title, keyword, or category. By selecting shows you have found using the guide, you can also record them with the touch of a button (for more information on recording shows, see Chapter 8, "Recording Shows You Find"). You can even choose to record an entire series of programs, so you'll never have to miss another important plot twist in your favorite soap opera, or the final installment of that blockbuster miniseries.

The basic EPG grid displays channel and network information in the first column, alongside title and scheduled broadcast times of shows you receive. When you highlight a show, by highlighting it with the remote control or by placing the cursor over the title using the mouse, a short description of the show appears at the bottom of the screen. (For instructions on viewing more detailed show descriptions, see Chapter 6, "Watching the Show.")

tip

Here's an interesting way to change your point of view. While looking at the program guide, instead of scrolling forward to view upcoming programs by pressing the Right (→) button on the remote, try pressing the Left (←) button and selecting the program-guide square that contains the channel number and call letters. Rather than getting the usual grid showing the time across the top and channels listed down the left side, you'll be able to see in detail what's playing on that particular channel for the next several hours (see Figure 7.1).

FIGURE 7.1

The channel-specific program guide view is a handy way to check the show lineup on a single channel.

Using the Program Guide

If you want to find out what's on TV, the way to start is by accessing the guide itself. The easiest way to get there is to press the Guide button on the remote control. However, you can also navigate to the guide by using Media Center's onscreen menus:

1. Press Start on the remote.
2. Select My TV.
3. Select Guide.

The guide's initial view (see Figure 7.2) shows the channel you are on, and the current listing for what's playing now. You can use the Right (→) navigation button on the remote to scroll ahead and view what's coming up in the next several hours. (Unfortunately, you can't scroll to the left past the channel listing itself. There is no support for viewing listings of shows that already aired—but what's the point of living in the past, anyway?)

FIGURE 7.2

The guide displays an hour and a half of programming on your current channel, and the next six channels in your local channel lineup.

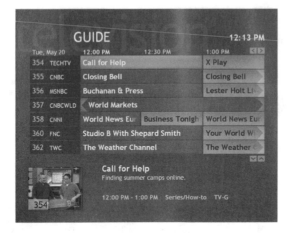

You can use the Up and Down navigation buttons to view listings on other channels, or you can press Ch/Pg+ or Ch/Pg- to scroll through the listings page by page (seven channels at a time). If you're using your keyboard instead of the remote, press the Page Up or Page Down keys to achieve the same effect.

When you find a show you want to tune to, just highlight the listing and press OK. My TV will change the channel and switch from the Guide view to full-screen mode.

Sorting the Program Guide

Here's a great undocumented feature of the guide that will help you zero in on exactly what you're in the mood to watch: While the guide is displayed onscreen, press the Guide button again. The program description at the bottom of the screen will be replaced by a series of categories: All Channels, Movies, News, Sports, Kids, and Music (see Figure 7.3). Select one of these categories and you will automatically sort your guide so that it displays only programs matching that description.

tip

Want to view listings farther into the future? Pressing the Right (→) navigation button only moves you ahead one-half hour at a time. To zoom ahead three hours in the program guide, press Fwd (Rew will take you back three hours). To skip ahead a full 12 hours, press the Skip button (Replay will move you back 12 hours).

tip

If you've been perusing what's coming up over the next several hours, and want to get back to seeing what's on right now, press Guide on the remote to return to the current time slot.

FIGURE 7.3

Pressing the
Guide button
on the remote
control twice
gives you access
to six ways to
sort the EPG by
program type.

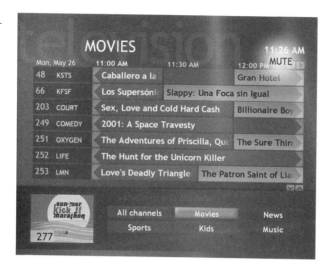

Customizing Your Program Guide

Now that you know how to get around in the program guide, you may want to take a minute and fine-tune your EPG listings. Among the things you can do:

- Hide channels you don't receive—or don't want—so they are no longer displayed on your program guide
- Reconfigure your EPG by changing your channel-guide lineup
- Force a fresh download of guide data from Media Center's EPG provider

Hiding Channels

When you come across listings for channels you don't actually receive from your TV programming service, or if you keep coming across listings for channels you can get but don't actually want, it's a simple procedure to hide those listings from view:

1. Press the MY TV button on the remote (on HP remotes, use the TV button).
2. Select Settings.
3. Select Guide Settings.
4. Select Edit Guide Listings.
5. From the Edit Guide Listings screen (see Figure 7.4), use the navigation buttons on your remote control to scroll through the list until you find a channel you want to hide.

6. Highlight the channel and press OK. That will clear the check box next to the channel number. Repeat the procedure until you have unchecked all the channels you want to hide. If you make a mistake, just select the channel and press OK again to replace the check mark.

7. When you've made all the changes you want to your channel listings, select Save.

FIGURE 7.4

Notice that as you go down the list of stations on the Edit Guide Listings screen, each channel you highlight is displayed in the inset TV window.

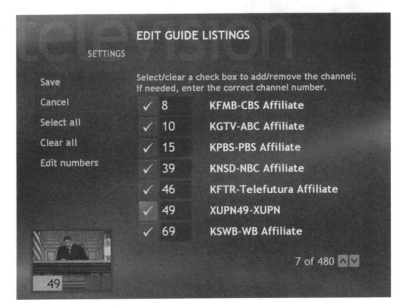

If you find that very few of the channels you receive are actually worth keeping, you may want to start from a clean slate by choosing Clear All and then placing check marks by the channels you want to appear in your listings. By the same token, you can choose Select All to add all channels back into your guide listings.

Finally, you can also use the controls on the Edit Guide Listings page to microman-age your channel numbers (see Figure 7.5). This will come in handy if there is a discrepancy between the downloaded listing data for your area and the actual channel where a particular TV station is received. To edit the channel number, just do the following:

1. Select Edit Numbers from the Edit Guide Listings menu.

2. Select the channel number you want to change.

3. Enter the correct value using the number keys on the remote, and press OK.

4. Select Save.

FIGURE 7.5

This screen allows you t o change individual channel numbers in the event of a discrepancy between the EPG and your TV service provider.

If you make changes that you later regret, you can always go back and choose Restore Default to wipe out your changes and return to the original EPG settings.

If Media Center detects a conflict between the new channel number you've entered and an existing channel, you'll be presented with a conflict resolution screen (see Figure 7.6) that offers several options for resolving the conflict.

FIGURE 7.6

This warning screen lets you know that the reassigned channel number is already in use.

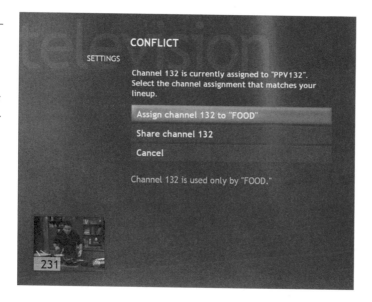

You can choose to go ahead and reassign the channel number—essentially overwriting the existing station listed at that number location—or you can have two stations share the same channel number. A third option is to cancel the operation altogether.

Changing Your Channel Lineup

Missing one or more channels? You may first want to check the Edit Channels screen as described in the preceding section, and make sure that you didn't accidentally deselect it from your channel list. If that doesn't solve the problem, it could be that you selected the wrong TV subscription package or programming provider when you did your initial setup (see the section "Setting Up Your TV Signal" in Chapter 3, "Getting Started and Taking the Tour"). It's also possible that your TV service provider has simply changed your channel lineup.

Whatever the reason, it may be time to go in and make some channel lineup changes of your own. Here's how:

1. Press Start on the remote.
2. Select Settings.
3. Select TV.
4. Reset Guide Lineup.
5. Follow the onscreen directions to select a new channel lineup.

Another option for adding a single channel that's missing from your lineup is to use the Add Missing Channels utility (see Figure 7.7), also available from the Television Settings menu.

caution

If you're not sure which program guide to select, take a look at the latest bill from your TV service provider for more information.

FIGURE 7.7

After entering the call letters for the TV station you want to add, using the text input buttons on your remote control, you'll be prompted for the channel number of the station.

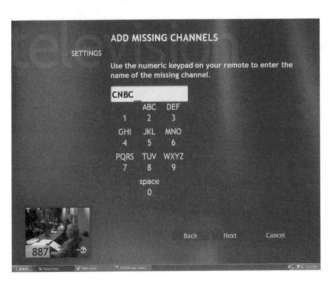

Downloading Guide Data

Although Media Center is designed to automatically download your guide data via the Internet from designated providers such as www.Zap2it.com, there may come a time when you want to initiate a download manually. For example, a manual download may be called for if you think that programming changes may have taken place since your last download occurred, or if you see discrepancies between your EPG data and program information published elsewhere.

Whatever your reason, here's how to make sure that your guide data is as up-to-date as possible. Follow the steps outlined previously to reach the Guide Settings menu. Then select Get Guide Data, and follow the onscreen prompts to complete the manual download process (see Figure 7.8).

tip

If you want to check out when your last download of guide data took place, you can view a guide-data information screen (see Figure 7.9) that will tell you not only when the guide was last refreshed, but also when it's due to be updated next. You'll also find details on your listing provider and guide data settings, and so on. Here's how to do it:

1. Press Start on the remote.
2. Select Settings.
3. Select TV.
4. Select Guide Settings
5. Select About Guide Data.

FIGURE 7.8

After you select Get Guide Data, you'll see this confirmation screen. Choose Yes to continue.

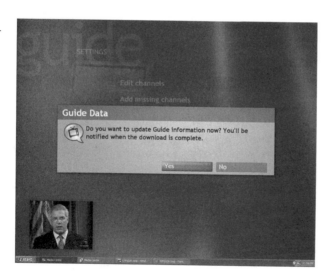

The actual download time can take many minutes or only a few seconds, depending on the speed of your Internet connection and how out-of-date your guide data is.

FIGURE 7.9

The About Guide Data screen also provides details about the version of the guide you are using and offers various information on your guide setup configuration.

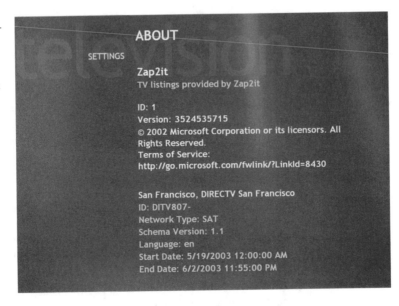

Searching with Your Remote Control

When you select My TV, then Search, you'll be greeted by the option to search by Categories, Title, or Keyword (see Figure 7.10). Let's look at each of these search methods individually.

FIGURE 7.10

Media Center's My TV main search page allows you to launch a programming search based on the genre, the program name, or a specific attribute contained in the show description.

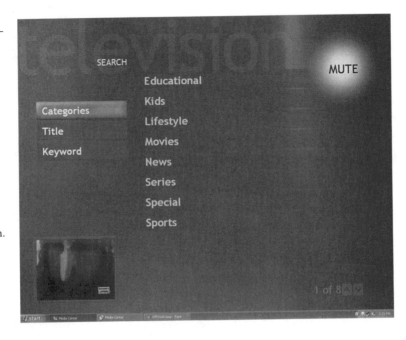

Searching by Categories

Selecting Categories brings up a set of eight initial search choices: Educational, Kids, Lifestyle, Movies, News, Series, Special, and Sports. Nested within each of these program genres are still more category choices. For instance, when you select the News category, you then need to choose All, Business, Current Events, Interview, Public Affairs, Sports, Weather, or Other.

In all, My TV search categories contain more than 80 topic areas. Table 7.1 offers a complete listing of search categories and subtopics.

TABLE 7.1   My TV Search Categories and Subtopics

Educational	Kids	Lifestyle	Movies	News	Series	Special	Sports
All	All	All	All	All	All	All	All
Arts	Adventure	Adults Only	Action and Adventure	Business	Action and Adventure	Awards/ Event	Baseball
Biography	Animated	Collectibles	Adults Only	Current Events	Children	Holiday	Basketball
Documentary	Comedy	Cooking	Children	Interview	Comedy	Music	Boxing
How-to	Educational	Exercise	Comedy	Public Affairs	Cooking	Religious	Football
Science	Special	Health	Drama	Sports	Drama	Sports	Golf
Other	Other	Home and Garden	Fantasy	Weather	Educational	Other	Hockey
		Outdoors	Horror	Other	Game Show		Outdoor
		Religious	Musical		How-to		Racing
		Other	Mystery		Music		Soccer
			Romance		Reality		Tennis
			Science Fiction		Soap Opera		Other
			Suspense		Talk Show		
			Western		Travel		
			Other		Other		

When you select a category and subtopic, Media Center will display the first page of items that fit within that category (see Figure 7.11). At the bottom right of the listings, Media Center displays the total number of listings available that meet the search criteria. At this point, you can sort the search results by name or date. Just select the corresponding Sort By tab.

FIGURE 7.11

This example shows a category search using the search terms Sports and Racing, sorted by date.

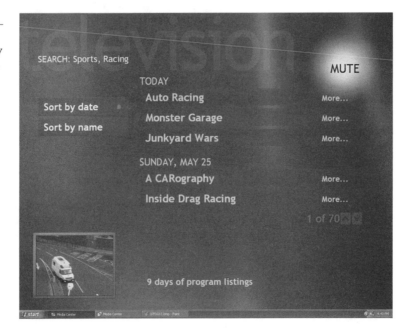

Searching by Title

Title search is probably the quickest way to find a specific program. Unlike the search features on dedicated PVRs—which require you to type in a full or partial title name and then select Done and wait for the search to run its course—Media Center begins searching as soon as you enter the first letter. This blazing-fast search method (compared to the rather sluggish speed of TiVo, ReplayTV, or UltimateTV searches) often completes the search and successfully finds your program before you can even finish entering the complete name of the show.

Entering text with your remote-control keypad is very similar to adding names to your mobile phone's address book, or navigating a company's automated phone system by entering the name of the party you're trying to reach. Number keys represent letters, beginning with the 2 key, which represents letters A, B, and C, and so on. Simply press once for A, twice for B—you get the idea.

Along with the number/letter input keys, the Media Center remote control offers two additional keys that are important to the text-entry process: Clear and Enter. Clear performs the same function as Backspace on your PC keyboard, erasing the last character you entered.

tip

Can't find the punctuation character you're looking for? Press the Ch+/Ch- button to switch between alphanumeric input mode and punctuation input mode.

Enter can be used to speed up the text-entry process by pressing it every time you find the character you want to use. That way, you can immediately proceed with entering the next character. Otherwise, you may have to wait a few seconds between entering characters—particularly when adjacent letters are both represented by the same number key.

To enter a space between words, press 0.

Searching by Keyword

Searching by keyword operates more or less the same way as searching by title—at least from the user's standpoint—however, the search itself is much more exhaustive. Instead of just looking at show titles for a match, Media Center compares the search term to the entire description provided in the program guide. Among other attributes, it will search for names of actors, directors, and characters in a particular show, along with subject matter, from Alaska to zebras. The more specific or obscure your search term, the fewer results you will get from your search. See Figure 7.12 for an example of keyword search results.

FIGURE 7.12

A keyword search for "judd" turns up listings with actors Judd Hirsch, Judd Nelson, Ashley Judd, and more.

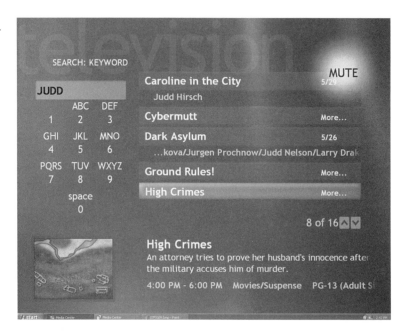

Searching with Your Mouse

To reach the search menus with your mouse alone, you'll need to start from the Media Center Start menu, selecting My TV and then Search. Unfortunately, to conduct a keyword or title search, you'll have to reach for your remote control or keyboard to perform any text entry. Although the text search interfaces display an onscreen keypad, it's there only for reference to your remote control's keypad and isn't mouse-enabled.

THE ABSOLUTE MINIMUM

In this introduction to navigating Media Center's EPG and search features, you've learned the basics for singling out the shows you want to watch from among the thousands of listings available to you. Among the key points to remember are these:

- It's worth taking time to clean up your program guide and customize it so that only channels you receive—and actually want to keep track of—are listed in your EPG. You can do this by using the procedure for hiding unwanted channels.

- Make sure that your program listings are fresh and up-to-date, and that they accurately reflect the offerings you receive from your program service provider, by changing your channel lineup and downloading new guide data.

- Media Center's My TV functions include powerful search features, allowing you to search by category, title, or keyword. Whatever you're searching for, Media Center gives you a way to find it.

- Search by category if you're not sure exactly what you're looking for but want to see everything that's available in any one of more than 80 subject areas.

- Search by title if you're sure that you know the name of the program you want to find. Media Center begins searching when you enter the first letter.

- Search by keyword if you want to find everything on a certain subject, or starring a certain actor, and so on.

8

RECORDING SHOWS YOU FIND

Does a procedure something like this sound familiar?

1. Set the VCR's clock to the correct time and date.

2. If you're using a cable box or satellite receiver, turn it on and tune it to the channel you want to record before the recording is to begin.

3. Insert a videocassette tape with its safety tab in place. Be sure that it is rewound and has enough tape to record the program.

4. Press the Menu button to display the VCR Main Menu.

5. Press the 2 button to choose Timer Recordings.

6. Press the 1 button to choose Create a New Program.

7. Select how often you want the program to record.

8. Using the number buttons, enter the channel number, as well as the start and end times (including AM or PM and the date), for the program you want to record.

9. Select the tape speed.

10. Press the Menu button to save.

That's the kind of lengthy, mind-numbing procedure most people in the world have to endure simply to record a TV show they like. Now compare that with the procedure for creating a "timed recording" using your Media Center PC's interactive program guide:

1. Highlight the listing for the show you want to record.

2. Press the Rec button.

Wait a minute—what happened to the other steps? There aren't any. This is the essence of the Media Center My TV experience: one-touch recording of any program.

In the VCR example, most consumers never get past step 1—setting the blinking LED on the recorder to the correct date and time. Each of the subsequent steps is also fraught with peril. The slightest misstep will cause the procedure to go awry, and another moment of television history will be lost forever (or at least until summer reruns begin).

It is a virtual guarantee that after you become accustomed to the one-touch recording capability of your Media Center PC, the old VCR style of recording will seem at best quaint, at worst like some primitive rite performed by a backward and superstitious people out of the ancient past.

Recording as You Watch

With all due respect to the VCR, recording the TV program you are currently watching is no simpler with a Media Center PC than it is with a videocassette recorder: Simply press the Rec button on the remote. The system will immediately start recording the show in progress. However, that's where the similarity ends.

Whereas a VCR can begin recording only from the moment you press the Rec button, Media Center makes use of its half-hour memory buffer to begin recording the show from the time it actually

> **note**
>
> To control live TV—to begin or stop recording, pause, and so on—you must select TV as the active window. You can do this by playing TV full-screen, or by highlighting the TV inset window.

started—up to 30 minutes before you got around to pressing the Rec button. (Of course, that will work only if My TV was tuned to that channel before you issued the record command.)

To stop the recording, just press Stop. However, unlike most VCRs, My TV will first ask whether you really want to stop recording (see Figure 8.1).

FIGURE 8.1

The Interrupt Recording message displays whenever you manually stop a recording in progress.

Recording from the Program Guide or Search Results

As described previously, My TV's one-touch recording feature (see Figure 8.2) is so simple that it hardly bears mentioning: Highlight the listing for the show you want, and press Rec. Just remember, though, that for My TV to successfully execute a timed recording based on your one-touch request, your Media Center PC needs to remain turned on, operating in either standby mode or hibernation mode (for details about standby and hibernation modes, see Chapter 4, "Navigating XP Media Center's '10-Foot' Interface").

Recording Manually

Sometimes you may need to override the program guide or search-based recording features, and set your Media Center to record manually. Manual recording also gives you more flexibility in deciding exactly what you record, and when. For example, if you want to record only the sports report on the local nightly news, you could manually set your Media Center to record just the last 10 minutes of the news program each night, and so on. All you need are the time and channel of what you want to record, and My TV will carry out your command to the letter.

Here's how to set up a manual recording session:

1. From the My TV menu, select Recorded TV.

2. Select Add Recording.

3. Select Create a Custom Recording with Channel and Time, and you'll arrive at the Manual Record setup screen (see Figure 8.3).

4. Specify the Channel, Frequency, Date, and Start Time.

5. Scroll down (click on the down arrow) and specify the values for Stop Time, Keep Until, and Quality (for details on these settings, see the section "Advanced Record").

FIGURE 8.3

Manual record
can be useful
when you know
that something
is going to be on
a certain chan-
nel at a certain
time—and your
program guide
doesn't—or if
you just want to
record a certain
portion of a
show.

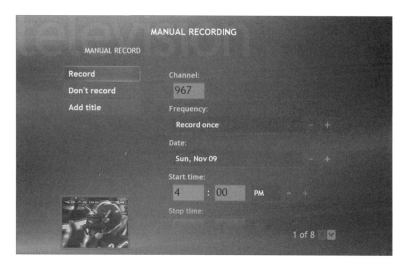

6. If you want, select Add Title to input a name for your recording, and then select Save.

7. Select Record.

Keyword Recording

Media Center also allows you to create a persistent program search that will track down and record shows automatically, based on search terms you define. These search criteria can include an actor's or a director's name, or keywords that represent subject matter or names that appear in the show titles or descriptions.

The beauty of this type of search-and-record mission is that it will keep looking for your shows until it finds what you want and records it for you.

Here's how to create a persistent keyword record command:

1. From the My TV menu, select Recorded TV.

2. Select Add Recording.

3. Select Create a Custom Recording with Keyword.

4. Now you have an opportunity to specify whether your keyword will appear as part of an actor's name, a director's name, a movie title, a TV program title, or just a Generic Keyword.

5. Select the type of keyword you want to use, and then enter the keyword using the remote control text-input buttons or your keyboard.

6. After you enter your keyword and select the matching term from the list, you'll reach the main keyword record settings page (see Figure 8.4). If you want, you can add a category to further refine your search, and set various other parameters, including Frequency, Show Type, Keep, Quality, Start time, and Stop time. (For more information on these record settings, see the section "Fine-Tuning Your Recordings," later in this chapter.)

7. Select Record.

FIGURE 8.4

From this keyword record session, Media Center will automatically record all kids' shows starring actor Rex Harrison.

Recording a Series

The capability to record a series of programs is another impressive feature that your old VCR will be hard-pressed to match. Whereas the VCR can be set to record any program that appears on a given day, at a given time, on a given channel, the computerized recording features in Media Center and other DVR devices use the show title to seek out multiple episodes of a series and store them on your hard disk.

You can record a series from the Guide or from Search. In this section, we'll look at each of these approaches individually.

Recording a Series from the Guide

If you liked the capability to record a show from the guide with one touch of the remote control, you'll love the capability to record an entire television series by simply pressing the Rec button a second time. To confirm your series recording command, the guide listing will display the multiple red dot icon (see Figure 8.5).

To cancel the scheduled recording, you can simply press Rec a third time, and the red dots will disappear, confirming your choice.

FIGURE 8.5

The symbol denoting a series recording command is visible both in the program guide grid entry and in the show description.

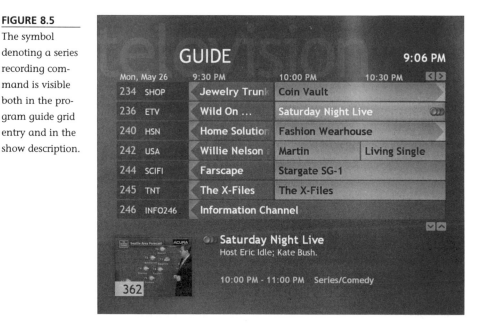

When you record a series from the program guide using the procedure noted previously, the recordings will reflect My TV's default Series Record settings. These defaults include the following:

- Both first run and rerun episodes will be recorded.
- If the show airs multiple times per day, My TV will record it every time.
- All episodes will be kept on disk, until space is needed for other, higher priority recordings.
- My TV will record using the "best" quality level.
- All recordings will start and stop on time, according to the program guide listing information for each episode.

As you can imagine, selecting an older and popular TV series, such as the *Saturday Night Live* example in Figure 8.5, would potentially yield many recordings per day, using the default series record settings. In addition to the first-run shows on Saturday evenings, *SNL* airs frequently in the form of reruns on multiple channels. We'll talk a little later in this chapter about how to fine-tune those record settings to avoid "episode overload."

Recording a Series from Search

First, conduct a search using the Categories, Title, or Keyword search options, following the steps outlined in the last chapter. Then do the following to record a series:

1. Use the navigation buttons on the remote control to scroll through the search results and select the show you want to record.

2. Multiple episodes are likely to be rolled up under the initial show listing, so your next view will display a list of upcoming episodes (Figure 8.6). You may need to select a title, and then select the title again to pick an episode that airs at a specific date or specific time. Depending on which episode air time you select, the series record features of My TV will schedule upcoming recordings that match your choice. For example, if you select a 10:30 PM air, My TV will record episodes at 10:30 PM each day and ignore other daily showings with the same episode title.

FIGURE 8.6

This search results page displays multiple episodes of a series.

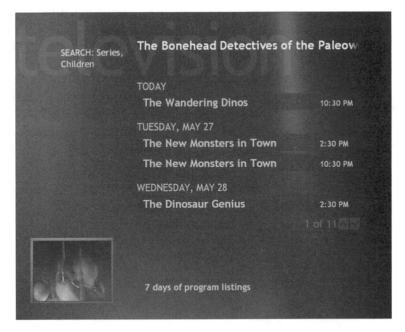

3. When you have the series episode you want highlighted, you can press Rec twice to record the series using default settings described previously.

4. As an option, you can select the series episode you highlighted previously, and select the Record Series option (see Figure 8.7).

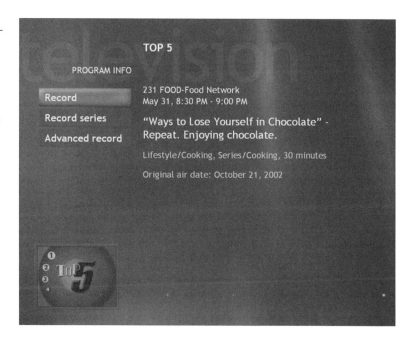

FIGURE 8.7

This Program Info page from search results offers another opportunity to record a series, a single episode, or access the Advanced Record menu.

Fine-Tuning Your Recordings

You have mastered the basics of recording single shows and series from live TV, search results, and the program guide, as well as recording manually and automatically. But there are many more options available to fine-tune your recordings, helping you maximize your enjoyment and minimize wasted time and disk space.

Advanced Record Features

In all the recording situations described previously, you have the opportunity to access Advanced Record features, which allow you to change the settings that Media Center uses to record your shows. The advanced record settings available to you may vary, depending on the type of recording you have selected, but you may be able to control some or all of the following attributes:

- **Frequency**: Choose Record Single Show for a one-time-only recording, or Record Series to instruct Media Center to record multiple shows on an ongoing basis.

- **Show Type**: (Available only when recording a series.) You can choose First Run or First Run & Rerun. With First Run, Media Center records only shows included in the new season. Choosing First Run & Rerun tells Media Center to record both new season episodes and shows that previously aired.

- **Record On**: (Available only when recording a series.) This setting lets you choose between the currently selected channel and the currently selected time, or the current channel at any time, or Any Channel, which allows Media Center to search on all available channels for the series you want to record.

- **Allow For**: (Available only when recording a series.) Tells Media Center how many shows to record each day. Choices are either One Per Day or Multiple Per Day.

- **Keep Up To**: (Available only when recording a series or from a keyword search.) Select the maximum number of shows in a series that you want to store on your hard drive at any point in time. Choose to keep from one to five episodes, or All Episodes.

- **Keep**: This setting tells Media Center when it can delete a recording from the hard disk. There are four options: Until Space Needed, Until I Delete, Until I Watch, or For 1 Week.

- **Quality**: Select from four image quality settings: Fair, Good, Better, or Best. Bear in mind that the better the image quality, the bigger the file size will be on the hard disk—meaning less room for your recordings. Thus, the default quality option—Best—will record TV with the clearest and most detailed image, but it will take the biggest bite out of your hard disk. (For a more in-depth discussion of recording quality levels, see "A Word About Quality and Quantity," later in this chapter.)

- **Start**: Sometimes being on time is still too late. For instance, if you have reason to believe that the program you want to record will actually start earlier than the guide schedule indicates, you can choose to begin recording before the show's scheduled start time. Choices include starting your recording On Time, 1 Minute Before, 2 Minutes Before, 3 Minutes Before, 5 Minutes Before, 15 Minutes Before, or 30 Minutes Before the scheduled start time of the show. The default setting begins the recording On Time.

- **Stop**: If you suspect that the show may run longer than its scheduled end time suggests, you can also choose to continue recording up to 3 hours after the scheduled

> **tip**
>
> To change Advanced Record settings, use the navigation buttons on the remote and OK to select the + or – symbols. Keep pressing OK to toggle through the various choices for each category. After you have made the desired changes, select Record to save your preferences. To cancel the changes, press Back on the remote.

stop time shown in the program guide. Choices include the default setting of On Time, or 1, 2, 3, 5, or 30 Minutes After the scheduled end time of the show. Alternatively, you can choose 1, 2, or 3 Hours After.

To reach the Advance Record settings page (see Figure 8.8) directly, follow these steps:

1. Press My TV on the remote.
2. Select Search or Guide.
3. Highlight a show you want to record.
4. Press the More Info button on the remote (for HP systems, press the Details button).
5. Select Advanced Record.

FIGURE 8.8
Advanced Record settings let you select from a multitude of options, from recording a single show to recording an entire series.

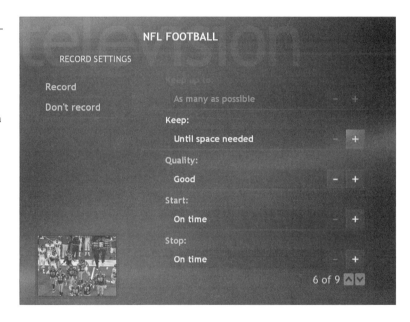

A Word About Quality and Quantity

Media Center recordings are stored in a new data file format called DVR-MS. This format uses the MPEG2 (Motion Picture Experts Group 2) compression technique to squeeze the video into as small a file as possible, without sacrificing too much video display quality. This balancing act between file size and visual quality represents the eternal struggle in handling video files on a computer.

As of this writing, there are no commercial software products that allow a DVR-MS to be edited or converted to other file formats (though Microsoft says it's working with third-party software manufacturers to make that happen). Although a few hand-coded shareware utilities have cropped up to permit these functions, their performance is unreliable and results can be disappointing. The upshot is that after the file is recorded, you're pretty much stuck with it—at least for now—so make your recording choices up front to ensure the results you want.

One of the most important choices is which quality setting to use. There are two factors to consider: quality and quantity. The quality setting you choose will directly impact the quantity of video you are able to store on your system's hard drive. Here are some points to consider when making your decision:

- **Quality** refers to actual video resolution, and it can be pretty subjective. Try recording programs at different quality settings to find out which setting gives you the most satisfactory results. If everything looks fine to you at "good" quality, don't waste disk space recording everything at the "best" quality level. You may also want to consider the type of show, and what you are watching it for. If it's a movie you've been waiting for, and you really want it to be a feast for the eyes, record it at a high quality level setting. If it's a show you are recording only in order to gather some information—such as the winning Lotto numbers—and you plan to immediately erase it afterward, there's no need to waste precious disk space. Consider recording it at the lowest quality setting.

- **Quantity,** in this case, refers to how large video files are after you record them. This is a direct function of the quality setting you selected, and the length of the show. Table 8.1 describes the difference in file sizes, measured in gigabytes per hour of video, for each of Media Center's four levels of recording quality: Fair, Good, Better, and Best.

Table 8.1   File Size Versus Recording Quality

Quality Setting	Approximate GB/Hour
Fair	1.0
Good	2.0
Better	2.5
Best	3.0

Recorder Settings

Now that you're familiar with setting the Advanced Record options for each program you record, you may want to make some changes to the basic default settings. This way, all your recordings will be set up with the same options and values you prefer—unless you decide to change them for a particular recording.

In addition to setting the recorder default values, the Recorder Settings menu (see Figure 8.9) also allows you to check your guide download history, and view or make changes to the video storage capacity on your hard drive.

FIGURE 8.9

The Recorder Settings menu lets you view and adjust detailed settings for hard disk video recording from My TV programming sources.

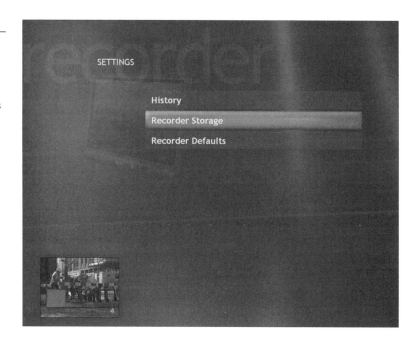

To reach the Recorder Settings menu, follow these steps:

1. Select My TV on the remote control.
2. Select Settings.
3. Select Recorder.
4. Select Recording Defaults.

Recorder Defaults

From this Recording Defaults screen (see Figure 8.10), you are able to fine-tune the default parameters for recording all TV programs on your Media PC. Using the procedures described earlier in this chapter, you can adjust the basic settings for all recordings in the following categories: Quality, Keep, Start, and Stop. You can also change the following default values for series recording: Show Type, Record On, Allow For, and Keep at Most.

After you have made your selections and changes, choose Save to put them into effect.

FIGURE 8.10

The Recording
Defaults page is
useful for chang-
ing the universal
settings that will
apply to every
TV program you
record.

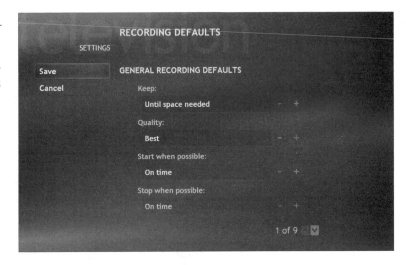

Recorder Storage

The Recorder Storage screen (see Figure 8.11) allows you to check the status of your hard drive's recording capacity, and adjust it to suit your storage needs. Here are some of the values you can check and control from this screen:

- **Record on Drive**: This setting allows you to select which disk drive Recorded TV will be stored on.

- **Disk Allocation**: This feature allows you to adjust the percentage of your disk drive that Media Center can use to store Recorded TV. Recorded TV files can never exceed the limit you set here.

- **Recording Quality**: Select Fair, Good, Better, or Best. Remember that the better the quality, the more disk space the recording will require.

- **Maximum Recording Time**: This displays the total video recording time available on your hard drive. Maximum Recording Time is calculated based on your disk allocation percentage, the size of your hard drive, and the default Recording Quality setting. If you change one or more of those values, your Maximum Recording Time will adjust automatically.

- **Unused Recording Time**: This displays the actual amount of recording time

caution

Media Center does not support Recorded TV storage on removable drives, network drives, or drives with less than 5GB of disk space.

currently left on your hard drive. As with Maximum Recording Time, the unused recording time changes based on your disk allocation percentage, drive size, and Recording Quality choices.

If you want to make any changes to your storage parameters, be sure to select Save and press OK on the remote control to apply the changes and return to the TV Settings menu.

FIGURE 8.11

As its default settings, Media Center allocates 75% of all disk storage to video, and records everything at the Best quality setting.

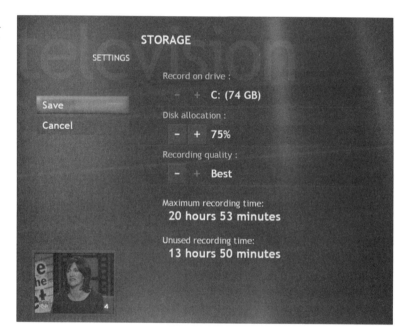

History

Media Center keeps track of your recording activities, and you can view this information by selecting History from the Recorder Settings menu (see Figure 8.12). You will be able to view explicit details of each recording attempt, including whether Media Center was successful. You can also choose one of the Sort By tabs to list all recordings by date, status, or name. Want to get a fresh start? Just select the Clear History tab to delete the current recording history information.

FIGURE 8.12

The History screen under Recorder Settings allows you to check Media Center's records, listing each recording event.

THE ABSOLUTE MiNiMUM

After you've gotten a taste of the ease with which Media Center My TV allows you to record television programs, the methods you previously used to record programs on VHS tapes will seem as antiquated as churning butter by hand. Some of the features we discussed in this chapter included the following:

- Recording the program you are currently watching is as simple as pressing the Rec button. And because Media Center stores the most recent half hour of live TV in memory, even if you start recording a few minutes late, you'll still be able to record your show from the beginning.

- You can set up a timed recording effortlessly from search results or the program guide. Just highlight the show you want and press Rec.

- You can also create a manual recording, or an auto-record session to capture an important show the next time it airs, even if the show doesn't currently appear on the program guide.

- Recording an entire series is as easy as pressing the Rec button twice. You'll never need to miss another episode of your favorite TV series.

- Media Center allows you to adjust many of its video recording parameters to customize copies of TV shows stored on your hard drive. You can apply your choice of settings to a single show, or change the default settings for all TV recordings.

PART III

My Videos

9

PLAYING AND ORGANIZING YOUR DIGITAL MOVIES

There's more to video than just television. In the preceding part of this book, we discussed Media Center's prowess in the area of television viewing and recording, but TV is only one potential source of video for your Media PC. Your system is also thoroughly proficient at handling video derived from other sources, including DVDs, the Web, and even your own camcorder.

In this chapter, we'll look at some of Media Center's basic video-handling capabilities regarding content that is not provided by your TV programming service. These features are not accessed through Media Center's My TV interface. Instead, you'll want to select the My Videos menu item from the Media Center Start page (see Figure 9.1).

FIGURE 9.1

The My Videos
section of Media
Center is the pri-
mary place to
play and organ-
ize your collec-
tion of digital
video files.

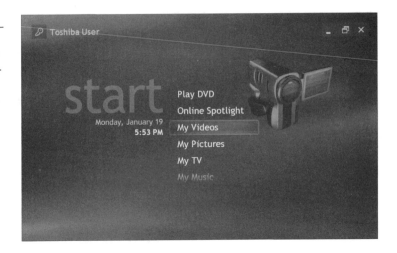

Navigating My Videos

When you launch My Videos by selecting it from the Start page (as shown in Figure 9.1), or by pressing the My Videos shortcut button on your remote control, you'll be greeted by a screenful of thumbnail images representing your digital video files, stacked on the right side of the screen (see Figure 9.2). You may also see thumbnails representing additional folders on your hard disk, where video may be stored.

On the left side of the screen, you'll see a menu, offering the following choices: Sort by Name, Sort by Date, My Videos, Shared Video, and Other Media. To move between the menu and the folders, use the arrow keys on the remote.

At the lower-right corner of the My Videos screen, you'll see a counter indicating how many videos are available in the current folder. Next to that, you'll find a pair of scroll arrows. These features are common to many Media Center display screens (in fact, you may have already noticed them on the search results pages discussed in previous chapters). If you have a large collection of digital video files, you can use the arrow buttons on the remote to

note

If you're just starting out and don't have any video files in your My Videos or Shared Video folders yet, you'll see the message "There are no files in this folder."

scroll up or scroll down, or click the onscreen scroll arrows with the mouse. These arrows will also indicate what direction you are scrolling in. If you have only a few video files, the arrows will be "grayed out," as shown in Figure 9.2.

FIGURE 9.2

This initial view of My Videos shows the video thumbnails organized on the right and menu items on the left.

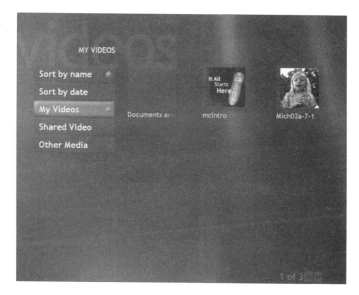

When you find a video you want to watch, simply select it by pressing the OK or Play button on the remote (or click on the thumbnail with the mouse), and it will begin playing in full-screen mode. When the video ends, My Videos will ask whether you want to see it again, or return to the My Videos home page (see Figure 9.3).

FIGURE 9.3

This screen appears when the digital video file stops playing.

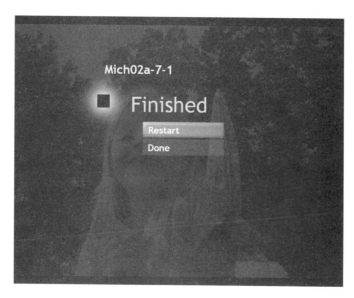

Organizing and Sorting Videos

Digital video files can be placed in My Videos folders manually or automatically. For example, when you capture digital videos from your camcorder directly into your Media Center PC, Windows stores them in the My Videos folder by default. (For more details on capturing video, see Chapter 10, "Capturing and Creating Videos with Media Center.")

Media Center's My Videos interface looks for video files in only three places: The My Videos folder, the Shared Video folder, and on Other Media, which refers to removable media such as CD-ROM disks or media cards. Each of these video destinations has a slightly different purpose and location.

My Videos Folder

The My Videos folder is physically located on your primary storage disk drive, usually at C:\Documents and Settings\Administrator\My Documents\My Videos. As mentioned previously, this is the default location for storing digital video files imported into your Media Center PC (this doesn't include shows recorded in My TV). Video files stored in this folder are accessible only to users who log on as the main administrator of your system. This becomes an important distinction if you plan to set up any passwords or additional identities (see Part VII, "Advanced Media Center Settings and Options," for more information) .

Shared Video

The Shared Video folder is also physically located on your primary storage disk drive, usually at C:\Documents and Settings\All Users\Documents\Shared Video. When videos are stored in the Shared Video folder, they will be accessible to all users of your system, as well as other users on your local area network, if you so choose.

Other Media

The Other Media tab in the My Videos interface refers to removable media, such as CD-ROMs containing video files. Some Media Center PCs may also offer built-in readers for Smart Media cards and other types of compact memory

caution

To avoid causing a software conflict, it's a good idea to exit from My Videos back to the Media Center Start page before ejecting a disk that you were accessing using Other Media. Otherwise, you are likely to get an error message indicating that the disk cannot be ejected because another application is still using it.

devices that are often used to store and transfer media files from cameras, music players, and other devices.

To access video files stored on a removable device using My Videos' Other Media capability, follow these steps:

1. While Media Center is running in full-screen mode, insert the disk and wait for the Media Inserted notification window to appear (see Figure 9.4).

2. Select whether the media you inserted contains video of picture files.

3. If you select video, Media Center will take you to My Videos menu so you can watch the media files.

FIGURE 9.4

This pop-up window appears when you insert a disk or another removable media device that contains media files.

Sorting Videos

Using the Sort By tabs on the My Videos page, you can quickly arrange your videos in alphabetical order, or by the date on which they were loaded onto your Media Center machine.

To sort your videos in alphabetical order, starting with the letter A (ascending order), select the Sort by Name tab.

To sort your videos by date order, starting with the oldest file, select the Sort by Date tab. To view more detailed information on when the file was created and modified, highlight the video thumbnail and press More Info on the remote control (see Figure 9.5) .

FIGURE 9.5
Along with file history, pressing the More Info button on the remote displays the file size and an onscreen Play button.

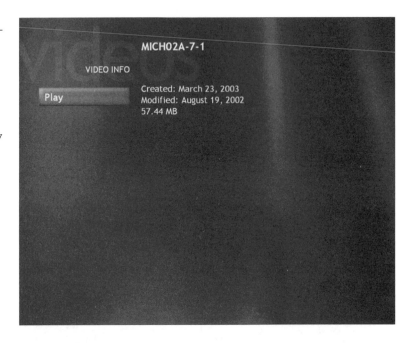

Watching Videos

You can watch various digital video types using Media Center's My Videos interface. A list of supported video file formats appears in Table 9.1.

Table 9.1 Supported Video Formats

File Type/Format	Filename Extension
Windows Media files	.wm, .asf
Windows Media A/V files	.wmv
Video files	.avi
Movie files	.mpeg, .mpg, .mpe, .m1v, .mp2, .mpv2

To launch a video file, just make sure that it's stored in one of the directories listed previously, or on a removable media device. If your video files are stored in hard drive folders other than the ones mentioned here, you can open Windows

tip

Media Center can support additional video file formats, but first you may need to install a new codec. According to Microsoft, *codec* stands for "compressor/decompressor" and refers primarily to software used to do just that: compress or decompress digital video. The filename extensions shown in Table 9.1 each represent different codecs that are already supported within Windows XP Media Center Edition.

Explorer (select Start, All Programs, Windows Explorer) and drag and drop the files into the My Videos or Shared Video folders.

Using the Transport Controls in My Videos

The transport controls on your remote—Fwd, Rew, Pause, Replay, Skip, and so on—may not all be supported when you play back files in My Videos. The degree of support varies depending on the file type. (For details on using the transport controls, see Chapter 4, "Navigating XP Media Center's '10-Foot' Interface.")

Sharing Videos

In most cases, when you capture video either directly from your camcorder or by using an add-on video capture device for digitizing video images, Windows XP Media Center edition will automatically store the file in your My Videos directory. My Videos is a good place to keep files that are only for your personal viewing, or that are "works in progress" which require additional editing.

However, if you want to make your videos available for other users of your Media Center system or your home network to watch, you'll need to copy them to the Shared Videos folder. The files then can be viewed by everyone who uses the Media Center computer, or who has access to your Shared Video folder via a connected PC.

There are several ways to move files from My Videos to Shared Video, but here is one of the simplest:

1. If you are within the Media Center interface, select Minimize.
2. Using the mouse, click the Start button on the Windows XP taskbar.
3. Click once on My Documents, and then click twice on My Videos.
4. Click once on the file you want to share, and hold the mouse button down to drag the object.
5. Drag the video thumbnail image over to the Shared Video folder link that appears in the left margin under the heading Other Places.
6. Release the mouse button, and the file will be moved into the Shared Video folder (see Figure 9.6) .

FIGURE 9.6

When a video
file is dragged
on top of the
Shared Video
folder link, the
thumbnail
image becomes
transparent so
you can view the
link underneath.

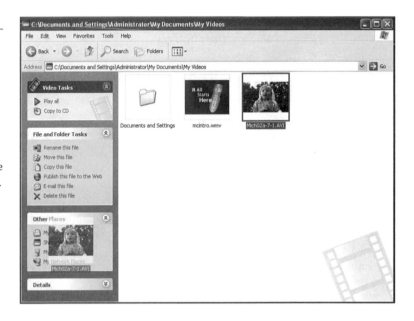

Using Shortcuts to Watch Videos

If you want to store your videos in folders other than My Videos or Shared Videos, but you still want to watch them using Media Center's My Video interface, there is an alternative to relocating the files. Rather than physically moving or copying your digital video files into the My Videos or Shared Videos folder, you can place shortcuts in those folders pointing to the videos, or to the folders where you keep them.

Say, for example, that your wedding video is located in a folder you have created, such as C:\Wedding\Videos. You can create a shortcut to that folder in the My Videos or Shared Videos folder so that when you go to the My Videos section of Media Center, you'll be able to select the shortcut and watch the wedding. Your shortcut can lead to a single video, or to a folder that contains multiple videos.

Here's how to do it:

1. From within Media Center, select Minimize to access the Windows XP desktop interface.

2. With the mouse, click the Start button on the taskbar, click My Documents, and then click on the My Videos folder.

3. If you want to create the shortcut in the Shared Videos folder, select the Shared Video link shown under Other Places, or browse to the Shared Videos folder, which is located at C:\Documents and Settings\All Users\Documents\ My Videos.

4. On the File menu, select New, and then click Shortcut.

5. This launches the Create Shortcut wizard (see Figure 9.7), which prompts you for the complete name of the video folder or file you want to link to. Enter the location, or click the Browse button to browse to the location of the folder or file.

6. Follow the onscreen instructions in the wizard, and select Finish.

Now when you return to Media Center's My Videos page, you'll see that a thumbnail is available for the video file or folder shortcut you created. You can select that image to launch the video or open the directory.

FIGURE 9.7

In the Create Shortcut wizard, be sure to enter the complete name of the directory or file you want to play from My Videos.

Troubleshooting My Videos

The My Videos section of Media Center is essentially a prettied-up file manager, specifically designed to give you access to video files from inside Media Center, using your remote control. Even though it's simple to operate, there are a few things that can occasionally go wrong. Following are some examples, and some explanations or suggestions for correcting the problems.

My Videos Displays the Wrong Thumbnail

Sometimes the thumbnail image in My Videos will not seem to match what you know is inside the video file itself. This happens when Media Center fails to identify an appropriate video frame for the thumbnail. In these cases, Media Center displays a generic thumbnail instead. It doesn't necessarily mean that your digital video file has a problem, or that it won't play properly, only that Media enter wasn't able to extract a thumbnail image from the video.

My Videos Won't Play the File

Sometimes the problem goes deeper than just being unable to generate a thumbnail. In cases in which the video file cannot be launched, it may be that the video data is corrupted or stored in an unsupported format (for a list of supported formats, see Table 9.1).

If this happens to you, here are a few things to try:

- Open the file with a video editor, such as Windows Movie Maker 2 (for details, see Chapter 10), and then resave it in a supported format.
- The problem could also be with the codec. Try using Windows Media Player to open the file, which may prompt Windows to download and install the necessary codec automatically. (For details on launching Windows Media Player, see Chapter 13, "Preparing Your Music Collection for XP Media Center.")

THE ABSOLUTE MINIMUM

When it comes to digital video on the Media Center platform, there's more that meets the eye than television alone. Digital video files are becoming increasingly easy and fun to create and share. That's exactly why Microsoft added a home for these files within Media Center. Media Center's My Videos allows you to switch effortlessly between home movies and other videos, and the stored and live TV programming available via Media Center's My TV interface. When you're using My Videos, here are some of the important things to keep in mind:

- Whereas My TV uses an electronic program guide and text listings to represent video programs, My Videos uses thumbnail images to help you navigate, organize, and launch video files. Get used to this type of interface, because you'll be seeing more of it as we explore entertainment features based on audio and still images in the coming chapters.

- Media Center looks for digital video files in only a few folders—the My Videos folder or the Shared Video folder. If you want to play your videos from within Media Center, you'll have to store your files—or at least create a shortcut—in one of those folders.

- My Videos is also designed to play back video files stored on removable disks and other storage media. Just be careful to exit from My Videos before you eject a disk containing video.

- My Videos automatically catalogs your video files, and allows you to sort them by name or date with the press of a button.

- Watching a digital video file is as easy as selecting the file and pressing Play. But if you want other users to be able to watch it as well, you'll need to place a copy or a shortcut in your Shared Video folder.

10

CAPTURING AND CREATING VIDEOS WITH MEDIA CENTER

If you own and operate a camcorder, one of the most satisfying experiences you're likely to have with your Media Center PC is capturing video you created, and then being able to simply and effectively display it and share it using Media Center's My Videos interface.

While the underlying operating system—Windows XP—does most of the heavy lifting in this exercise, there's something wonderful about using the Media Center remote control to switch effortlessly from a movie made by Spielberg or Scorsese to one made by you. Yes, your audience may notice some subtle differences in the production values, but they'll have to admit that home movies have come a long way from the days of dimming the lights and firing up the old Super 8 projector.

Connecting to Your Camcorder

The first step in making your masterpiece is to move your "raw footage" from the camcorder to your Media Center PC. Start by taking stock of your connection situation. This means literally taking a hard look at your camcorder to determine its video output options, and then scrutinizing your Media Center PC to check out its video input capabilities. Obviously, the goal is to find a match.

Most, if not all, Media Center PCs support a FireWire (IEEE-1394) high-speed connector for just this purpose. If you have a reasonably recent model of camcorder, chances are that you will have a match in terms of a 1394 input on the PC (see Figure 10.1) and a 1394 output on the camera (see Figure 10.2). If you do, count your blessings, because you're about to find out what great engineering is all about.

FIGURE 10.1

This close-up of the IEEE-1394 FireWire input port on a Media Center PC is your best bet for high-quality, high-speed transfers of video from your camcorder.

FireWire technology, first introduced on PCs made by Apple, is more than just a superfast serial bus connection. When you connect a new device using FireWire, the system automatically recognizes the device, and generally knows what to do with it. You'll see that in action a little later in this chapter.

However, if you don't have FireWire connectivity, you'll probably need to establish an analog connection to transfer video from your camcorder to your PC. Find yourself a match (camcorder output, PC input) using RCA type connectors, coaxial cables, or S-Video. (For examples of these connector types, see Figure 2.2 in Chapter 2.)

note

Remember that if you connect your camcorder video to your PC using an S-Video cable, you will still need to connect an audio cable of some kind—unless you have decided to capture the spirit of the Silent Movie Era. You may opt for a cable that connects the twin RCA-type audio output jacks to a 1/8-inch stereo plug (see Figure 2.4 in Chapter 2 for an example of a 1/8-inch-to-RCA Y-patch cable).

FIGURE 10.2

This close-up of the IEEE-1394 FireWire port on the back of a JVC Digital CyberCam (marked "DV IN/OUT") provides a perfect match for transferring digital video data to the FireWire port on a Media Center PC.

Making the Connection

The first thing you'll need is the right cable. If you are lucky enough to be able to connect directly and digitally via FireWire, you'll need a 1394 cable, such as the one shown in Figure 10.3.

FIGURE 10.3

A 1394 FireWire connector cable like this may or may not be included as standard equipment with your camcorder or your PC.

Plug one end of the cable into the 1394 receptacle on your camera, and the other end into its counterpart on the PC, and you're in business.

Capturing Video

After you have the cables connected, do the following:

1. Switch the camcorder on. In a moment, the PC will sense the new device and display a pop-up window such as the one shown in Figure 10.4.

FIGURE 10.4

This What Do You Want Windows to Do? window allows you to establish a video capture connection between your camcorder and a video editing application.

2. With your mouse, select Capture Video Using Windows Movie Maker. If you're reasonably sure that you'll want to do the same thing every time you connect your camcorder, you can also check the box that says Always Perform the Selected Action.

3. Click OK.

4. In the following pop-up screens, select your camcorder device, and specify a name and location for your captured video. The default video storage location is the My Videos folder.

5. The Video Capture Wizard will then ask you to pick a video capture rate (see Figure 10.5). The recommended setting is Best Quality for Playback on My Computer, which captures the video using an eye-pleasing 640-by-480-pixel resolution and 30 frames per second.

note

Although Windows Movie Maker is a free program that comes bundled with Windows XP, many other excellent video capture and editing programs are available for the Windows platform from third-party software developers such as Adobe, Ulead, and Roxio. If you do decide to stick with the least expensive option (it's hard to beat free), make sure that you've got the most up-to-date version of Windows Movie Maker by visiting www.microsoft.com/windowsxp/mo viemaker and downloading the latest revision.

FIGURE 10.5

If you are planning to edit your video on the PC, and then record your final movie back to tape on your camcorder, Windows Movie Maker recommends selecting the DV-AVI video setting.

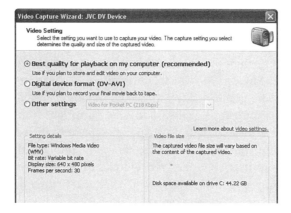

6. Choose between capturing the entire tape automatically and capturing parts of the tape manually. The simplest method is simply to capture the entire tape. You can always edit it down to size after it has been stored on your PC.

7. Click Next, and Movie Maker will begin capturing your video.

After the video capture is complete, Windows Movie Maker will open a project page displaying your video as a series of scenes (see Figure 10.6). Now you're ready to begin the editing process and create your movie.

FIGURE 10.6

Windows Movie Maker automatically divides your video into segments, or scenes, so you can drag and drop them onto the storyboard.

Using Windows Movie Maker

Although more expensive and full-featured video editing products are available, your Media Center PC includes a very capable program that covers all the basics, and quite a bit more. Windows Movie Maker is designed to let you edit and share your home movies—all on your desktop with drag-and-drop ease. You can also add various transitions, special effects, music, and even narration. Finally, your Media Center PC allows you to display your finished masterpiece to friends and family right in your entertainment center, or use the communications features of Movie Maker to distribute your movie via the Web, email, or removable media. (You can also create DVDs from your movie, which we'll discuss in greater detail in Chapter 12, "Creating DVDs on an XP Media Center.")

Creating Your Video

The basic idea of editing video involves deciding which stuff to take out, and which to leave in, and then putting it all together in just the right order. At the professional level, it is an art form that can take a lifetime to perfect, and the top craftsperson in the field is honored each year with an Academy Award. Well, everyone has to start somewhere, and dragging and dropping together a montage of family scenes is as good a way as any.

Editing Your Clips

Movie Maker has already separated your video into clips, or scenes, based on changes in the video itself. You'll find that the clips are usually of various lengths, and seem to start and end in ways that correspond to events that occur in the video, such as switching from one location to the next.

You can preview individual clips by selecting them with your mouse or remote control. With the mouse, play the clip by clicking on the Play arrow in the transport controls provided at the bottom of the preview window (see the close-up in Figure 10.7). With the remote, you can highlight the clip and press OK to play it.

FIGURE 10.7

In addition to the Play button, the transport control bar in Movie Maker has buttons for Stop, Back, Previous Frame, Next Frame, Forward, Split and Still Picture.

If you want to use the clip as-is, just drag it to one of the empty Storyboard squares at the bottom of the screen to place it in your movie. If you want to modify the clip, here are some options:

- **Combine clips**—To turn two or more contiguous clips back into one longer clip, hold down the Ctrl key and select the clips you want to combine, and then open the Clip menu and click on Combine.

- **Split clips**—To separate a single clip into two discrete clips, preview the clip and pause it at the point where you want to split it. Then click on the Split button in the transport controls (see Figure 10.7).

- **Trim clips**—This procedure is done from within the Timeline view. Drag a clip into the Storyboard, and then click on Show Timeline. Then, by dragging the Trim Handles (see the illustration in Figure 10.8) at the beginning and end of each clip, you can include or exclude portions of the video.

> **tip**
>
> A shortcut for selecting multiple contiguous clips is to click on the first clip, then hold down the Shift key while you click the last clip in the series. To select one clip at a time, hold down the Ctrl key while you click on each clip.

FIGURE 10.8

This close-up of the Timeline view shows where the Start and End Trim Handles are located. Just click and drag them to lengthen or shorten your clip.

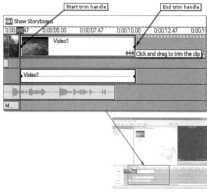

Adding Transitions

Video transitions knit your clips together, and can make the difference between a series of disjointed clips strung together and a cohesive cinematic experience. Best of all, they make it very easy to dress up your home movies and give them a professional flair.

You can place transitions in your movie project in various ways. Here's one of the simplest, which you can perform while in the Storyboard view:

1. Select Tools.

2. Select Video Transitions. Movie Maker will replace your palette of clips with a screenful of transition choices (see Figure 10.9).

3. Click on the transition you want, and drag it to the transition cell, which is a small box that separates any two clips on the Storyboard.

4. Click on Play in the preview window to see how your transition looks.

tip

You can try out as many transitions as you want. Just keep dragging and dropping them on the transition cell until you find a keeper.

FIGURE 10.9

Windows Movie Maker offers you 60 transitions, from Bar to Zig Zag.

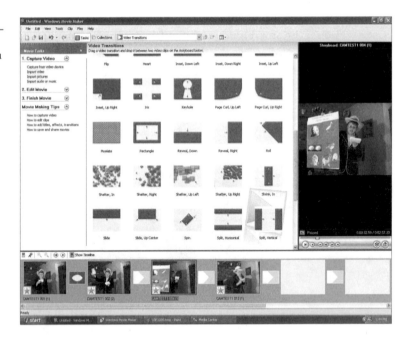

Adding Titles

Titles are another way to give your homemade video a professional touch. Here's how to use them:

1. Select Tools.

2. Select Titles and Credits.

3. Movie Maker will display the question Where Do You Want to Add a Title? Select the appropriate answer.

4. Movie Maker will display a text input box (see Figure 10.10). Type your text. Anything you type in the lower of the two title boxes will appear in smaller type, below the main title, and will fade in slightly after the primary title appears. When finished, click Done, Add Title to Movie.

FIGURE 10.10

As you type the title text, Movie Maker will display it in the preview window..

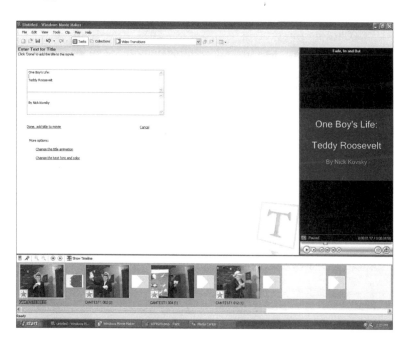

You can also choose Change the Title Animation, or Change the Text Font and Color, to further customize your titles.

Adding Effects

Video effects are available to provide various interesting visual enhancements to your clips, from fading in or out, to giving your video a sepia tone, or even a watercolor look. Simply choose Video Effects from the Tools menu, and then drag and drop the desired effect onto the clip you want to change.

Adding Audio

Creating a music soundtrack or adding audio effects is another way to add interest and depth to your movie project. The right tune or noise at just the right moment can turn a humdrum production into a comic or dramatic masterpiece—or at least help keep your viewers from falling asleep on the sofa.

To import music or other audio files, follow these steps:

1. Select Import Audio or Music from the Movie Tasks pane, or choose Import into Collections from the File menu.

2. Browse to find the directory that contains your audio file, and select it.

3. Click on Import.

4. Movie Maker will display a Collections page containing the audio you imported (see Figure 10.11). You can import multiple files, if you want.

5. Drag and drop the audio file you want onto the Timeline. You can place it wherever you want and use the Trim Handles to adjust the length. You can also right-click on the clip and make additional selections, such as fade in or out, adjust its volume, or mute it.

tip

You can also add narration to your video. Just plug a microphone into your Media Center PC, and select Narrate Timeline from the Tools menu. Click Start Narration to begin. Using headphones when narrating your video is a good idea, because playing the audio of your movie through the Media Center PC's speakers while you are recording may cause the audio to be recaptured as part of your narration, creating unnecessary background noise.

FIGURE 10.11

The Collections screen displays files you have imported into your movie project.

Saving and Storing Your Movie

Perhaps the most important part of creating your movie project is saving it. Because there are various options, Windows Movie Maker provides a Save Movie Wizard (see Figure 10.12) to help you navigate the process.

FIGURE 10.12

The Save Movie Wizard will guide you through the procedure for finalizing your movie, and storing it in various ways to suit your needs.

Choices provided in the Save Movie Wizard include the following:

- **My Computer**—Lets you save your movie to your local computer hard drive, or to a shared network location.

- **Recordable CD**—Lets you save your movie to a recordable or rewritable CD (CD-R or CD-RW). This option, naturally, requires that your Media Center PC is equipped with a CD-R or CD-RW drive, and a blank disk.

- **Email**—Lets you save your movie as an attachment to send in an email message. This option is a good way to share smaller movies with family or friends, by attaching the file to an email using your default email program.

- **The Web**—Lets you send your movie to a video hosting provider on the Web. This option will allow you to save your movie so that family and friends can watch it via the Internet—anywhere, at any time.

- **DV Camera**—Lets you record your movie back onto a tape in your DV (digital video) camera. This option requires that you have a DV camera connected to the PC via an IEEE 1394 port.

To start the Save Movie Wizard, just select Save Movie File from the File menu, and follow the onscreen prompts. The final page of the wizard will give you an option to play the movie when you click Finish.

Using AutoMovie

If you want a fast and hassle-free way to create your movie, Microsoft has provided a feature called AutoMovie. It will automatically take a collection of video clips, audio clips, still pictures, and music, and combine them into a finished movie project.

To make an AutoMovie, this is what you do:

1. Create a collection containing all the elements you want to use. Or select an existing collection by clicking on Collections in the View menu. This will open the Collection pane and allow you to click on the collection you want to use.

2. From the Tools menu, select AutoMovie.

3. Choose an AutoMovie editing style. These include Highlights Movie, Music Video, Old Movie, and others.

4. Under More Options, click on Enter a Title for the Movie.

5. Under Enter Text for Title, type the text you want to appear as the title for the AutoMovie.

6. Under More Options, click Select Audio or Background Music.

7. On the Audio and Music Files selection page, choose an audio or music file from the drop-down list, or click Browse to import an audio or music file stored elsewhere on your hard drive.

8. Select Done, Edit Movie to begin creating the AutoMovie.

The amount of time required to make the AutoMovie will vary, depending on the length and number of the audio and video clips you chose to include in your movie.

When the AutoMovie is finished, it will appear in the storyboard/timeline in your Movie Maker project. You can preview the AutoMovie from within Movie Maker, but it will be necessary to save the movie using the procedure outlined previously (see the preceding section, "Saving and Storing Your Movie") before it can be viewed outside of Movie Maker.

THE ABSOLUTE MINIMUM

Nothing worth watching on Media Center's My TV? That's not a problem, because your Media Center PC offers all the tools to create your own video entertainment—from scratch. When you capture and create your own videos, remember these points:

- An IEEE 1394 FireWire connection is the best bet for getting your camcorder and your Media Center PC to talk to each other. In most cases, Media Center will recognize your camera immediately, making the transfer of video onto your PC's hard drive a snap.

- Windows XP's built-in video editing software, Windows Movie Maker, is both serviceable and free with your system. To ensure that you have the latest version, visit the Movie Maker Web site at www.microsoft.com/windowsxp/moviemaker.

- When you choose the option Capture Video Using Windows Movie Maker, the program will automatically store your video on disk, and divide it into clips for easy editing.

- Mix and match clips on your Storyboard or Timeline, and then add titles, transitions, audio, and visual effects. When you're finished, Movie Maker will guide you through the process of saving your movie for viewing within Media Center, or for sharing with others in various ways.

- Don't forget, if you want to watch your movies via Media Center's My Video interface, you must store them in either the My Videos folder or the Shared Video folder. (For details, see "Organizing and Sorting Videos," in Chapter 9, "Playing and Organizing Your Digital Movies.")

PART IV

PLAYING AND RECORDING DVDs

11

WATCHING DVDs ON AN XP MEDIA CENTER PC

One of the most seductive qualities of the Windows Media Center machine is its chameleon-like capability to take on the characteristics of so many different devices, effectively eliminating your need for numerous standalone entertainment components such as a home stereo system, a television, and, not least, a DVD player.

The basic DVD playback features of Media Center are designed to be as simple and straightforward to operate as those of any conventional DVD player. However, many of these standalone players have expanded their resume in recent years, adding advanced capabilities to fine-tune your DVD watching experience.

The problem is that these devices are limited in how they allow you to access these advanced features. Generally, a dedicated button is required for each feature, from Menu to Skip. As a consequence, their remote controls are bristling with buttons, and most consumers will never take the time to ascertain the functions or learn the use of most of them.

Media Center has the upper hand in this design conundrum. Simple playback tasks are assigned to dedicated buttons on the remote control, but because that remote is communicating with a sophisticated multipurpose multimedia machine, it also gives you access to underlying layers of software menus that let you thoroughly customize your viewing experience. The result is that it's much easier to unlock those hidden features that are often difficult to fathom and configure using today's standalone DVD players.

Of course, you can also climb into the "cockpit" of your Media Center and manage your DVD playback with mouse and keyboard. It's just a matter of personal preference, and how much control you want to exert over your home theatre experience.

Basic DVD Playback

One of the admirable qualities of the Media Center design is that it knows when to lay back and keep a low profile. You just want to relax and watch a movie? Slip the disc into the DVD drive and let Media Center do the rest.

Watching Full-Screen

When you put a DVD in the drive while Media Center is displayed, it will automatically begin playing. The entire Media Center screen will be used

caution

If you insert a DVD disc when the Windows XP desktop is displayed, such as when the Media Center interface is not running or has been minimized, Windows should open an option window and ask whether you want to play the disc. More insidiously, the disc manufacturer may have included a DVD player application of its own that automatically opens a setup window and asks whether it can begin installing the software.

Choose carefully! For one thing, you already have a very capable default DVD player application within Media Center, so there's really no need to install an additional one. Also, that third-party DVD player application may turn your machine into a remote "client" for the DVD maker, including launching Web-enabled applications designed to entice you into a marketing relationship with the manufacturer. Unless you want to register with the company that made the movie you're about to watch, and participate in its online promotions and marketing plans, it may be that you should "just say no."

to display the DVD movie. If you are using Media Center in a window on your Windows XP desktop, you may want to switch to full-screen viewing mode to maximize the visual playback quality.

If you insert a DVD when Media Center is not running, Windows XP will prompt you to see what you want to do with the disc (see Figure 11.1). Choose Play DVD Video Using Media Center.

What do you do if you inadvertently make the wrong choice in the What Do You Want Windows to Do dialog box and, for instance, choose to always have Windows open a DVD movie disc using Windows Media Player? If you want to change your AutoPlay choices at any point for any reason, it's not hard to do. Just open My Computer from the Windows XP Start menu, and right-click on the DVD drive icon. Choose AutoPlay from the menu (see Figure 11.2), and make your new selections.

tip

If you want Media Center to be launched every time you insert a DVD movie disc, check the box for Always Do the Selected Action in the What Do You Want to Do dialog box that Windows XP displays when you insert the disc. (This occurs only if Media Center is not running when you insert the DVD.)

FIGURE 11.1

In this pop-up window, you can select Media Center to watch your DVD.

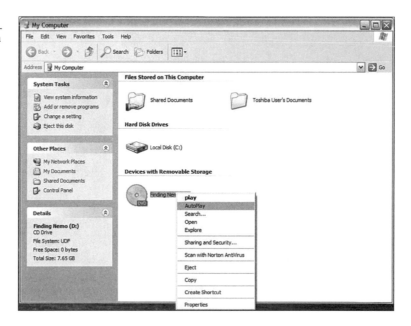

Playing a DVD That Is Already in the Drive

To launch a previously loaded DVD, follow this simple procedure:

1. Press Start on the remote.
2. Select Play DVD to display the default DVD menu.
3. Select Play to begin viewing the DVD.

Controlling DVD Playback with the Remote Control

In addition to the Media Center remote control's basic transport features—play, stop, fast-forward, rewind, skip forward, and skip back (for details, see Chapter 4, Table 4.1)—there are a few special functions you may want to use when operating your Media Center DVD player with the remote control. Table 11.1 lists them.

Table 11.1 Remote Control Commands for DVD Playback

To	Press
Access the DVD's on-disc feature menu	DVD Menu
Display the "chapter" or section of the DVD that is currently playing	More Info
Advance to the next chapter	Skip
Reverse to the last chapter	Replay
Zoom	More Info

Controlling DVD Playback with the Mouse and Keyboard

Most of the transport controls—shown in Figure 11.3—are also available with the mouse (see Chapter 5, "Navigating XP Media Center's '2-Foot' Interface") and the keyboard (see Table 5.5).

Although there are keyboard shortcuts for the skip forward and skip back features (Ctrl+F and Ctrl+B, respectively), skipping is not supported with the mouse alone. Likewise, the mouse does not give you a direct way to display the DVD's on-disc menu, though after the menu is opened using the remote control or keyboard, you can easily navigate and choose menu options with the mouse.

tip

To access the on-disc DVD menu from the keyboard, press Ctrl+Shift+M.

FIGURE 11.3
While the DVD is playing, just move the mouse and the cursor, and transport controls will be displayed.

Playback Preferences: Changing DVD Settings

There are several ways to customize your DVD playback experience using Media Center by changing the options available in the Media Center Setting menu. To reach it, press the green Media Center button on the remote to launch the main menu screen, and then select Settings and then DVD (see Figure 11.4).

FIGURE 11.4

If your DVD is already playing when you switch to the Media Center Settings menu, the video will continue to play in the inset window.

Language Settings

Using Windows Media Center's language settings menu, you can choose an exhaustive list of languages, ranging from Afrikaans to Vietnamese. You can also individually set the language preferences for Subtitle, Audio Track, and Menu (see Figure 11.5).

To change the language setting with the remote control, do the following:

1. Use the navigation buttons to select the attribute you want to change: Subtitle, Audio Track, or Menu.

2. Highlight the – or +, and then use the OK button to change the language that is displayed.

3. When you're satisfied with your selections, highlight Save and press OK.

If you are currently watching a DVD, each time you store your language preferences, the DVD will restart from the beginning.

caution

Changing your "global" language settings to Macedonian or Malayalam (which is the principal language of the South Indian state of Kerala, in case you were wondering) won't magically create a DVD soundtrack or subtitles in that language—the languages you've chosen as your preferences are subject to what's available on the DVD disc itself. Your choices can also be overridden by selections you make in the DVD's default on-disc menu.

FIGURE 11.5

If you or your guests speak or read a language other than English, Media Center is ready to accommodate you.

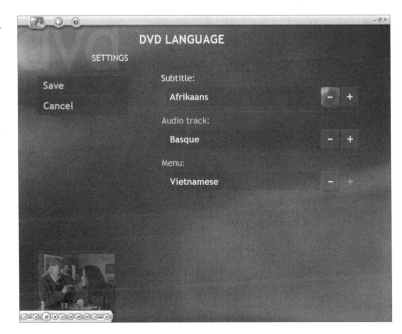

Audio Settings

You can also customize your audio settings for DVD playback. You'll need to have your mouse and/or keyboard handy to complete this maneuver. The audio controls are configured using a utility which is not part of the Media Center interface, but according to the Windows driver files supplied by the manufacturer of the playback hardware and software inside your Media Center PC. As a result, your Media Center remote control will be of little use in this exercise.

An example is the nVidia nV DVD audio device control panel application that shipped with many Media Center PCs (see Figure 11.6).

The nV DVD audio control panel lets you do the following:

- Choose a dynamic range control. Choices include Normal, Late Night, or Theatre.

- View the bit rate (Kbits/sec) for the currently playing DVD.

- Perform speaker setup. You can specify whether your Media PC is connected to computer speakers, headphones, or a receiver. Audio options change depending on which output mode you choose.

Try a range of output options and listen to the differences to determine which ones work best for your room acoustics, and which ones simply sound more pleasing to your ears.

FIGURE 11.6

The nV DVD driver control panel allows you to choose from a range of options to create the perfect audio playback experience.

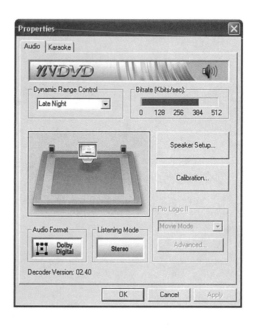

Troubleshooting DVD Playback

Although inserting and playing a DVD should be dead simple, a surprising number of things can go wrong. General error categories include problems involving the DVD disc and hardware (optical read errors), the software, the video playback, and the audio playback.

Hardware Problems

If you receive an error message such as "Unable to read drive *X:*" (substitute the logical letter for your DVD drive), chances are there is a physical problem with your disc or your DVD drive. Here are a few things to try before demanding a replacement from your video store or computer retailer:

- **Clean the disc**—Either use a commercial disc cleaning kit or wipe the silvery side of the disc gently with a soft, lint-free cotton cloth. Don't wipe it in a circular motion, but brush outward from the center of the disc toward the edge. Avoid the urge to use a paper towel or tissue, because these can leave tiny scratches on the delicate plastic surface of the disc.

- **Try the disc in another machine**—Make sure that the new drive has a DVD logo on the front panel. Insert the disc and see whether it plays. If it works there, but not in your Media Center machine, you know that the disc itself is not causing the problem.

■ **Clean your DVD drive**—If you've ruled out a problem with the disc, it could be that your drive needs cleaning. Clean the drive using a commercially available CD-ROM or DVD drive cleaning disc. Cleaning discs are available at most computer and home electronics stores.

Software Problems

There are many things that can go wrong when it comes to software, not the least of which is a simple memory shortage caused by trying to run too many applications at once. To see whether that's causing your problem, start by quitting all unnecessary applications. Sometimes that's all it takes to stabilize your system and get it to stop misbehaving. Here's how to do it:

1. Quit the programs you know are running which you don't need.

2. Right-click the items in your system tray and close or disable each one.

3. Press Ctrl+Alt+Delete to access the Windows Task Manager (see Figure 11.7). This will reveal all the software programs currently running on your system.

4. Selectively close programs to recapture your processing resources (don't close Explorer.exe—that's part of Windows) .

FIGURE 11.7

The Processes tab of the Windows Task Manager shows everything going on inside your Media Center PC.

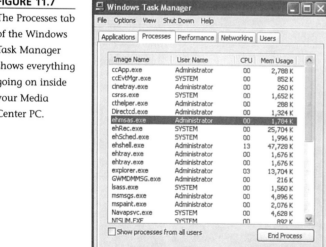

Video Problems

If you can hear the audio but can't see the video image, chances are it's a problem with your video hardware drivers. First, check all of your video cable connections, just to be sure. Then check the hardware documentation that came with your machine or call the manufacturer to find out how to update your display drivers.

If you are the hands-on type, you can also view the driver properties for your display adapter by opening the device manager from the Windows Control Panel (you'll find it in your Windows XP Start menu). After you launch Control Panel, choose the System icon to access System Properties (lower left), and then select the Hardware tab to open the Device Manager window (upper right). Finally, double-click on your display adapter to open its control panel, and choose the Driver tab (lower right). Many display adapters, such as the nVidia GeForce4 MX series, provide an Update Driver option (see Figure 11.8).

tip

Another common complaint among Media Center movie-watchers is that the TV image is too dark. The monitor brightness setting that's often perfect for your PC applications may not be bright enough for video images. If your DVD playback image is too dark, you may want to adjust your monitor settings to lighten the screen image.

Some high-end monitors even let you store "profiles," groups of settings that are optimized for different viewing modes. If your hardware supports this capability, you may want to set up separate profiles, one for using software applications and one for watching video.

FIGURE 11.8

This image shows the pop-up windows that will lead you to your display adapter's driver options.

Audio Problems

The cure for most common audio problems is often simply a matter of getting everything plugged in and turned on properly, so try the following before you call your hardware manufacturer to complain about low (or no) audio levels:

- It sounds like a no-brainer, but before you get on your hands and knees to crawl behind your Media Center system, try turning up the volume. Also check the system-level volume, which you can access through Windows Control Panel (see Figure 11.9). To reach the Audio Devices Properties window, select Sounds and Audio Devices from the Control Panel main screen.

- Check to see whether you have activated the Mute button.

- Now it's time to escalate things. Are your speakers properly configured, plugged in, and turned on? To be absolutely sure, try plugging headphones into your Media Center. If you hear everything with the headphones, and nothing from the speakers when the headphones are unplugged, there's definitely a problem with your speaker system. You can also confirm that your speakers are okay by connecting them to an alternative sound source, such as a boom box or portable CD player.

- After you've ruled out the easy stuff, you may need to update your audio drivers (see Figure 11.10) .

FIGURE 11.9

You can access the system-level volume through the Windows Control Panel.

FIGURE 11.10

From Control Panel you can access screens that let you check on your drivers for specific audio hardware devices.

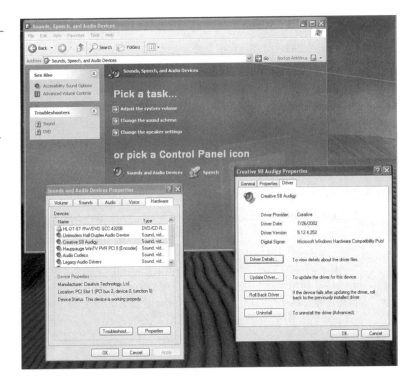

Troubleshooting Digital Audio

If the audio card in your PC is equipped for digital audio, and so are your speakers, there's no reason not to start living the good life and enjoying the best sound quality your Media Center has to offer.

Properly configuring Media Center's digital audio for DVD is a somewhat involved process, however, because it requires making choices from both the Media Center interface and the Windows Control Panel. Here's how it's done:

1. Open the DVD Audio Settings screen in Media Center, as described earlier in this chapter.

2. In the control panel for your audio device, choose the S/PDIF Digital Output option.

3. Click Apply, then OK.

4. Now minimize Media Center and launch the Windows Control Panel. Use the procedure described previously to reach the system volume controls (see Figure 11.9).

5. Under Speaker settings on the Volume tab, click Advanced.

6. In the drop-down list under Speaker setup, pick 5.1 Surround Sound Speakers (see Figure 11.11).

7. Click Apply, then OK.

FIGURE 11.11

Whether or not you have a 5.1 surround-sound speaker system, you will find this screen useful for optimizing Media Center for your audio system.

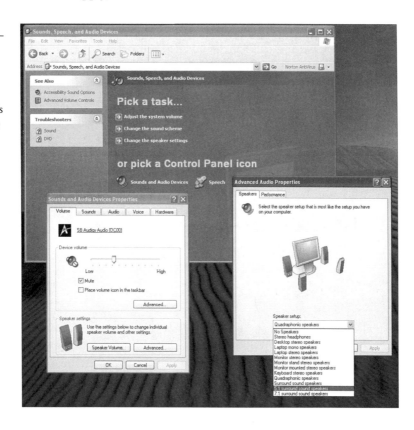

THE ABSOLUTE MINIMUM

Playing a DVD on your Media Center PC should be every bit as simple and enjoyable as using a conventional standalone DVD player. However, there are a few significant differences to bear in mind:

- Whereas your standard DVD player has two means of operation—pressing buttons on the remote control or pressing buttons on the face of the player itself—Media Center adds two more input modes: the mouse and the keyboard. Depending on how, when, and even what you like to watch, you could eventually find yourself using a combination of all four input styles to control your DVD playback experience.

- Media Center lets you set a wide variety of language and audio preferences to get the most out of every DVD you watch.

- The language settings support no fewer than 70 languages, along with settings for Title Default and None. You can make separate language choices for Subtitle, Audio Track, and Menu.

- Audio settings vary depending on the hardware manufacturer. Additional settings are available under Windows Control Panel.

12

CREATING DVDs ON AN XP MEDIA CENTER PC

Microsoft's Media Center software provides many entertaining experiences —but one thing it does not support is the capability to record DVDs directly from Media Center. Whether you want to create—or "burn"— a DVD using video you captured from a camcorder, footage downloaded from the Internet, or video recorded from your TV via Media Center, you will have to go outside Media Center to get the job done.

Choosing Your Tools

Let's look at the three types of DVDs you can create, and talk about the software tools you'll need to get the job done.

Creating Data DVDs

Data DVDs can be created using Windows XP, without the need to buy additional software. In general, XP supports the capability to copy files to a recordable DVD disc so that you can access them on another PC. DVDs recorded in this way will not allow you to pop them into a standard DVD video player, however, because they contain only computer data. The main benefit of using a DVD in this manner, versus using a recordable CD, is the size: A typical DVD-R disc will hold 4.7GB of data, compared to the measly 700MB capacity of a CD-R disc. If you want to store large files, or even lots and lots of small ones, there's no contest.

To create a data DVD using Windows XP, do the following:

1. Minimize or exit Media Center.
2. Insert a blank DVD disc into your PC. If XP opens a dialog box, select Take no Action.
3. Click on Start, then on My Computer.
4. Right-click on the recordable DVD drive icon (see Figure 12.1), and then select Format.
5. Follow the onscreen instructions to format the disc.
6. Copy, move, or drag and drop files onto the formatted DVD disc using My Computer.

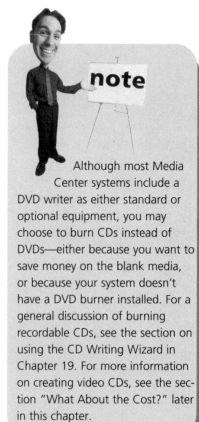

note

Although most Media Center systems include a DVD writer as either standard or optional equipment, you may choose to burn CDs instead of DVDs—either because you want to save money on the blank media, or because your system doesn't have a DVD burner installed. For a general discussion of burning recordable CDs, see the section on using the CD Writing Wizard in Chapter 19. For more information on creating video CDs, see the section "What About the Cost?" later in this chapter.

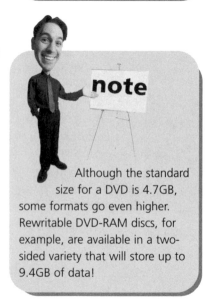

note

Although the standard size for a DVD is 4.7GB, some formats go even higher. Rewritable DVD-RAM discs, for example, are available in a two-sided variety that will store up to 9.4GB of data!

FIGURE 12.1

This view of My Computer shows the icon for a shared DVD/CD-RW drive, which supports rewritable disc media.

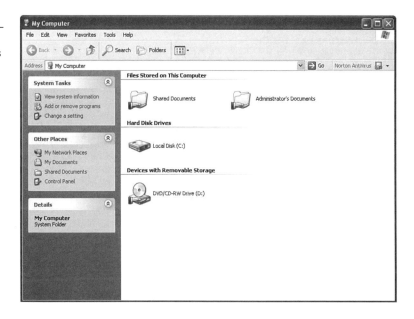

Creating a DVD from Video Files

To create a basic video DVD disc that can be played back on a PC or in a typical video DVD player, you'll need some specialized DVD editing software and recording software. Check and see whether your Media Center PC came with any bundled DVD authoring software. Some typical ones that PC manufacturers bundle include the following:

- ShowBiz from ArcSoft
- Expression from Pinnacle
- VideoStudio from Ulead
- VideoWave from Roxio
- Sonic MyDVD

There are many others as well. Most of these programs allow you to edit your video, create a DVD menu system, and record the video to a DVD disc. Another software package you may want to consider—primarily because at the time of this writing, it is being offered free—is Microsoft's Windows Movie Maker. This program may come already installed on your Media Center Machine.

tip

For details on how to edit your video and prepare it for burning to a DVD disc, see the section "Using Windows Movie Maker" in Chapter 10, "Capturing and Creating Videos with Media Center."

If you need to download a copy, visit the Web site www.microsoft.com/windowsXP/moviemaker and look for the "Download Windows Movie Maker 2" link (see Figure 12.2).

FIGURE 12.2

This section of the Movie Maker home page contains two links to download the free software: one at the center of the screen and one to the right.

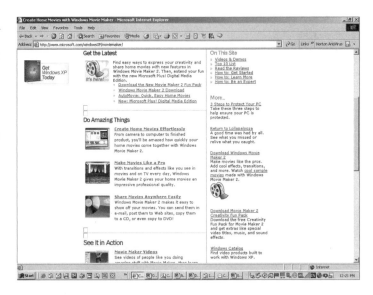

Windows Movie Maker has one major drawback, at least as far as this chapter is concerned: It does not support recording your finished movie to a DVD disc. Instead, you can choose to create a Video CD (VCD), which provides many features similar to a true DVD disc. But because it records using a blank CD instead of a DVD, the finished disc is limited in terms of the quality and size of the video you can store. In addition, the interactivity features you can add for use in a DVD player device are limited.

Creating a DVD from Recorded TV Programs

This is probably the most interesting, and least supported, DVD recording project available to owners of Media Center PCs. As of this writing, the only company that fully supports the capability to create DVDs from programs and movies you recorded from your TV signal in Media Center is Sonic. The company offers two products with this capability: MyDVD and PrimeTime.

note

Like Windows Movie Maker, ArcSoft ShowBiz doesn't directly support the capability to burn a DVD-R disc. The program is integrated with Sonic's MyDVD, however, so you can edit your video project in ShowBiz and then turn it over to MyDVD for the actual creation of the DVD disc (see Figure 12.3) .

FIGURE 12.3

To create a DVD-
R from a movie
you edited in
ShowBiz, click
on Create, and
then select
MyDVD Project.

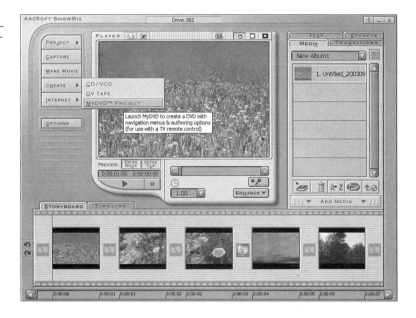

MyDVD

Sonic's MyDVD was the first DVD recorder software to support Microsoft's proprietary DVR-MS file format. This allows Media Center users to create DVDs from shows they have recorded on their Media Center, providing one of the easiest methods for transferring TV content onto a removable disc. The discs you create can be played not only in a PC, but also in most consumer DVD players.

To create a DVD from TV shows you recorded in My TV, follow these steps:

1. Close or minimize Media Center.

2. Insert a blank DVD disc that is compatible with your DVD burner.

3. Open the MyDVD program from the Windows Start menu.

4. Click on Get Recorded TV Shows. MyDVD will display a list of programs you previously recorded using the My TV interface in Media Center (see Figure 12.4). Media Center stores all recorded programs as .DVR-MS video files.

5. Select the program (or programs) you want to add to the disc, and click OK. MyDVD will display an Importing Media window with a progress bar that will gradually turn green as the file is prepared for use in the DVD project you are creating. Be patient—this can be a lengthy process.

6. Edit the text on the title screen.

FIGURE 12.4

When you select
Get Recorded TV
Shows, MyDVD
displays a list of
files in your
C:\Documents
and Settings\All
Users\Documents
\Recorded TV
directory.

7. Click the red Burn button. MyDVD will display the Make Disc Setup window
   (see Figure 12.5). Make any necessary changes to the settings displayed, and
   click OK.

8. MyDVD will create the disc and eject the disc when it's finished.

FIGURE 12.5

The Make Disc
Setup window
allows you to
select the record-
ing device, num-
ber of discs, and
write speed (if
you are record-
ing a VCD).

PrimeTime

For Media Center users, PrimeTime takes the DVD burning experience one step further by actually integrating it within the Media Center My TV interface. Instead of
making you exit Media Center and mouse around in a completely separate desktop
software application, PrimeTime enables you to record programs onto removable
DVD discs with remote-control ease.

To use PrimeTime, install it from the CD in Windows XP. Reboot your machine and launch Media Center. PrimeTime will have been added to your Media Center main menu (see Figure 12.6).

FIGURE 12.6

The Create DVD option has been added to the Media Center main menu, indicating that PrimeTime has been installed.

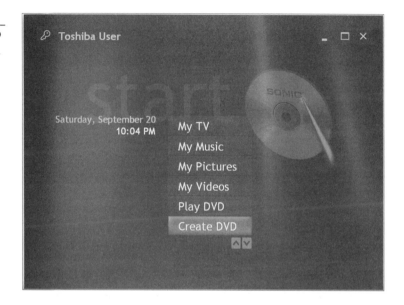

Recording a DVD with PrimeTime is simple. Select the Create DVD option from the Media Center menu to launch PrimeTime. After a setup screen is displayed, while PrimeTime identifies your DVD recording device, the main PrimeTime screen will be displayed (see Figure 12.7). From here you can choose the recorded program you want to use and then select Burn DVD to complete the process.

FIGURE 12.7

A feature of PrimeTime is that the interface has been designed to preserve the Media Center look and feel.

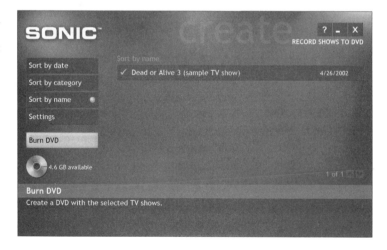

Copying and Copyrights

This capability to very simply create perfect digital copies of TV shows and movies on removable DVD discs brings up an important question: Is it legal? The answer is, predictably, yes and no.

The Digital Millennium Copyright Act (DMCA) is generally held to give consumers the right to make copies of copyrighted works that they have purchased, for their own personal use. If you are worried about it, consult a lawyer. If you're willing to let common sense be your guide, then as long as you are not making thousands—or even dozens—of copies and distributing them to friends, neighbors, family, or complete strangers, you are probably acting within your rights. If you are distributing someone else's copyrighted works in quantity, without the permission of the copyright holder, you probably should get a lawyer—and of course, you should stop doing it immediately. Not only is it probably illegal, but it also is not fair to the people whose hard work is reflected in the creative works you are copying. (For more discussion of the DMCA and its impact on you, see the section "Ripping CDs" in Chapter 13, "Preparing Your Music Collection for XP Media Center.")

Troubleshooting the DVD Burning Experience

As with burning CDs, there are many things that can go wrong when you're creating home-made DVDs—probably too many to mention in a book this size. In the interest of time and saving trees, let's look at some of the problems you're most likely to encounter when burning DVDs of TV shows recorded in My TV.

Choosing the Right Media

The first obstacle in a series of potential show-stoppers is choosing the right type of blank discs for your DVD burner.

Matching Media with Your DVD Burner

There are at least five popular categories of DVD media available now: DVD-R (pronounced "DVD *minus* R") and DVD+R (you guessed it: "DVD *plus* R"), DVD-RW and DVD+RW, and DVD-RAM—and the list seems to keep growing. All have slightly different properties and price points. Some will work with your PC's DVD burner but not your living room's DVD player—and vice versa.

So how do you choose the right media for your DVD burner? Theoretically, you should be able to look at the logo on the drive door of your DVD device (for examples, see Figure 12.8 and Figure 12.9) and determine its compatibility. Alas, if only it were that simple. In reality, you will probably need to determine the exact make and model of your DVD burner, and then try to match it with the appropriate media using online resources, such as those published at Web sites like www.dvdrhelp.com.

To determine the make and model of your PC's DVD drive, do this:

1. Right-click on the My Computer icon on your XP desktop or in the Windows Start menu.

2. Choose Properties to open the System Properties window.

3. Choose the Hardware tab, and then click on Device Manager.

4. Scroll down the list until you see the DVD/CD-ROM drives entry, and click on the adjacent + symbol.

5. Write down the model number.

Now you can do an online search to get more information. For example, the "HL-DT-ST RW/DVD GCC-4320B" identified in the System Properties menu in a Gateway Media Center PC (see Figure 12.10) was revealed to be an LG Electronics combo drive, which an online search determined has write compatibility with DVD-R and DVD-RW discs.

FIGURE 12.8

This logo on your DVD burner's drive door indicates that the device supports 4.7GB write-once DVD-R disc media.

FIGURE 12.9

If your DVD burner bears this logo, it supports rewritable DVD+RW technology, which is designed for maximum compatibility with home DVD players.

FIGURE 12.10

This view of the hardware properties of a Gateway Media Center PC lists an LG Electronics 4320B combination CD-R/DVD-RW drive.

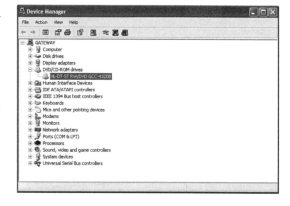

Matching Media with Your DVD Player

Let's assume that you've successfully purchased blank DVDs that are compatible with your PC's DVD burner. Congratulations are in order. Unfortunately, that's only half the battle. Even if you can now burn a DVD, you still may not be able to produce a disc that your DVD player will recognize. You'll need to get the specs on your playback deck as well, and match that up with other online compatibility lists.

If all else fails, try calling the manufacturers of your Media Center PC and your DVD player, or visiting their respective Web sites, to gather more information on their DVD format compatibility.

Your Video Is Too Big for the Disc

Another common problem you may run into is that your video file may exceed the size of your recordable disc. Using MyDVD's standard settings, only about one hour's worth of video will fit on a standard DVD disc. One way to adjust this is by tweaking the bit rates, which refer to the number of bits of data needed to display each second of video.

Some of the DVD authoring applications mentioned earlier in this chapter allow you to make changes to the bit rate (selecting a lower one will let you pack more video onto a DVD, but at some cost to the quality of the video). Unfortunately, MyDVD and PrimeTime do not allow you to change the bit rate of shows recorded using Media Center My TV. Your best bet for recording long programs in that fashion will be to use the Trim Video feature in MyDVD (see Figure 12.11) to reduce the size of the file you are burning to disc. If necessary, you can use this feature to burn separate volumes, to create a multipart set of discs.

> **tip**
>
> How can you fit a full-length movie onto a blank DVD in PrimeTime? You can't. However, you can record the movie at a lower bit rate. To do this, choose advanced recording features from the recording menu in My TV, and change the settings for the recording quality. The default level is Best, so try knocking it down to Better, or even Fair, to make a recording that will fit on a standard 4.7GB DVD disc.

FIGURE 12.11

You can drag the start and end handles, and click the forward and reverse arrow buttons to nudge the trim handle backward or forward a few frames at a time.

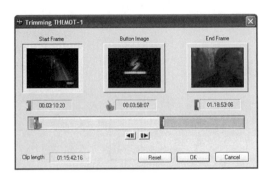

To trim the video file down to size, do the following in MyDVD:

1. Click on Tools.

2. Click on trim movie.

3. Drag the green handle on the left side of the movie timeline to the starting point you want.

4. Drag the red handle on the right side of the movie timeline to the ending point you want.

5. Click OK to accept the changes to your DVD project.

What About the Cost?

Blank DVD discs have come down significantly in price, but even on sale, they still usually run at least a few bucks each. Recordable CD discs, however, are dirt cheap—in the range of pennies per disc, especially if you buy in bulk. As a result, you may want to experiment with recording video programs as VCDs rather than DVDs, if for no other reason than to save some cash. You will lose a lot of quality, so don't use the VCD technique to record a movie that you want to keep for posterity. But if you just want to burn a quick disc of your favorite sitcom to watch on your laptop during your next layover in Denver, a VCD disc might be just the answer. And when you're finished with it, you won't feel bad about just dropping the disc in the trash.

note

To save a My TV recording as a VCD rather than a DVD using PrimeTime, do this:

1. Choose Settings from the main PrimeTime menu.

2. With the General tab selected, choose Recording Devices.

3. For the Type of Disc setting, select the – (minus) symbol, and PrimeTime will change the value from DVD to Video CD (see Figure 12.12).

4. Click OK.

FIGURE 12.12

Along with changing the disc type, this settings screen in PrimeTime lets you specify which recording device you prefer to use.

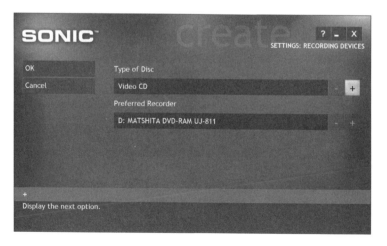

THE ABSOLUTE MINIMUM

Burning your own DVDs is one of the coolest features supported by your Media Center machine. It can also be one of the most frustrating. Here are a few pointers to keep in mind:

- There are essentially three types of DVDs you can create with your Media Center PC: data DVDs, video DVDs using digital video stored on your PC, and video DVDs using video recorded by Media Center.

- Media Center recordings use a special format created by Microsoft. Lots of software packages will let you record video DVDs, but as of this writing, only Sonic's MyDVD and PrimeTime software allow you to burn DVDs from Media Center recordings.

- TV and movie studios take copyright restrictions very seriously these days. Feel free to copy video for your personal use. Just make sure you got the video through legal means, and refrain from distributing copies en masse.

- You may need to do some homework to buy the right blank discs for your DVD burner. A profusion of competing formats has made a mess for consumers. Bottom line: When you buy blank DVD media, be sure to save your sales receipt.

- When it comes to burning recorded TV programs onto DVDs, size matters. Fitting a full-length movie onto a DVD can be tricky. Try recording with a lower quality setting to reduce the bit rate.

- Want to save some money? You might want to burn a VCD instead of a DVD. Most recording software supports both formats, and a lower-quality VCD can be made on an inexpensive CD-R disc.

PART V

MY MUSIC

13

PREPARING YOUR MUSIC COLLECTION FOR XP MEDIA CENTER

We've covered some of the great things Media Center does for your eyes--so what about your ears? Don't worry, the other half of the audio-visual experience has not been neglected. In fact, Media Center was created to let you take full advantage of the online digital audio revolution that is transforming the way we acquire and consume music around the world.

Supported File Formats

Many types of audio files are available, and not all are supported by your Media PC's My Music interface. The primary file types you can listen to from My Music are shown in Table 13.1.

TABLE 13.1 Audio File Formats Supported by Media Center

File Type (Format)	Filename Extension
CD audio	.cda
Windows Media audio files	.asx, .wm, .wma, .wmp, and .wmx
Windows audio files	.wav
MP3	.mp3 and .m3u

tip

As with video files (see "Watching Videos," in Chapter 9), Media Center can support additional audio file formats, but first you may need to install a new codec. The filename extensions shown in Table 13.1 each represent different codecs that are already supported within Windows XP Media Center Edition.

Putting the Music into My Music

As noted in Chapter 3, My Music relies heavily on the Windows Media Player program in Windows XP (see Figure 3.8). In fact, when you open My Music for the first time, you will be prompted to first use Windows Media Player to populate your media library.

Like a media vacuum cleaner, Windows Media Player scours your system and sucks in all the audio files so that they're available for playback in My Music.

Importing Music from Your Network

One of the first places you may want Windows Media Player to look for additional audio files is on other computers in your home network. Here's how to do it:

caution

Occasionally, Media Center will display a codec error when playing back a digital audio file. If this happens to you, try opening the file in Windows Media Player, launched from the Windows XP desktop. You may need to configure Windows Media Player to automatically download codecs, but if the correct codec is available online, your file should play.

1. Close or minimize Media Center and open Windows Media Player from the Windows XP Start menu.

2. Select Media Library from the tabs in the left margin (the Features Taskbar) of the player.

3. Click Add, and choose By Searching Computer.

4. Click to the right of the Search On box and select <User-Selected Search Path> from the drop-down menu.

5. Click the Browse button, and navigate to the network PC on which you want to search for media. Then click OK.

6. Select any search options you want to use (see Figure 13.1), and then click on Search.

FIGURE 13.1

Several useful options are available when you view the Add to Media Library by Searching Computer control panel.

Importing Music from the Web

This is an area about which volumes could be (and, in fact, have been) written. Millions of free audio files are available on the Internet, easily accessed free through file-sharing services such as Kazaa, Morpheus, and iMesh.

Unfortunately, much of this music has been illegally copied and is being traded without the consent of the recording artists, or the distribution companies that support their art. In the past few years, some commercial music download services have emerged that allow you to acquire music files legally (see Figure 13.2). Unlike the earliest offerings in this space, these services are backed by major record labels-- and, consequently, they offer access to major music libraries. Prices are coming down and selection is expanding, making these commercial services a better value proposition for consumers.

Media Center's My Music is also configured to present you with commercial "pay to play" download opportunities. Simply choose the Buy Music menu item when it appears next to a song in the My Music audio library (see Figure 13.3), and you will be redirected to a Web search page where you can find music files similar to the one you were playing, offered for sale by an online vendor.

caution

When you select Buy Music, you are redirected to a Web page that provides search results for media files you can buy online. However, the Web pages may not support Media Center's "10-foot experience," that is, the capability to view them from the sofa and navigate using your remote control. If this is the case, Media Center will display the error message shown in Figure 13.4. When this occurs, you can either move closer to the screen and take control with mouse and keyboard (choose View Now), or have Media Center create a shortcut on your desktop so that you can go back to the Web page later (choose View Later) using Media Center's "2-foot" user interface.

FIGURE 13.2

Clicking on the Premium Services tab in Windows Media offers links to content providers that have partnered with Microsoft.

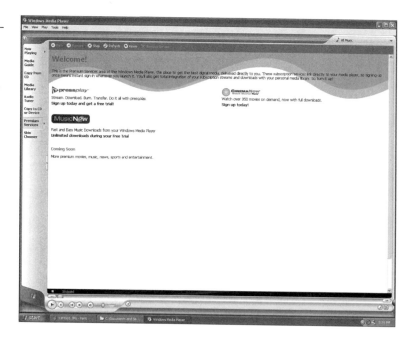

FIGURE 13.3

The Buy Music option is displayed on the Song Details page, which you reach by selecting a tune with the remote control, keyboard, or mouse.

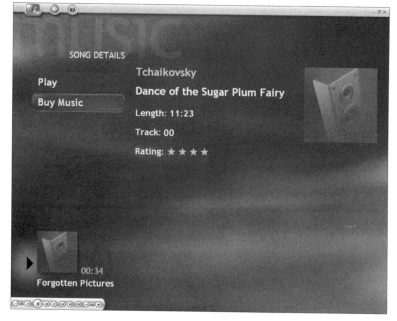

FIGURE 13.4

The Not Designed for Media Center error screen is shown when you are being directed to a Web site that doesn't support the "10-foot" interface.

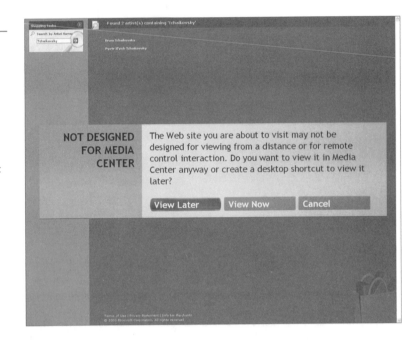

Ripping CDs

Possibly the safest and most rewarding way to get audio into your Media Center PC (so you can enjoy it using the My Music interface) is to import music directly from your personal CD collection. This copying process, commonly called ripping, is perfectly legal *as long as you do not share the resulting files with others who have not paid for the content.*

One of the things that has contributed to the abuse of sharing CDs is how very easy it is to rip them. Simply insert an audio CD into your Media Center machine and watch what happens. If you are in the Windows XP desktop, a pop-up screen will appear with a list of options (see Figure 13.5). The first item on the list is Copy Music from CD Using Windows Media Player.

Ripping a CD from the Windows XP Desktop

If you select the option to copy the CD using Windows Media Player, you'll be asked whether you want to add copy protection to the audio files you are about to create.

If you choose not to, you'll be forced to check the box next to a not-so-subtle reminder of Microsoft's interpretation of the DMCA. If you choose to make copies without adding copy-protection code to the files, you'll need to check the box indicating that you are aware of your responsibility to ensure "the appropriate use" of the copies, with respect to copyright law.

Ripping a CD from the My Music Interface

If you place a CD in your computer while the Media Center My Music interface is being displayed, the audio will immediately begin to play. Select the CD's listing from the My Music main screen, and one of the prominent options you'll find is Copy CD (see Figure 13.6).

Choosing the Copy CD option from within My Music will conjure up a screen offering to allow Media Player to add anticopying code to prevent unauthorized use--and advising you of your responsibilities if you don't choose the copy-protection option.

> ### caution
>
> What about sharing the tunes you ripped with a few friends? Or with a few strangers? There is a rather ambiguous law on the books called the Digital Millennium Copyright Act (DMCA), which has been generally interpreted as making it legal to copy material for personal use. However, distributing that copied material free or for money to strangers-- whether you post the files on a peer-to-peer file-swapping service or start stamping out counterfeit CDs in your basement--is generally viewed as a violation of the copyright law. Suffice it to say, this can get you into hot water--possibly even into jail. Proceed at your own risk!

FIGURE 13.5

To rip a CD, you simply choose Copy Music from CD Using Windows Media Player. What could be simpler?

FIGURE 13.6

From the Now
Playing screen
in My Music,
ripping the
entire CD is a
simple matter.

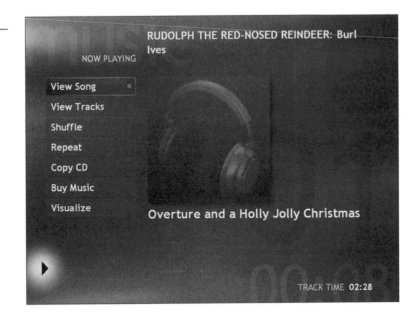

Next, you'll be advised of different codecs you can choose, and how to change your
encoding options within Media Player (see Figure 13.7). The Windows Media Audio
Variable bit rate codec makes files smaller but may skimp a bit on the audio quality.
The Windows Media Audio Lossless codec preserves every nuance of the audio,
though you'll pay a higher price in disk capacity required to store the file. Choose
Finish, and then confirm that you want to copy the disc into your Media Library by
selecting Yes.

After you've navigated past these screens--which won't be repeated the next time
you choose to copy a CD--My Music will display a progress screen (see Figure 13.8)
showing you each track as it is stored to the My Music folder on your hard drive. In
fact, My Music creates a new folder for each album you copy, bearing the same
name of the album, and stored in your My Music data directory.

FIGURE 13.7

This screen lets you know that Media Player offers you a choice of codecs for encoding the CD Audio.

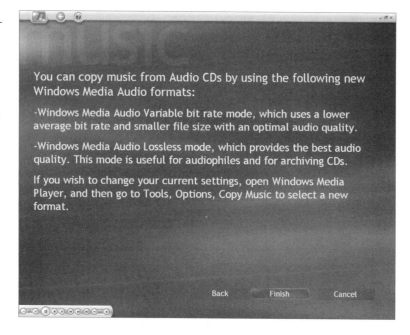

You can copy music from Audio CDs by using the following new Windows Media Audio formats:

-Windows Media Audio Variable bit rate mode, which uses a lower average bit rate and smaller file size with an optimal audio quality.

-Windows Media Audio Lossless mode, which provides the best audio quality. This mode is useful for audiophiles and for archiving CDs.

If you wish to change your current settings, open Windows Media Player, and then go to Tools, Options, Copy Music to select a new format.

Back   Finish   Cancel

FIGURE 13.8

This Now Playing screen displays a spinning disc next to the track being copied, and a check mark next to the completed tracks.

NOW PLAYING

View Song	One Week	2:49
View Tracks	It's All Been Done	3:26
Shuffle	Light up My Room	3:36
Repeat	I'll Be That Girl	59%
Copy CD	Leave	3:23
Buy Music	Alcohol	3:43
Visualize	Call and Answer	5:48
	In the Car	3:53
	Never Is Enough	3:23
	Who Needs Sleep?	3:44

00:01
One Week

4 of 13

Metadata Tags and You

How are My Music and Windows Media Player able to almost instantly and infallibly recognize any commercially manufactured CD, and automatically display the name of the artist, song, and album? The answer lies in the metadata available through online databases to identify the disc. This data can then be attached as metadata tags to identify the digital music files that are created in the ripping process.

This metadata can contain practically any information about digital media content that you might find printed on the CD cover, even including lyrics, track length, genre, producer, and more.

The metadata displayed in My Music is limited to just the basics (Figure 13.9), including the name of the artist, song, and album, along with the track number and length. The date and publisher are also shown, if available online, and the pièce de résistance: the actual album cover art. It is this data that allows you to sort music copied from CDs by artist, album or song title, genre, and so on. Much more information is often included in the online listing, but to view it, you need to use other software, such as Windows Media Player (see Figure 13.10) .

FIGURE 13.9

The Song Details screen displays metadata downloaded from an online database.

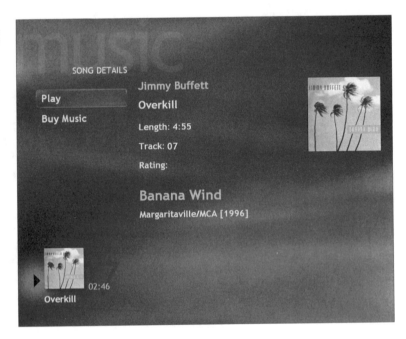

FIGURE 13.10

The Tag
Information
screen in
Windows Media
Player displays
a wealth of
information
culled from the
comprehensive
All Music Guide
(AMG) data-
base.

Editing Media Tags

Although the automatic identification and clas-
sification of your CD audio content is an
admirable feature, it works best with popular
music tracks that have been recognized and ver-
ified thousands of times. If your musical tastes
run a little farther from the beaten path--or if
some files have wandered into your collection
that are unlabeled or contain incorrect meta-
data--there is a way to go in and manually edit
the tags using your Media Center's Advanced
Tag Editor software. Here's how to do it:

1. From the Media Player Features taskbar,
   choose Media Library.

2. From the Details pane, right-click the item
   you want to edit. Choose the Advanced
   Tag Editor.

3. Using the dialog box (see Figure 13.11),
   enter or change the media information as
   necessary.

tip

In addition to editing basic
information on the song and
artist, the Advanced Tag
Editor lets you add lyrics, pictures, and comments. You
can even synchronize the
lyrics to the music, or add
links to related Web sites. And if
you have a whole collection of
tunes you want to edit at once,
Advanced Tag Editor allows you to
enter information for several items
in a single operation. To do this,
use the Contents pane on the left
side of the screen. Hold down the
Shift key while selecting to choose
a range of items, or hold down
the Ctrl key to select non-adjacent
items. Make the changes you
want in the dialog boxes on the
right, and then click Apply or OK.

FIGURE 13.11

With the Windows Media Player Advanced Tag Editor, you can add or correct detailed track and artist information.

THE ABSOLUTE MiNiMUM

Now that you have searched and selected, downloaded, ripped, and edited your audio collection using Windows Media Center, you're ready to open My Music in Media Center and let the good times--and the good tunes--roll. Before you do, remember these things:

- You're operating in a Microsoft-only world when you're in Media Center. Many file formats are accepted, but competing technologies such as RealMedia and Apple QuickTime need not apply, as far as Microsoft is concerned. To enjoy music encoded in those formats, you'll have to download a third-party player and listen outside of Media Center's My Music interface, without benefit of your Media Center remote control.

- My Music is designed for listening to audio, not necessarily for acquiring or managing media files. For most of those tasks, you'll need to rely on the Windows Media Player program.

- When it comes to importing media files from the World Wide Web, remember that the music industry frowns on file-swapping. Look for a legal means of obtaining the media files you want, or beware the wrath of the RIAA (Recording Industry Association of America).

- Ripping CDs is an area where a lot of people run into trouble with copyright laws, such as the DMCA. As long as you're copying audio that you own, for your own use, you have nothing to worry about.

- The miracle of metadata allows My Music and Windows Media Player to instantly recognize the contents of your audio CDs and display many details. You can manually edit the information on any digital recordings that you make using the Advanced Tag Editor in Windows Media Player.

14

PLAYBACK TIME: SORTING, VIEWING, AND CONTROLLING YOUR MUSIC

Now that you've got a handle on the basic tools for building a music collection on your Media Center PC, we'll spend some time learning about the ways to listen to that music while getting the most enjoyment from it. You'll quickly find that Media Center allows you to do things with your music collection that you never dreamed of with your old 4stereo. Prepare to be spoiled!

Playing Audio CDs with Your Music Center PC

Naturally, the easiest way to launch the audio playback experience on your Media Center PC is to simply insert an audio CD. First, be sure you have opened the Media Center interface on your PC. Media Center will detect that an audio CD is present, and will immediately switch to My Music's Now Playing screen, while simultaneously starting disc playback.

Initially, the Now Playing screen will show generic track numbers and song lengths (see Figure 14.1). However, even while you're still listening to Track 1, Media Center is already busy searching the metadata stored in an online music database (see the section "Metadata Tags and You," in Chapter 13, "Preparing Your Music Collection for XP Media Center") to gather detailed information about the new disc. Within moments of recognizing the CD, My Music will substitute the generic track information with actual song titles (see Figure 14.2) .

FIGURE 14.1

As My Music begins playing your CD, it simultaneously searches for metadata containing specific details about the disc.

NOW PLAYING		
View Song	Track 1	4:44
View Tracks	Track 2	4:09
Shuffle	Track 3	2:43
Repeat	Track 4	3:59
Copy CD	Track 5	4:38
Buy Music	Track 6	4:09
Visualize	Track 7	2:30
	Track 8	4:54
	Track 9	2:45
	Track 10	3:39
00:07		
Track 1		1 of 12

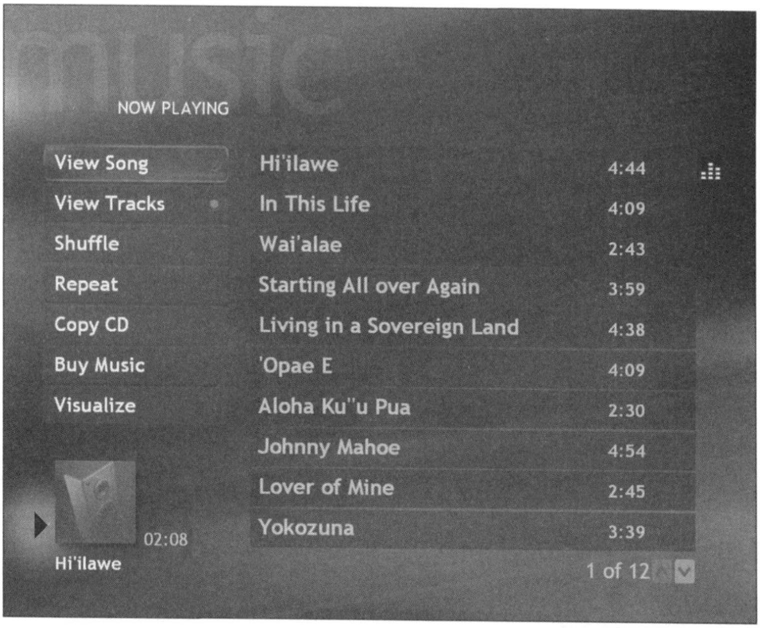

FIGURE 14.2

Without skipping a beat—literally or figuratively—the My Music Now Playing page will update to include actual song names instead of generic track numbers.

Making Media Center Your Default CD Player

What happens if you insert a CD when the Media Center interface isn't running? Typically, Windows XP will simply present an Audio CD control panel (see Figure 13.5 in Chapter 13). If you'd like to have your PC launch Media Center's My Music interface every time an audio CD is inserted, simply do the following:

1. Insert an audio CD.

2. Using your mouse, select the option Play Audio CD Using Media Center.

3. Check the box labeled Always Do the Selected Action.

4. Click OK.

tip

If you have already configured autoplay options with another player—such as Windows Media Player—the dialog box won't appear now. You can access the menu and reconfigure autoplay at any time by opening My Computer from the Windows XP Start menu and right-clicking on your CD drive icon. You then select Properties from the list, and click on the AutoPlay tab.

Sorting Your Collection

One of the most powerful features of Media Center's My Music interface is the capability to manage a large music collection using a wide variety of sorting and search techniques. From the My Music main menu, you can automatically sort your music collection by the following criteria:

- Album name
- Artist name
- Playlist name
- Song title
- Musical genre
- Keyword

Simply choose your sorting preference from the default Recent Music page (see Figure 14.3), which displays the audio you have most recently listened to.

FIGURE 14.3

The Recent Music display in My Music shows various items reflecting your most recent musical selections.

To sort by album, artist, playlist, song or genre, choose the corresponding tab on the left of the My Music screen. Each choice will reveal additional options for viewing and filtering the contents of your digital music collection.

Albums

Choosing the Album tab provides a list of the albums stored on you Media Center PC (see Figure 14.4). You can choose from the following options:

- **Play**—This immediately begins playback of the currently listed items. Playback will occur in the order shown onscreen. When you select Play, the screen will change to the Now Playing display (see Figure 14.2).

- **Shuffle**—This begins playback of the listed items in random order. The Now Playing screen will be displayed.

- **View by List**—This is the default view for the Albums screen.

- **View by Cover**—Shows your album collection using thumbnails of the album cover art (see Figure 14.5) that Music Center was able to retrieve from metadata stored online.

FIGURE 14.4

The dot that appears on the View by List tab indicates that My Music is displaying a list of all your albums.

Artists

Choosing Artists will display the initial Artists screen (see Figure 14.6), listing every artist on every track of every album in your collection—or at least all of those that were identified in Media Center's online metadata search.

FIGURE 14.5

When My Music is unable to locate an album cover graphic, it displays a generic graphic such as the picture of a stereo speaker shown here.

FIGURE 14.6

The Artists screen lists recording artists in alphabetical order based on the first name, or the first word in the name of a music group.

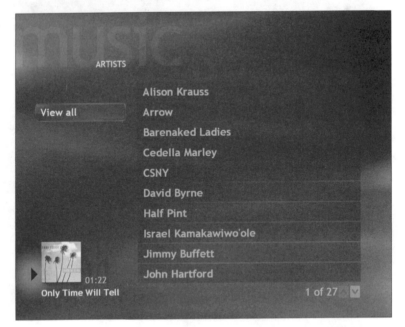

If you select the View All tab from the Artists display page, My Music will show the
View by List screen (see Figure 14.7). This screen also permits you to choose View by
Cover, which will display a different view of Album cover thumbnails (see Figure 14.8).

FIGURE 14.7

The View by List
screen shows all
your albums,
sorted by the
artists' names.

FIGURE 14.8

The View by
Cover screen
shows thumb-
nails of all your
album covers,
but this time
they are sorted
in alphabetical
order according
to the artists'
names.

Playlists

Sorting with the Playlists tab will bring up a list of the playlists you have created using Windows Media Player (see Chapter 16's section "Working with Playlists" for more details). As long as you have the most current version of Windows Media Player installed, you'll also have the option of choosing Auto Playlists, which displays a list of choices for playing back portions of your music collection (see Figure 14.9). The list offers an imaginative array of options to experience your songs in ways that only a computerized audio companion like Media Center can provide. These are the 15 Auto Playlist choices:

- Favorites—4 and 5 Star Rated
- Favorites—Have Not Heard Recently
- Favorites—Listen to at Night
- Favorites—Listen to on Weekdays
- Favorites—Listen to on Weekends
- Favorites—One Audio CD Worth
- Favorites—One Data CD-R Worth
- Fresh Tracks
- Fresh Tracks—Yet to Be Played
- Fresh Tracks—Yet to Be Rated
- High Bitrate Media in My Library
- Low Bitrate Media in My Library
- Music Tracks I Dislike
- Music Tracks I Have Not Rated
- Music Tracks with Content Protection

Songs

Selecting the Songs tab will sort your audio collection by track. From the Songs page, you can select Play to listen to all the tracks in alphabetical order, or Shuffle to listen in random order.

note

The Auto Playlist function is dynamic. It constantly changes as you add new items to your music library. While it continuously notes these changes to your audio content, it's also keeping tabs on your listening habits, observing which tracks you listen to and when, as well as which ones you always skip over.

So what do you do if you like an Auto Playlist you've heard, and want to preserve it—knowing full well that the next time you try it, it may be completely different? Just follow this procedure:

1. Close or minimize Media Center.

2. Open Windows Media Player from the Windows XP Start menu.

3. Choose Media Library from the menu on the left.

4. Select Auto Playlist in the directory tree pane to display all the choices.

5. Right-click on the Auto Playlist you want to keep.

6. Select Save as New Playlist, and a New Playlist dialog box will appear (see Figure 14.10).

7. Enter a name for the new playlist, and click OK.

FIGURE 14.9

The Auto Playlists menu gives you an interesting set of ways to listen to your music collection.

FIGURE 14.10

After you've saved your new playlist from the Auto Playlist choices in Windows Media Player, it will be added to the list of My Playlists.

Genres

The Genres tab brings up the Genres page (see Figure 14.11), displaying a list of the major categories into which My Music automatically sorts your audio collection, based on metadata for each track. The genres displayed will reflect the actual music content stored on your Media Center system, but here are some of the categories you may encounter:

- Classical
- Country
- Easy Listening
- Jazz
- Misc
- Other
- Rock
- Soundtrack
- World

tip

Want to speed up your search? Think about the word—or even just the part of a word—that's most unique to the song, artist, or track you are looking for. Remember: When you're doing a keyword search, less really is more.

Keywords

To sort your audio collection by searching for a keyword in the album title, track, or artist name, select the Search tab and enter a word using your keyboard or the text-entry keypad on your remote control (see Figure 14.12).

The Music Search page displays a guide to the alphanumeric keys on your remote control. Just press the button that corresponds to the letter you want to enter. Each button represents three letters—press once for the first letter, twice for the second letter, and three times to enter the third letter.

note

The Music Search feature looks at the entire contents of each listing to find a match for your search term, and it begins searching the moment you enter the first letter. As a result, you'll initially see items that contain only the first character you entered in the search field. For example, enter the letter Q, and Music Search will display all items that contain the letter Q. Enter an additional letter—such as a U—and the display will show only the items that have those two letters in sequence, and so on. As you enter more letters, Music Search continues to narrow the search results.

FIGURE 14.11
From this view of the Genres display, simply click on the category you want.

FIGURE 14.12
If you're kicking back on the couch, there's no need to pull yourself up to your PC's keyboard just to do a keyword search in My Music.

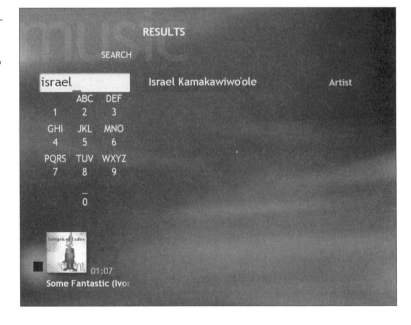

Controlling My Music Playback

After you have located the songs you want to hear using the techniques discussed previously, Music Center allows you full control of the playback experience with your remote control, your mouse, or your keyboard:

- **Remote control**—To play, pause, skip forward or backward, and so on, use the transport controls as described in Chapter 4 (see Figure 4.1).
- **Mouse**—Just move the mouse to make the audio transport controls appear onscreen (see Figure 5.1 in Chapter 5).
- **Keyboard**—To control audio functions, use the keyboard shortcuts for audio controls, as described in Chapter 5 (see Table 5.5) .

Additional Audio Options

My Music gives you several additional ways to customize your listening experience, including the capability to repeat and visualize audio tracks.

Repeat

Along with the Play and Shuffle playback options offered in My Music, you can also choose to repeat a track. Just select the Repeat tab, available from the Now Playing screen (see Figure 14.13). Place a check mark next to the tracks you want to repeat. When you've finally gotten your fill of that particular musical selection, just press OK again on your remote control to clear the Repeat command.

Visualize

Microsoft has incorporated into the My Music interface the ability to choose from various visualization schemes that let you experience your audio collection in a new and very interesting way. The results range from a primitive—and perhaps a little hokey—synchronized graphic that looks as though it was created with a Hasbro Spirograph and some colored pens, to sophisticated full-color effects worthy of the psychedelic light travel sequence in *2001: A Space Odyssey* (see Figure 14.14). Don't be surprised if you find yourself mesmerized!

FIGURE 14.13

When you select Repeat, My Music will show your choice by placing a check mark in the Repeat tab.

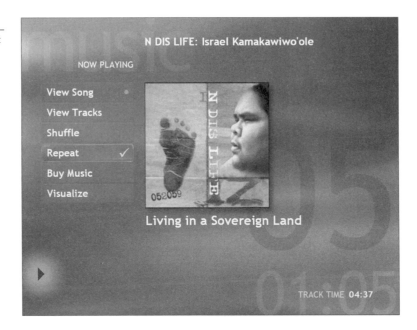

FIGURE 14.14

After you select Visualize, you can use the Ch+/Ch- buttons on your remote control to scroll through the various visualization schemes.

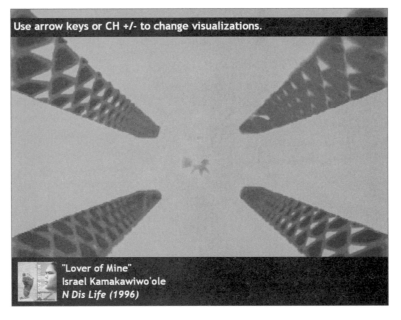

THE ABSOLUTE MINIMUM

Your old stereo is about to hang its head in shame. The My Music interface in Media Center allows you to manage and take pleasure in your music using technology your traditional home audio system never dreamed of.

To get the most out of Media Center's music playback features, be sure to do this:

- Set Music Center to be your default music player for audio CDs. This way you'll always be able to control CD playback with your remote.

- Your days of playing "name that tune" to find music tracks on your PC are over. My Music lets you slice and dice music metadata, allowing you to sort songs by album, artist, song title, or genre.

- My Music includes a powerful search engine. Search by any keyword—or even a particular letter—to find exactly the music you want, every time.

- Choose your weapon—remote control, mouse, or keyboard—to manage music playback. Whichever way you are most comfortable interacting with your computer system, Media Center supports it.

- Sample some of the interesting graphic visualizations Media Center provides, and select the perfect optical accompaniment to each musical selection.

15

RADIO

How many times have you been listening to the radio and wished you could rewind it and hear that last song—or the DJ's shocking statement—just one more time? It's never before been possible with an off-the-shelf consumer radio. Strangely, several years after the capability to delay, or time-shift, television was introduced in products like TiVo and ReplayTV, the much less technically challenging capability to time-shift live radio has finally made it to the consumer market. Thanks to the most recent version of the Media Center software, you can now treat FM radio transmissions in much the same way as TV programs.

There are some limitations to Media Center's Radio capabilities. For example, at present, you cannot save radio programs to play back later.

As noted previously, anything you can do with video data is generally even easier to do with audio-only files, so it stands to reason that these record-and-store capabilities were left out intentionally, probably because of the outcry that would ensue from broadcasters and record labels if we could all suddenly make perfect digital recordings of radio broadcasts with ease.

There are still a few wish-list items for Radio features, which Microsoft or enterprising third-party developers can address. However, the core Radio capabilities in Media Center grant us a wish that has been unfulfilled since the invention of the wireless broadcast medium itself: the ability to go back and rehear a radio program, even as the broadcast continues.

note

Technically, Media Center's FM Radio features do not support rewind, but you can use the Replay button to move backward or the Skip button to jump forward within the radio memory buffer.

Setting Up Radio

If you just purchased a Media Center PC, and Radio is included in the main Media Center menu (see Figure 15.1), very little setup is involved. All you need to do is attach an external antenna and start cranking up the audio.

However, Media Center PCs sold or configured before the introduction of the most recent upgrade to the Media Center software (code-named Harmony) did not include a radio-equipped tuner card. And not all manufacturers plan to offer the capability in their more current models, either.

If you do not see Radio in your Media Center menu, first make sure you have an FM radio antenna input connector on your tuner card. Typically, this will appear as a second male coax connector labeled "FM" protruding alongside the TV-Out connector on the back of your Media Center PC. If you have confirmed that you have a radio-equipped tuner card and still don't see the Radio menu choice in Media Center, try upgrading to the latest version of the Media Center software, and reboot your system. If this does not correct the problem, contact your PC manufacturer.

FIGURE 15.1

Close inspection of the animated radio icon reveals that it's tuned to the fictitious FM station KRAM 108.8.

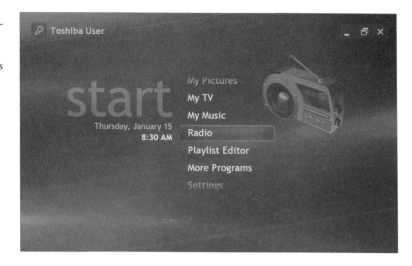

Connecting an External Antenna

If your Media Center PC has an FM tuner on board, but the manufacturer did not supply you with an external FM antenna, you're going to need one to get any reception at all. Fortunately, this doesn't need to be a big investment. You can find a serviceable external FM antenna for well under $10 at just about any electronics store. If you live in a remote area, or in a place that features rugged terrain, you may want to investigate a more sophisticated, powered antenna. Even a top-of-the-line model from a respected manufacturer such as Terk Technologies, maker of the FMPRO 50 antenna (see Figure 15.2), for example, should be available for well under $100.

FIGURE 15.2
Terk's FM Pro antenna, also called the FM50, is engineered to provide clear and powerful reception for both distant and nearby FM stations.

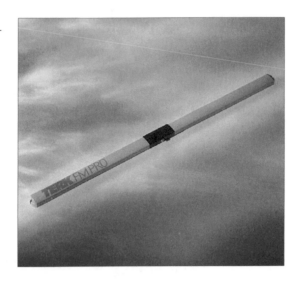

Finding Radio Stations

After you have your antenna configured, you're ready to start playing the radio inside your Media Center PC. When you select Radio, you'll be greeted by the main FM Radio screen (see Figure 15.3). These are the main features:

- The Start FM button
- The Settings button
- Spaces for nine station presets

FIGURE 15.3
The current frequency dominates the display, flanked by a Save button and resting atop twin Seek and Tune buttons.

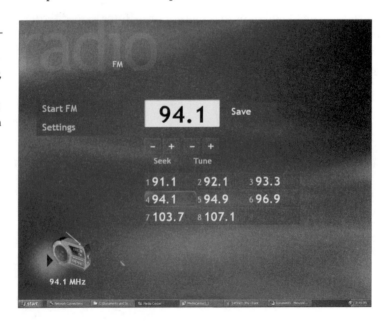

If you know the "dial" location of the station you want to tune to, select the – or + Tune button with the remote control or your mouse, and advance to the desired frequency.

If you want to tune "by ear," you'll need to select the Start FM button to begin hearing audio. If you are not already tuned to a strong FM signal, you should hear static.

You can also tune in stations by pressing at least three digits on the remote control's numeric keypad, or by using the – or + Seek buttons on the screen to automatically advance to the next strong signal. If you like what you hear, select Save to store the station in the next available preset location.

tip

Another way to navigate the FM dial with your remote is to use the Ch+ and Ch- buttons to tune up or down to the next dial position. If you are in the United States, pressing the channel button will scroll up or down in increments of 0.2 megahertz (MHz). In other countries, you'll be able to move in 0.1MHZ increments.

Using Presets

Nine preset locations are available. If you try to exceed that number, Radio will indicate that you need to make some room before you can store additional stations (see Figure 15.4).

FIGURE 15.4
When you exceed the number of preset slots, you'll have to delete one before you can add another.

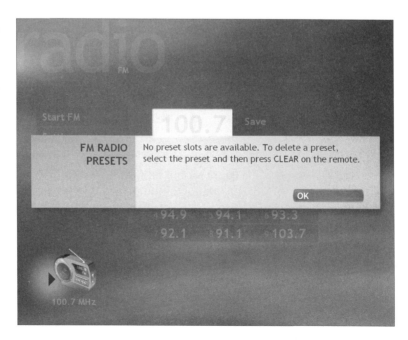

FM RADIO PRESETS

No preset slots are available. To delete a preset, select the preset and then press CLEAR on the remote.

OK

To delete a stored preset, select the preset by using the navigation arrows on the remote, or by using the numeric keypad on the remote to enter the preset number, and then press the Clear button. Radio will ask you to confirm the action (see Figure 15.5). Press OK to complete the process.

FIGURE 15.5

This confirmation message gives you an opportunity to back out and keep the station presets as they are.

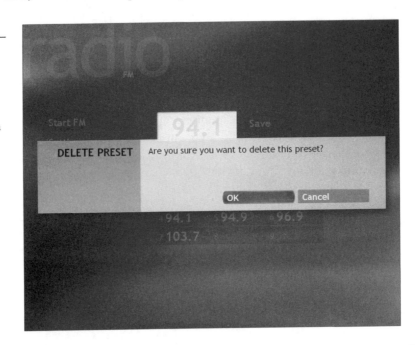

Using Pause, Play, Replay, and Skip

Now for the fancy stuff. As with many of Media Center's most powerful features, time-shifting radio transmissions is deceptively easy. Here's how it works:

■ **Pause**—To stop the radio reception in its tracks, just press the Pause button on the remote control, click the Pause button in the on-screen transport controls using the mouse, or press the keyboard shortcut Ctrl+P. Radio will let you pause the broadcast for up to 30 minutes. A progress bar will be displayed, as shown in Figure 15.6.

caution

Although selecting the Start FM button onscreen to resume airplay of your broadcast will technically do the job, it will also erase the memory buffer. That's fine if you want a fresh start and don't care about losing the ability to replay the previous 30 minutes of audio. If that matters to you, just use the Play button to resume.

FIGURE 15.6

FIGURE 15.6

When you pause the broadcast, Media Center automatically displays a progress bar, showing how much memory buffer is available.

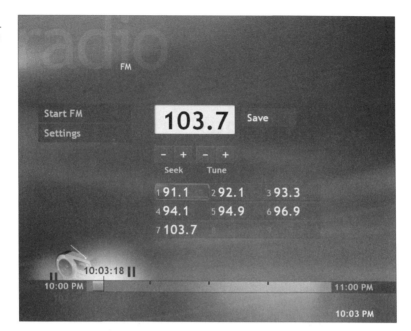

- **Play**—To resume playing the broadcast with the remote control, press the Pause button again, or press the Play button. The same principle applies to the mouse and keyboard commands. You can also select Start FM from the FM Radio screen.

- **Replay**—Although you can't actually use the Rew and Fwd buttons in Radio, you can accomplish the same thing by pressing the Replay and Skip buttons to reverse or advance through the memory buffer. Replay skips back 7 seconds. If you are paused when you press the Replay button, the audio will remain paused at the earlier point. Press Play or select Start FM to resume the broadcast from that point. Press Replay repeatedly to reverse up to 30 minutes into the broadcast.

tip

As you might expect, you can stop the broadcast at any time by pressing the Stop button on your remote, or by clicking the square Stop icon on the transport control. What you might not realize is that Media Center will continue to record the audio from that point. If you resume playing the radio again within the next 30 minutes, it will continue playing from the point where you left off.

■ **Skip**—The Skip button will advance through the memory buffer in 29-second increments, until you reach the end of the buffer. As with pressing Replay, if you are paused when you select Skip, you'll remain paused until you press Play, press Pause again, or select Start FM.

Adjusting Radio Settings

Choosing the Settings button on the FM Radio screen gives you some options for organizing and grooming your station presets (see Figure 15.7). For each of the nine preset locations, you can move the preset to a new location in your station list, or delete it to make room for other presets.

FIGURE 15.7

Selecting the ˆ or ˇ symbol next to a station preset in the Settings screen tunes it up or down to the next preset.

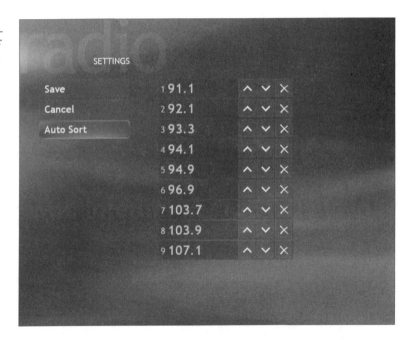

The Auto Sort button allows you to have Media Center reorganize your presets so that they appear in ascending or descending order. Press Auto Sort again to change the order. Select Save when you get it organized they way you want it.

Using Radio with My TV

Because Media Center PCs with FM Radio capability use a single tuner card for TV and radio reception, it's an "either/or" situation: You can listen to radio *or* watch TV, not both at once. Because most human beings aren't set up to multitask in that manner, either, this typically doesn't present much of a problem.

However, if you were hoping to listen to the radio while Media Center's My TV features record video programming for you to watch later, you're going to be disappointed. When Media Center approaches a TV recording session you previously scheduled, a message will appear in the lower screen advising you that you have a choice to make (see Figure 15.8). You can either keep listening to Radio or let My TV record the video program.

FIGURE 15.8

When the time comes to choose either Radio or My TV, Media Center will display a message like this.

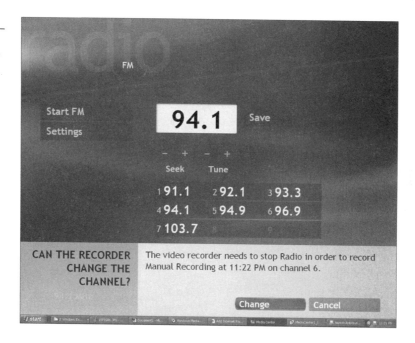

THE ABSOLUTE MINIMUM

Media Center provides something that just about anyone who listens to the radio has wished for at one time or another: the ability to go back and hear something a second time. Or a third time. Now you'll be able to control radio broadcasts as if they were on tape—without having to actually tape the broadcast.

As you get ready to kick the tires on the next-generation digital radio inside your Media Center PC, remember these points:

- The FM Radio features aren't available with every Media Center PC. Check to make sure your system has a built-in FM tuner. If there's no tuner, the Radio menu item won't appear on the Media Center start page.

- You'll need some kind of external antenna to get any FM reception. Remember that PCs can give off some significant radio emissions of their own, so if you hear too much static, try moving the external antenna well away from your PC.

- As long as you have decent reception, finding broadcast stations is a snap. If you know the station's location, you can punch in the numbers using the keypad on your remote control, or select the +/– buttons on the screen to tune to the exact frequency.

- Media Center also offers a Seek capability to automatically tune to the strongest radio signals in your broadcast area. After you find the stations you like, use Save to store the station as a preset.

- You can use the Pause, Play, Replay, and Skip capabilities to control the radio programming, just as you would a digital video program in My TV.

16

CUSTOMIZING THE MEDIA CENTER AUDIO EXPERIENCE

With the introduction of Windows XP Media Center Edition 2004, the Media Center audio experience was expanded from only listening to digital audio stored on your PC, and limited capabilities to access streaming Internet stations, to a full-on audio arsenal that includes rewindable FM radio and fully supported Internet audio.

In this chapter, we'll look at some of the ways to customize and personalize that expanded audio experience, to make it really "sing."

Working with Playlists

We discussed how to use the Auto Playlist feature in Chapter 14, "Playback Time: Sorting, Viewing, and Controlling Your Music." You may not have realized it at the time, but creating on-the-fly playlists based on what tunes you play, and when, is a capability that Media Center borrows from its sister application in Windows XP, the Windows Media Player.

Playlists are a powerful feature that allow you to play the role of Big-Time Music Producer, deciding which tracks make it into the final mix, and which ones don't. You can also pick the order in which songs are played, and create new "compilation albums" that mix and match songs from any combination of artists that happens to suit your musical fancy.

There are two ways to work with playlists on your Media Center PC: by using Windows Media Player outside of the Media Center Interface, and by working within Media Center using the Media Center Playlist Editor.

> **tip**
>
> As an alternative method to creating a playlist from Windows Media Player, you can open the My Music folder from the Windows XP Start menu, and right-click on the songs you want to add. Choose Add to Playlist, and then choose an existing playlist from the drop-down box, or select New (see Figure 16.1).
>
> If you want to add multiple songs at once, hold down the Ctrl key while you click on them, and then right-click on one of the selected files to complete the procedure.

Creating Playlists with Windows Media Player

To create a playlist using Windows Media Player, launch the player from the Windows XP desktop, and do the following:

1. Click on Media Library, and then click on File, New Playlist, or use the keyboard shortcut Ctrl+N.

2. In the blank provided, type the new playlist name, and click OK.

3. Your new playlist has been added to the My Playlists folder. Select it in the left pane, and the empty playlist will be displayed on the right.

4. To add items to the playlist, click on All Music in the left pane to display a complete list of the available audio tracks.

5. Right-click each item you want to add, and select Add to Playlist. Choose the new playlist from the drop-down menu. (You can also just drag and drop the tune directly onto the selected playlist, if you prefer.)

FIGURE 16.1

In this view of
the My Music
folder, multiple
tracks have
been selected,
using the Ctrl
key, for adding
to a new
playlist.

After you've completed the playlist creation process, you'll be able to launch Media Center and choose the new playlist from within the My Music interface. (For details on playing playlists in My Music, see Chapter 14.)

Creating Playlists with Media Center Playlist Editor

If the idea of setting down your precious remote control and exiting Media Center to the Windows XP desktop is utterly abhorrent to you, take heart: There is a way to create and manage playlists without leaving the Media Center interface.

To make use of this capability, however, you'll have to download the Playlist Editor PowerToy from Microsoft's Web site, as described in the "Special Media Center Downloads" section of Chapter 24, "Downloads and Enhancements." Admittedly, you will have to wander outside of Media Center to actually get the PowerToy file, but as soon as it's installed, you can put your mouse safely back on the shelf.

Here's how to create a playlist using the Media Center Playlist editor:

1. From the More Programs menu in Media Center, select Playlist Editor.

2. Choose Create Playlist.

3. Choose how you want your songs to be sorted, by selecting Albums, Artists, Songs, or Genres.

4. Select the items you want added to the new playlist by pressing the OK button on each item. This will place a check mark in the item listing (see Figure 16.2).

FIGURE 16.2

The Playlist
Editor PowerToy
for Media
Center lets you
select the songs
you want, and
then add them
to a new, cus-
tom playlist.

5. When you have selected all the songs for your new playlist, highlight Add Items, and press OK on the remote control.

6. A text entry box will appear, allowing you to input the name of your new playlist using the text entry keys on the remote control. Press the up arrow to type in uppercase, and the down arrow to return to lowercase. (For more information on the fine points of text entry with your remote control, see the section "Searching by Title," in Chapter 7, "Finding Shows to Record.")

7. When finished, press OK on the remote, select Done, and then select Exit.

Now go to My Music and select Playlists. Your new playlist will appear, sorted with other playlists into alphabetical order. Select the new playlist and press the Play button on the remote control to enjoy the fruits of your labor.

Working with Internet Radio Stations in Media Center

Tired of your own music collection and hankering for something new? Try to resist the urge to download "pirated" songs from an online file-swapping service, and instead try tuning in the fresh sounds of Internet radio.

These stations run the gamut from commercial radio stations that take their pro-gramming right off the airways and stream it live over the Net, to tiny operations that are little more than a solitary music enthusiast with a PC, a Web connection, and arguably too much time on his hands.

The result is a musical mish-mash of global proportions, and an endless opportunity to sample new sounds and styles. All you have to do is locate these virtual radio stations on the Web, and add them to your Media Center music collection. There are various ways to accomplish this task, and we'll take them in turn.

In general, there are two places in Media Center where you can access Internet radio: My Music and Radio.

Adding Internet Radio Stations to My Music

Until the 2004 version of Media Center came along, with its support for FM radio, My Music offered the only means of accessing Internet radio stations from within Media Center. The process is fairly simple, but not very intuitive, and it does require that you leave the Media Center interface and do all the dirty work using Windows Media Player. Here's how it's done:

1. In Windows Media Player, click on the Radio Tuner button.

2. Select a station by clicking on one of the links, such as Featured Stations, Find More Stations, Search, or one of the categories listed on the left side of the screen (see Figure 16.3).

FIGURE 16.3

The Radio Tuner in Windows Media Center allows you to locate hundreds of Internet radio stations from all over the world.

3. Find a radio station you want to play, and then double-click the radio station link to view details. Click on Play or Visit Website to Play.

4. After you hear the station start playing, open the File menu in Media Player, highlight Add to Media Library, and click on Add Currently Playing Playlist.

5. Type in a name for the new playlist, and click Save. The streaming radio station is now stored under Playlists in Media Center's My Music (see Figure 16.4).

FIGURE 16.4

This view of My Playlists in My Music shows the entry "WKSU Folk," which actually consists of a link to a streaming audio station.

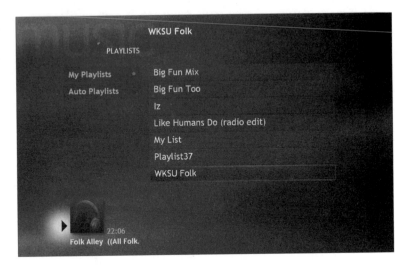

Adding Internet Radio Stations to Radio

Although the process previously outlined is reliable, storing a radio station as a playlist doesn't make as much sense as simply saving it as a preset in the Radio section of Media Center. However, there are a few things to consider before you can make this work.

First of all, if you don't have an FM radio-capable tuner card installed in your Windows XP Media Center 2004 PC, you may well be wondering, *What Radio section?* As described in Chapter 15, "Radio," you must have the latest version of the operating system and a working FM tuner card for the Radio menu item to automatically appear in the Media Center main menu. There is an exception, however. If you add an Internet radio station preset in a format that Media Center recognizes, the Radio menu will magically appear—even if you don't have a radio tuner card.

> **caution**
>
> Make sure that the Internet radio station you selected is actually playing in Windows Media Player. Some stations use their own custom player, leaving Windows Media Player out in the cold. In such cases, you won't be able to store it as a Media Center playlist.

Unfortunately, adding a streaming radio station using the My Music playlist process previously outlined won't have any effect on the Radio features of Media Center. For a radio station to show up in the Radio menu (and to make the Radio menu itself show up, if you don't have an FM tuner), the station must be stored as a Media Center radio preset, not as a playlist.

The easiest way to accomplish this task is to access a Media Center–compatible streaming audio service, such as Live365.com. This service is available from the Online Spotlight menu in Media Center, and the process of adding a radio station preset in this fashion is fully described in Chapter 23, "XP Media Center and Your Internet Connection."

Unfortunately, relatively few Internet radio stations have gone to the trouble of providing the Media Center integration necessary to add a radio preset as smoothly and simply as Live365.com has done. The selection is likely to increase as the Media Center audience grows. And in the meantime, Live365.com boasts a massive library of streaming audio stations to choose from. But what if you want to add an Internet radio station that doesn't support Media Center's Radio presets?

Creating Internet Radio Presets from Scratch

There is a workaround that allows Media Center owners to create their own Internet radio station presets, but beware: It's a tricky process, and one that Microsoft doesn't support for consumer-grade customers—only developers. If you're feeling reckless, and ready to dig in "under the hood" of your Media Center, here's how to do it.

First, you need to copy the Internet address of the radio stream that you want to add to your Radio menu in Media Center. The easiest way to do this is to use your browser to find a Web link that causes the radio station to start playing in Windows Media Center when you click on it. After you've tested it, right-click on that link and select Copy Shortcut. Then open a blank Notepad file (choose Start, All Programs, Accessories, Notepad) and paste the shortcut there for safekeeping.

Now all you need to do is create the MCL file. Here's a sample MCL file, which creates a link to the Rudolph Radio streaming radio station:

```
<application name="Rudolph Radio"
url="http://www.radiorudolph.com/rudolph.asx"
<capabilitiesrequired directx="false" audio="true"
video="false" intensiverendering="false" console="false"
```

All you need to do is copy the preceding into a Notepad window, substituting the name of the station in quotes in the name line, and the link to the radio stream (which you previously copied into another Notepad window) in quotes in the url line. When you're done, the file should look something like what's shown in Figure 16.5.

Now you need to save the file to the correct folder on your Media Center machine, making sure that you use a filename that ends with the .mcl suffix. The correct folder is as follows:

```
C:\Documents and Settings\YourUserName\Start Menu\Programs\Accessories\
Media Center\Media Center Programs\Radio
```

FIGURE 16.5

This MCL file for the Rudolph Radio station is actually a series of simple statements that tell Media Center where to find what it needs.

Now when you open Media Center and select Radio, you'll see the new radio station link that you created listed under Internet (see Figure 16.6). Just select the preset you created and press the Play button on the remote control. And as sweet music fills the air, go ahead and pat yourself on the back for a job well done!

FIGURE 16.6

The preset for Rudolph Radio is flanked by a hand-made preset for RadioMargarita ville.

THE ABSOLUTE MINIMUM

In this chapter, we discussed ways to truly customize your music experience in Media Center. As you get ready to try these things for yourself, remember the following:

- Use playlists to create audio programs of multiple audio files. In a few minutes, you can create a playlist that you and your friends will enjoy for hours.

- If you prefer not to venture outside of Media Center any more than is absolutely necessary—or if you just like the feel of the remote control in your hand—you can download the Playlist Editor for Media Center.

- Internet radio stations offer a refreshing break from tedious commercial radio stations, and from your own tired music collection. You can add streaming stations to My Music by saving them as playlists in Windows Media Center.

- It's a bit more complex, but you can also write .MCL files that will allow you to create custom presets for streaming audio stations and have them appear in the Media Center Radio interface.

PART VI

MY PICTURES

17

IMPORTING AND STORING YOUR DIGITAL PHOTOS

Digital cameras are getting smaller, better, and cheaper practically every day. They aren't just replacing our film cameras (the day is fast approaching when some youngster will ask you, "Film? What's that?"), but digital cameras have become so compact and affordable that they are cropping up in everything from mobile phones to PDAs.

As we trade in our old film canisters and cartridges for reusable memory devices, the whole process of picture-taking begins to change. Shooting scores of photos to get the one perfect shot used to be a trade secret of the professional photographer, but no more. If you own a digital camera, there's no incremental cost associated with taking three dozen rather than just one. You may run out of room on your removable memory card temporarily, until you delete the photos you don't want to keep, but you won't start running up your bill until you begin making hard copies.

Therein lies the Shakespearean "rub" in digital photography: printing. Although consumer-grade color printers and related software continue to improve, they have not reached the point where the process can match the ease and convenience of dropping your film off at the one-hour photo shop or corner drugstore. In fact, many of us have shelled out hundreds—even thousands—of dollars in digital photo equipment and supplies, only to find that we have essentially become our own one-hour photo technician. In fact, count yourself lucky if you can actually produce a set of quality prints from your digital camera in only an hour. Most of us find ourselves spending much longer, and still end up frustrated with both the process and the results.

Surely there must be a better way? There is. Why print photos at all when you can easily share them with family and friends electronically? Email and Web pages provide effective ways for showing off your photos over long distances, but for displaying them in your own home, nothing beats the television screen. Here's where the whole idea of Windows XP Media Center Edition's My Pictures feature set really starts to shine.

My Pictures lets you display your photos individually or as a virtual slide show. You can sort your pictures in various ways, and browse through them using the remote control, or your mouse and keyboard. Your digital photos never had it so good, and the one-hour photo guy will have to find somebody else's pictures to leaf through in his spare time.

Transferring Your Photos

To put My Pictures to work for you, the first step is moving your photos from your digital camera into your Media Center PC. As with connecting your video camera to the Media Center (see the section "Connecting to Your Camcorder," in Chapter 10, "Capturing and Creating Videos with Media Center"), you'll need to start with an inventory of the types of outputs your camera supports, and then compare that list to the types of inputs your PC supports.

Connecting to Your Digital Camera

The process of transferring photos from a digital camera to a PC used to be a tedious one. Serial cables were usually involved, along with TWAIN (believe it or not, it stands for "Toolkit Without an Interesting Name") drivers and other abstruse bits of software. However, camera and PC designers have come together in recent years over interfaces such as USB (Universal Serial Bus), which, along with Windows XP's Plug and Play features, can virtually eliminate the headaches that used to accompany the process of establishing a connection between your camera and your computer.

Although the oblong USB connector on your PC is pretty easy to spot (see Figure 17.1), its counterpart on the camera is apt to look quite different.

> **tip**
>
> Chances are that your Media Center PC will not have just one USB receptacle, but several to choose from. The design goal of USB was to make it, well, universal—so that anything plugged in to any USB port should be recognized automatically by the host system. As such, it shouldn't matter which USB port you plug your camera into. However, because it's likely to be an intermittent connection, used only when you have fresh photos to download, it's probably most convenient to use a USB port located on the front of your computer (see Figure 17.3), rather than one in back. Use the less-convenient, rear-facing receptacles for "permanent" peripherals, such as a USB-equipped mouse, keyboard, printer, or monitor.

FIGURE 17.1

The oblong USB plug that connects to the PC is quite distinctive, making it easy to identify.

Some USB plugs for cameras and other input devices are small and rectangular, some are vaguely bell-shaped, and some have shapes that simply defy description. A collection of USB connectors supported by various digital devices is shown in Figure 17.2.

In most cases, your digital camera will come equipped with an appropriate connection cord, so all that remains to be done is find the correct receptacles on the camera and the PC, and plug everything in.

FIGURE 17.2

The USB connector that attaches to your camera can come in various forms, including any of the four configurations shown here.

FIGURE 17.3

The HP Media Center features a drop-down door in the front bezel that conceals ports for connecting digital still and video cameras.

The first time you connect your camera to your PC, Windows will tell you it has detected new hardware, and in most cases, it will ask you to install the proper software drivers. However, some cameras make use of drivers that Windows XP already has installed. Follow the screen prompts, as well as your camera manufacturer's recommended procedure, to set up the camera connection properly the first time.

After Windows recognizes your camera, transferring photos becomes quite easy. In fact, the process is essentially the same whether you are plugging in a camera or just inserting a removable media card from your camera into a memory-card reader on the PC.

tip

With all the USB peripherals proliferating around your PC, even a desktop that's generously endowed with USB ports may eventually come up short. If you find yourself in that predicament, consider investing in a USB hub, such as the one shown in Figure 17.4.

FIGURE 17.4
Inexpensive USB
hubs, like this
four-port model,
can cost as little
as a few dollars.

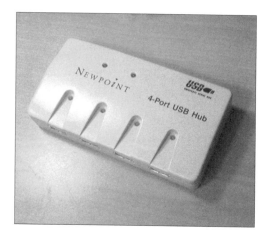

Using Media Cards

Media cards come in an array of shapes and sizes, and all of them work in pretty
much the same way: Insert the card into the camera and store images on it. When
you're done, remove the card and insert it into a card reader, and then transfer the
photos to your PC's hard disk. The only variable to worry about is whether your PC
comes equipped with a memory-card reader at all, and if it does, whether that
reader accepts the type of memory card your camera uses.

Some Media Center PCs are configured with no built-in card readers whatsoever,
whereas others are "loaded for bear" in that department. Systems that fall into the
latter category include the HP Media Center PC 864, which boasts support for four of
the most popular media card formats (see Figure 17.5) .

FIGURE 17.5
The HP Media
Center PC 864
has built-in
readers for
SmartMedia,
CompactFlash
(Type I and Type
II), Multimedia
Card/Secure
Digital Card,
and Sony's
Memory Stick.

Media Card Adapters

If your Media Center PC does not include any slots for reading memory cards, never fear. Various external adapters are available (see Figure 17.6), most of which plug conveniently into a USB port on your PC and allow instant access to a wide selection of memory-card formats.

FIGURE 17.6
External card readers provide an inexpensive way to expand your PC's repertoire when it comes to accepting removable memory devices.

Getting Your Photos into Media Center

Typically, plugging in your camera or a media card will produce the same result: opening a pop-up window that offers you various action choices (see Figure 17.7). This gives you a variety of ways to access your photos and make them available to your Media Center's software applications.

FIGURE 17.7
This pop-up window allows you to choose which action to take when a camera or removable memory card is recognized by the Media Center PC.

These are the choices:

- Copy Pictures to a Folder on My Computer Using Microsoft Scanner and Camera Wizard
- View a Slideshow of Images Using Windows Picture and Fax Viewer
- Print the Pictures Using Photo Printing Wizard
- Open and Edit the Pictures Using Microsoft Picture It! Photo 7.0
- View Pictures in Media Center Using Media Center
- Open Folder to View Files Using Windows Explorer
- Take No Action

To open your photos directly using Media Center's My Pictures interface, select the Using Media Center option.

Now you're looking at the photos stored in your camera or on your removable media card using the Media Center My Pictures interface (see Figure 17.8). You have several options at your disposal for viewing, sorting, and navigating to other places where My Pictures typically looks for photos.

Storing Your Photos

We'll go into detail about the cool things you can do with your photos using the My Pictures interface in subsequent chapters. First let's talk about something you *can't* do while using My Pictures: store your photos. If you ever want to view these photos in My Pictures a second time, you will need to store them in a file folder where My Pictures will look for them. There are two to chose from: the My Pictures folder and the Shared Pictures folder. (The Other Media tab will look for photos stored on removable media.)

> **note**
>
> The option to open and edit pictures using Microsoft Picture It! appears only if you have downloaded the free software from Microsoft's Web site. Details on using the photo editing application are discussed in Chapter 20, "Customizing the My Pictures Experience with Microsoft Picture It!"

> **tip**
>
> Many digital cameras automatically format removable media cards using a file structure that you may not recognize when Media Center initially opens and allows you to view the contents of the card. If you at first see a file folder as opposed to your actual photos, try double-clicking on the folder until you find where the pictures are stored.

FIGURE 17.8

Selecting the
View Pictures in
Media Center
Using Media
Center option is
the quickest way
to open your
photos using the
My Pictures
interface.

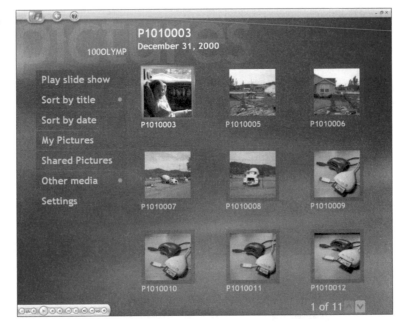

The idea behind these two default folders for use
with the My Pictures interface is that each user
on the Media Center System has her own My
Pictures folder that only she can access, and she
can choose to share pictures with other users by
storing them in the Shared Pictures folder.

The easiest way to store your photos in one of
these folders for later viewing in Media Center's
My Pictures interface is to go back to where you
attached the camera or inserted your media
card. This time, instead of choosing the option to
open them using Media Center, choose the
option Copy Pictures to a Folder on My Computer
Using Microsoft Scanner and Camera Wizard.

tip

The selection screen in the
Scanner and Camera Wizard
also shows you buttons to
rotate photos 90 degrees to
the right or left, or to view
the properties of a particular
image.

Using the Scanner and Camera Wizard

When the Scanner and Camera Wizard launches, it will display an opening screen
to advise you of its purpose. Click Next to view a catalog of your photos (see Figure
17.9). Now place a check mark next to the photos you want to transfer.

FIGURE 17.9

The wizard automatically selects all the photos to be transferred. You can click on a photo to remove it from the list.

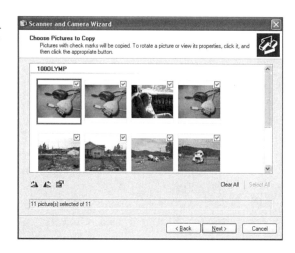

When you have selected the photos you want to store on your hard drive, click Next. The following screen (see Figure 17.10) allows you to choose a folder and subfolder to store the photos in. Choose the default location—the My Pictures directory—or use the drop-down box to select Shared Pictures, the other directory to which the My Pictures interface in Media Center has access. Checking the box to automatically delete the transferred files from your media card is a handy way to perform a little routine housekeeping, keeping your media cards uncluttered and ready for your next photo shoot.

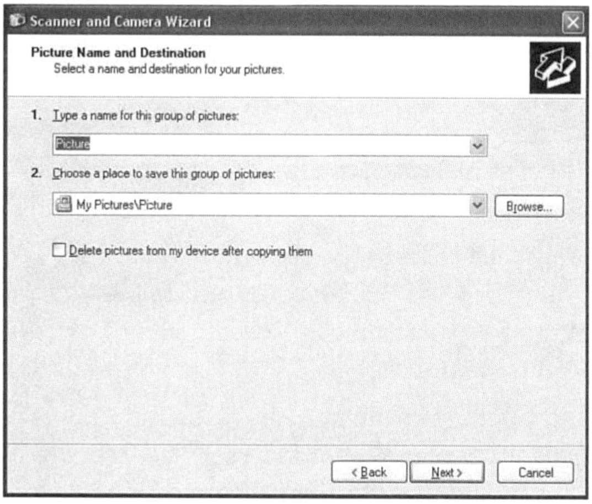

FIGURE 17.10

This wizard screen allows you to automatically delete files from your media card after they have been transferred to your PC.

After you select Next, the wizard will perform the file transfers as you requested. The final screen gives you the following three options:

- Publish These Pictures to a Web Site
- Order Prints of These Pictures from a Photo Printing Web Site
- Nothing. I'm Finished Working with These Pictures

Choose the last option and click Next. A summary screen will be displayed. Click Finish.

THE ABSOLUTE MINIMUM

Now you're ready to return to the My Pictures interface from the Media Center main menu, and begin viewing and sharing your photos using the extremely easy and accessible tools that My Pictures places at your disposal. But first, remember these points:

- The first step is to load your digital photos onto your Media Center PC. This can be accomplished by establishing a direct connection between your camera and the PC, or by removing the media card from your digital camera and accessing it from the PC using a media card reader.

- Most digital cameras come with a USB cord for establishing a simple and stable connection with your PC for transferring files.

- Your Media PC may or may not come equipped with a built-in card reader that supports the type of memory card your camera uses. If it doesn't, you can pick up an inexpensive external card reader at most electronics and computer stores.

- After the connection is established, your Media Center will provide you with several options for transferring, manipulating, or simply viewing your photos. One option is to open them directly using Media Center.

- Media Center's My Pictures photo viewing interface does not allow you to store photos. You may want to open your photos initially using the Scanner and Camera Wizard so that you can tuck the photos away on the hard drive of your PC for future reference.

- If you want your photos to be available from within My Pictures the next time you start Media Center, you need to save the shots in a directory that Media Center recognizes: My Pictures or Shared Pictures.

18

CREATING SLIDE SHOWS

In the preceding chapter we successfully transferred photos to Media Center from a camera. You could just as easily have scanned them in with a desktop scanner (just use the Scanner and Camera Wizard, as described in the section "Storing Your Photos") or downloaded them from a Web site, and so on.

Now that you have your digital image collection loaded into your Media Center machine, the next order of business is to explore the interesting ways Media Center allows you to organize and enjoy those images. In short, it's time to get organized.

Selecting Pictures

To enter the My Pictures interface, start Media Center from the Start menu using the mouse, or press the green Start button on your remote.

As with the other features of Media Center, the My Pictures interface lets you use any of your Media PC's input devices—remote control, mouse, or keyboard—to select and manipulate your images.

You'll get the same results whether you

- Use the arrow buttons on your remote to navigate to the picture you want to view, and then press OK.
- Use the arrow buttons on your keyboard to highlight the picture, and then press Enter.
- Click on the picture using the mouse.

Either way, My Pictures will switch to a full-screen view of the image you selected.

Zooming In on a Picture

Here's where Media Center gives your remote control some added "oomph." If you click on the photo with your mouse, nothing happens, but if you press OK again on the remote control, you automatically zoom into the image. Press OK one more time, and you'll enlarge the photo to an even greater magnitude. Press OK a third time, and you'll be returned to the normal full-screen view.

While you are zoomed in, press the arrow buttons to scroll the picture in any direction you want. This allows you to scrutinize every area of the image to your heart's content.

Returning to the Thumbnail View

To go back to the thumbnail view (which displays up to nine photos per page), press Back on the remote control, or Backspace on the keyboard. If you are navigating with the mouse, click on the green arrow icon near the upper left of the screen. Repeat the process to return to the folder-level view (see Figure 18.1). Note that My Pictures displays small thumbnails of the images stored inside the folders, allowing you to "see into" the folders and get a better sense of their content.

tip

You can also use your keyboard to zoom and scroll the image. Just use the Enter key to zoom, and the arrow keys to scroll up, down or sideways.

FIGURE 18.1

The folder view allows you to see multiple folders, or collections of images, as well as single images stored on your hard drive.

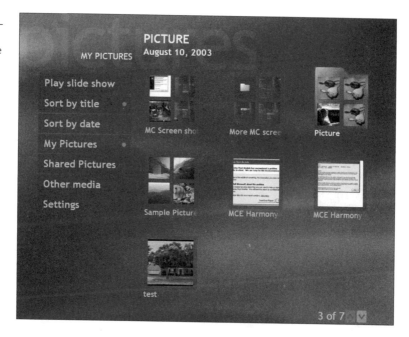

Organizing Your Pictures

My Pictures provides several ways for simply and effectively organizing your image collections at a touch of the button. These include tabs that do the following:

- Sort by name
- Sort by date
- Change subdirectories

Let's look at how these work, and how they can make even a very large collection of images easily accessible.

Sort by Name

Sort by Name is the My Pictures default method of sorting your images: alphabetical order (see Figure 18.2). My Pictures applies this sorting method to either folder or thumbnail views. If you have named your photos and folders individually using descriptive titles (and this is

tip

My Pictures will remember where you last looked for image files when you exit to the Media Center main menu. It will automatically go back to the same subdirectory, or to Other Media, the next time you use My Pictures.

recommended if you want to be able to find images easily as your collection grows), and if you tend to categorize your images by subject matter, you'll find the Sort by Name feature very useful.

FIGURE 18.2

This shows a typical folder full of photos, placed in alphabetical order by using the default Sort by Name feature.

Sort by Date

Selecting the Sort by Date tab changes the pecking order of your images, instantly rearranging them into chronological order. Note that the date now appears in the beginning of the title under each photo, allowing only four or five characters of the image file's name to be displayed (see Figure 18.3).

This sorting method is preferable if you are viewing the results of a typical outing with your digital camera. Similar to scrolling through a set of prints (or perusing a "contact sheet," if you happen to be photographically inclined), the pictures are arranged in the same order in which you snapped them.

caution

If no picture files are stored in the subdirectory you have chosen, or if no removable media is available when you select the Other Media tab, Media Center will display the error message shown in Figure 18.4.

FIGURE 18.3

This thumbnail
view of photos
in My Pictures
shows how the
same images (as
in Figure 18.2)
appear when
you're using the
Sort by Date tab.

FIGURE 18.3

This thumbnail view of photos in My Pictures shows how the same images (as in Figure 18.2) appear when you're using the Sort by Date tab.

Changing Subdirectories

As mentioned in Chapter 17 (see the section "Storing your Photos"), My Pictures is set up to look in only three places for image files: the My Pictures subdirectory, the Shared Pictures subdirectory, and on Other Media, meaning removable storage devices, such as memory cards. Select the appropriate tab to locate your pictures.

Linking to Other Image Locations

What if you have images stored elsewhere on your hard disk, in a place where My Pictures stubbornly refuses to look? Here's a workaround that allows you to create a link to your alternative image location.

For the sake of this example, let's assume that you have image files stored in your My Documents directory, and you want to access them from within the My Pictures interface, but you don't want to actually change the physical location of the image files. Just do the following:

1. Minimize Media Center and click on the Start menu in Windows XP.

2. Click on the My Pictures folder icon to view the content of the My Pictures directory (see Figure 18.5).

FIGURE 18.4

If you select a location to search for image files, and no pictures are stored there, you'll see this error message.

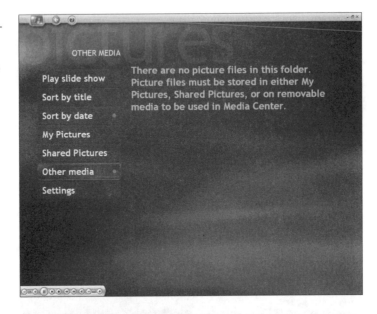

FIGURE 18.5

This view is useful for exploring and organizing the contents of your My Pictures subdirectory.

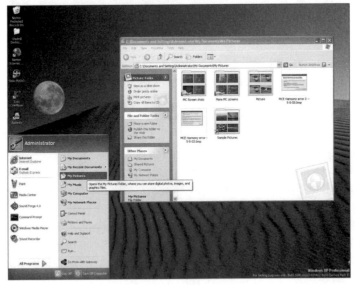

3. Right-click inside the contents window. Click on New, then Shortcut (see Figure 18.6).

4. The Create Shortcut Wizard will open and prompt you to type the location of the item you want to link to.

5. Click on Browse, select My Documents, and click OK (see Figure 18.7).

FIGURE 18.6

This view shows the location of the Create Shortcut Wizard.

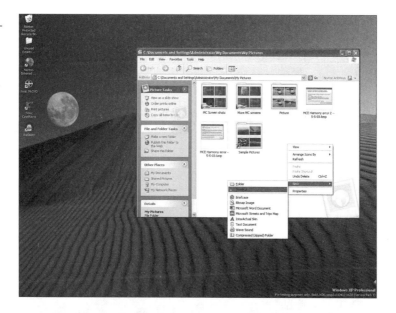

FIGURE 18.7

Using the Browse feature in the Create Shortcut Wizard, you can navigate and link to any location on your Media Center.

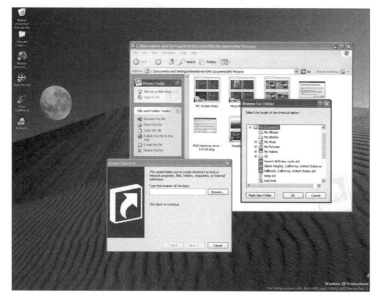

6. Select Next in the wizard, and then click Finish. Close the My Pictures contents window.

A new shortcut now exists in the My Pictures subdirectory. When you return to Media Center and open the My Picture interface, if you select the My Pictures subdirectory tab, a My Documents folder icon will be visible (see Figure 18.8). Just click on it to access the image files stored there.

FIGURE 18.8

The result of your labor: The link to the new image folder is now visible from within the My Pictures interface.

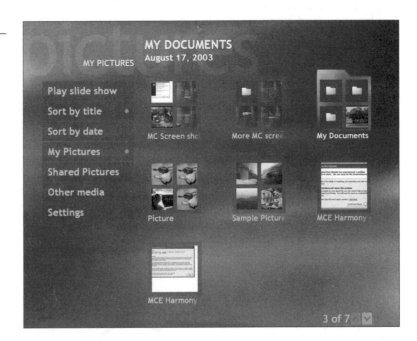

Launching a Slide Show

One of the things that is most impressive about the slide show feature in Media Center is how easy it is to use—particularly with the remote control. Simply do this:

1. Select the folder containing the images you want to view, and press OK.

2. Now press Play.

Media Center does the rest. What makes the slide show display so compelling is that Media Center doesn't just flash static images, one after another. One image may pan languidly from right to left, and the next one may slowly zoom into the center of the photo, and so on. The result is subtle, yet mesmerizing. The pictures actually seem to come alive, right out of the computer screen. This simple animation is done so skillfully that it instantly elevates even the most mundane snapshots so that they appear fascinating and strikingly professional.

Launching a Slide Show with Your Keyboard or Mouse

The procedure for launching a slide show is slightly different with your mouse. From the thumbnail view, you must click on a picture and display it in full-screen mode before you can launch the slide show. Then just click on the triangular play icon in the onscreen transport controls to launch the slide show. Use the square stop icon in the transport controls to end the slide show.

To launch and control a slide show using your keyboard, refer to the My Pictures–related keyboard shortcuts listed in Table 18.1.

Table 18.1 Keyboard Shortcuts for My Pictures Slide Shows

To	Press
Start My Pictures	Ctrl+I
Play a slide show	Ctrl+Shift+P
Pause a slide show	Ctrl+P
Stop a slide show	Ctrl+Shift+S
Skip back to the previous picture	Ctrl+Shift+B
Skip forward to the next picture	Ctrl+Shift+F
Zoom a picture in full-screen mode	Enter

Adding a Music Background

Now it's time to add some real pizzazz to your visual display by delighting the ears as well as the eyes. Once again, Media Center makes it easy. Here's all that's required to add a soundtrack to your instant slide show:

1. Press Start on the remote (or click on the green Start button icon at the upper left of the screen) to exit My Pictures and return to the Media Center main menu.

2. Select My Music, and then choose the music you want to use as your slide show background. Press Play.

3. As the music begins to play, return to the main Media Center menu and select My Pictures. Information about the music that's playing will be displayed in the inset window (see Figure 18.9).

4. Start your slide show as described previously.

tip

Want to create a longer soundtrack for your slide show? Use the features discussed in Chapter 16 to create a playlist, and then launch that before playing your slideshow.

Admittedly, this procedure is a bit kludge. Don't be surprised if Microsoft creates an even easier way to achieve this effect in a subsequent revision of the Media Center software. The capability to store your music preference and launch a "scored" slide show with one or two button presses would also be a welcome enhancement.

FIGURE 18.9

The inset window in My Pictures displays the title and length of the music track you have selected to accompany your slide show.

Selecting Transitions and Durations of Photos

Although the default settings for slide shows in My Pictures are pretty pleasing, you may want to make some changes to suit your tastes.

Using the My Pictures Settings menu, you can control the transition time between pictures in a slide show. You can also tweak the display order for your pictures.

Selecting Transitions

The default transition setting is Animated, producing the varied transition effects described earlier in this chapter (see "Launching a Slide Show"). You can also choose a simple-yet-elegant Cross Fade effect, or reject any kind of transition effect by choosing None.

Simply choose Settings from the My Pictures menu tabs, and then scroll down to the option you want and click on it or press the OK button on the remote control (see Figure 18.10). When you're satisfied with your choices, select Save to return to the My Pictures main display.

FIGURE 18.10

This view of the Settings controls for My Pictures shows Cross Fade selected as the preferred slide show transition effect.

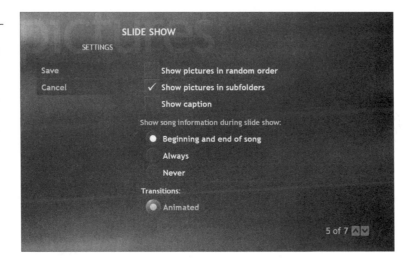

Changing Transition Times

The default display period for an image in a My Pictures slide show is 5 seconds, which seems just about right for taking in an image and then moving on to the next. But what if you want to really shake it up, such as by synchronizing your slide show to the staccato beat of a particular up-tempo tune? Or what if you are displaying highly detailed images that you want to savor and explore individually before moving on to the next?

Simply use the Settings menu to create a custom Transition time for your slide shows. Select the +/- buttons shown on the My Pictures Settings screen (see Figure 18.11) to choose a new value between 2 seconds and 60 seconds.

FIGURE 18.11

One minute is the maximum length of time a picture can be displayed in a slide show, and 2 seconds is the minimum.

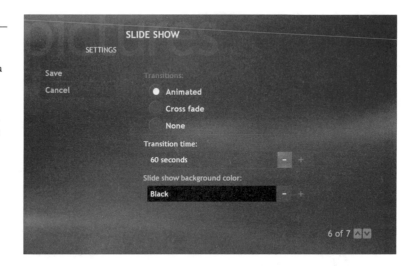

Setting the Display Order for Your Slide Show

When it comes to the display order, My Pictures lets you choose from three settings:

- Show Pictures in Random Order
- Show Pictures in Subfolders
- Show Caption

The random-order setting quite literally selects the next picture without rhyme or reason. This setting will override any other order selection you may have made, such as Sort by Title or Sort by Date (see the section "Organizing Your Pictures").

The option Show Pictures in Subfolders deals with how My Pictures handles things if you launch a slide show from the folders view (as opposed to the thumbnail view). For example, if the Show Pictures in Subfolders option is not checked and you launch a slide show from the My Pictures subdirectory, only those pictures stored in the My Pictures folder

note

What happens if the Show Pictures in Subdirectories option is unchecked, but all the pictures are stored in subdirectories? Media Center will ignore the option, and launch a slide show displaying pictures in the subdirectories.

will be used, and pictures stored in subfolders will be ignored. If the option Show Pictures in Subfolders is checked, all photos in the My Pictures subdirectory will be used in the slide show, regardless of whether they are stored in subdirectories inside My Pictures.

Additional Slide Show Options

Among the other ways to customize your slide shows using the Settings menu in My Pictures are the following options:

- **Show Song Information During Slide Show**—Choose between Always displaying and Never displaying song specifics, or choose to show them only at the beginning and end of each song.
- **Slide Show Background Color**—The default choice is black, but you can also select white, or any of nine shades of gray.

THE ABSOLUTE MINIMUM

For many of us, the idea of "watching a slide show" still conjures up images of unpacking the old carousel projector, unfurling the big white screen at one end of a darkened room, and then being subjected to hours of the photographer's droning monologue while the slides click by with a rhythmic "ka-shoonk, ka-shoonk." The very thought of it is enough to make the eyes glaze over and chill the heart with a sense of impending doom.

Media Center changes that by taking your digital images and allowing you to instantly create professional-looking results that can resemble anything from an award-winning PBS documentary to a fast-paced montage set to the latest hip-hop tune. Here are some of the things you'll need to remember, as you get your slide show ready for "primetime" viewing:

- Selecting pictures and viewing them individually is a snap, whether you use the remote control, mouse, or keyboard.
- My Pictures give you several ways to sort and organize your image collection.
- You can launch a slide show instantly by pressing the Play button on the remote control. The My Pictures default slide show options make the most of your photos with minimum effort on your part. Add some background music for an even more entertaining display.
- You can customize your slide show even further by using the Settings menu to change the order, duration, transition style, background color, and more.

IN THIS CHAPTER

- Get your digital images ready to share

- Access the Picture Details menu in My Pictures to view information about and make changes to your pictures

- Use the Touch Up process to let Media Center take the headaches out of photo enhancement

- Learn how Touch Up can instantly fix red-eye and contrast problems with your digital pictures

- Use the Picture Tasks menu in Windows XP to access additional options for repairing and outputting your images

19

PREPARING AND SHARING DIGITAL IMAGES

The My Pictures interface provided by Media Center seems at first glance to be all about displaying your photos easily and attractively—and it is. But if you get under its skin, you'll also find access to a rich set of tools for refining and repairing your digital images.

Accessing Picture Details

The fastest and easiest way to start fixing and finessing your photos is to highlight the image you want to work with in the thumbnail view within My Pictures, and then press the More Info button on the remote control (Details, if you have an HP system). This works equally well if you are displaying the photo in full-screen mode or in a slide show, or simply have it highlighted in the thumbnail view. You'll instantly be presented with the Picture Details screen (see Figure 19.1), which includes the following choices:

- Play Slide Show
- Rotate (left)
- Rotate (right)
- Print
- Touch Up
- Next
- Previous

FIGURE 19.1

The Picture Details screen is the control center for moving and manipulating images from within the My Pictures interface.

Using the tabs on the left side of the Picture Details screen, you can launch a slide show, rotate the image, print it, fix it, or click to view a different image. Let's take a look at some of these controls individually, beginning with the most interesting and powerful.

The Touch Up Control

When you select the Touch Up option from the Picture Details screen, Media Center may present you with a range of options for correcting common problems associated with digital photos (see Figure 19.2).

FIGURE 19.2

This screen gives you an opportunity to tweak your digital images.

The business end of the Touch Up menu gives you a choice of the following common procedures for doctoring up your digital images:

- Red Eye
- Contrast

In addition, you'll also have options to save or cancel these operations.

Red Eye

This is another prime example of how the ease of using Media Center's simple push-button features can lull you into thinking that nothing very special is going on. With remote-control ease, you can instruct Media Center to scrutinize your image and automatically apply the fix your photo needs.

To remove red-eye distortion, simply highlight the Red Eye tab and press OK on the remote (see Figure 19.3).

What is red-eye, anyway? In this case, it's not an optical disease, but a visual distortion that occurs when the light from your flash hits the subject's eyes at just the right angle, causing a bright red reflection from the blood vessels in a person's retinas. If you seem to have a bigger problem with red-eye when you take pictures of kids, it's no accident. Children's pupils are larger and have less coloring than adults, compounding the problem. People with blue or gray eyes also tend to reflect more light to the lens.

Luckily, the Touch Up feature does a pretty good job of repairing red-eye distortion, but if you want to try to avoid having red-eye occur in the first place, here are a few things to try:

- Turn on all the room lights. This should make the subject's pupils contract, reducing red-eye reflections.

- Ask the subject to look at a bright light just before they say "cheese."

- Ask your subject not to look directly at the lens, but slightly away from it.

- If your flash is detachable, move it away from the camera lens.

FIGURE 19.3

The check mark next to Red Eye indicates that Media Center's Touch Up feature has corrected the red-eye in your image.

Contrast

The Contrast tab allows you to automatically optimize the light and dark areas of your image. If you want to compare the image before and after the contrast fix, select the tab to remove the check mark. If you prefer the way the picture looks with the contrast optimized, select Contrast again. The check mark will be replaced and you can then select Save (if you try to exit without saving, you'll be confronted with the warning screen shown in Figure 19.4).

After selecting the Contrast option and saving the image, you'll automatically be returned to the Picture Details page.

caution

Be sure that you want My Pictures to make the changes before you select Save, because there's no going back! After the changes are made, you won't be able to undo them.

FIGURE 19.4

If you make changes using the Red Eye or Contrast controls, Media Center asks whether you want to save them before allowing you to exit.

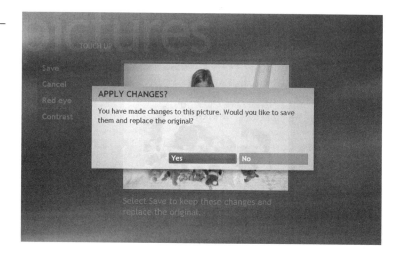

Save or Cancel

As discussed previously, you need to save the changes made during the Touch Up process to make them permanent. If you decide to cancel, you can always change your mind and fix your photos later.

The Play Slide Show Control

The Play Slide Show option on the Picture Details screen launches the slide show display, starting with the selected photo and progressing through every photo in your directory. (It will also include subdirectories if you have chosen the Show Pictures in Subfolders feature in the Settings menu, as described in Chapter 18, "Creating Slide Shows.")

The Picture Rotation Controls

With this readily accessible feature, Media Center has addressed one of the major annoyances of digital photography: the inability to easily rotate a photo from a vertical to a horizontal orientation, and back again. Anyone who has rotated his camera to take a vertical photo, and then tried to view it on his PC and been frustrated by the picture being cocked sideways, will appreciate the ease with which Media Center My Pictures has integrated the ability to rotate your photo into the "right side up" position.

The Picture Navigation Controls

The Picture Details screen makes it easy to view, rotate, and repair multiple images in assembly-line fashion by using the Next and Previous tabs to quickly navigate from one picture to another.

The Print Control

If you want a quick route to printing a full-screen hard copy of your image, simply select the Print tab from the Picture Details screen (see Figure 19.5). You'll be given only two choices: print a full-page photo using your default printer, or cancel the process. More full-featured printing options are available elsewhere on your Media Center machine (see "Print This Picture," later in this chapter).

FIGURE 19.5

This pop-up message is displayed when you select the Print tab from Picture Details.

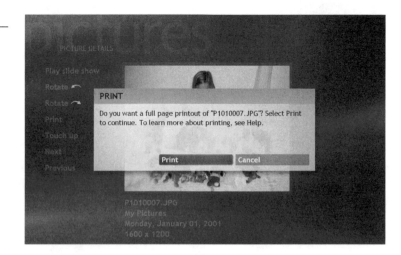

Additional Windows XP Photo Features

Now that you have mastered the image-related capabilities inside the My Pictures interface, you may want to venture outside Media Center to take advantage of some of the expanded image manipulation and output tools that your Windows XP operating system places at your disposal.

Picture Tasks

To get started, exit or minimize Media Center and select My Pictures from the Start menu in the Windows XP desktop.

The Filmstrip View

A handy way to use the photo-handling features provided by XP is via the Filmstrip view (see Figure 19.6). This view allows you to view thumbnail images along the bottom of the screen while simultaneously viewing a large image (nearly 900×700 pixels) at the top center of your screen.

FIGURE 19.6

The My Pictures folder in Filmstrip view offers various photo-handling options not available within the Media Center interface.

This large picture is the active image, and any of the options you select on the screen will be applied to that image file. The options available include icons that advance to the next or the last image in the directory, alongside icons that will rotate the image 90 degrees to the right or left. These icons, centered directly below the large image, work exactly as the controls in the My Pictures Picture Details screen described earlier in this chapter.

The more interesting options are located along the left margin of this screen, under the heading of Picture Tasks. The tasks listed may actually vary, depending on the extent to which your PC manufacturer has customized the menu. Hewlett-Packard, for instance, typically includes various advanced image-handling capabilities on the Picture Task menu (see Figure 19.7).

Although your actual results may vary, the more common picture tasks available from the My Pictures display generally include the following:

- View as a Slide Show
- Order Prints Online
- Print This Picture
- Set as Desktop Background
- Copy to CD

FIGURE 19.7

This example from the My Pictures display on an HP Media Center includes options to create fun backgrounds and greeting cards with your pictures.

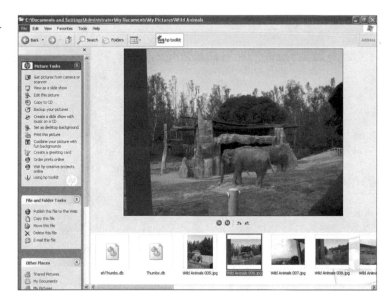

View as a Slide Show

The slide show option in Picture Tasks is convenient, but rather rudimentary compared to the slide show capabilities found in Media Center's My Pictures interface. The most obvious feature lacking here is the choice of transitions, particularly the animated transition (described in Chapter 18). However, as a tool to quickly view and inventory the images placed in your My Pictures folder, the slide show feature available here is quite adequate.

Order Prints Online

When you select the Order Prints Online option, Windows XP immediately launches the Online Print Ordering Wizard (see Figure 19.8). This wizard guides you through the process of designating print size and quantity, choosing a company to print your photos, and providing that company with your billing and delivery address information. Prices are generally comparable to having prints made at a retail camera shop or drug store.

Print This Picture

Whereas the Print Picture option in My Pictures only allows you to print one full-size copy on your currently selected default printer, the Print This Picture feature in Windows XP gives you access to a full range of printing options. These are presented via another wizard, aptly called the Photo Printing Wizard. By following the onscreen prompts, you'll be able to select the photo or photos you want to print (see Figure 19.9), choose and configure the printer you want to use, and set your printing preferences. You can choose the images you want to print individually, or click on Select All.

FIGURE 19.8

When you choose to order prints online, this wizard screen appears to help you send your photos out via the Web.

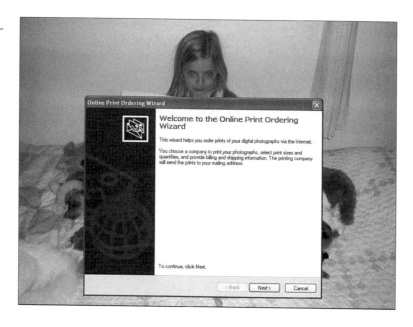

FIGURE 19.9

The Photo Printing Wizard begins by showing you thumbnails of the available images in your My Pictures folder.

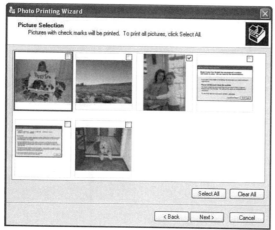

In the Printing Preferences menu, you'll be able to select from several layouts, ranging from a full-page shot, to a contact sheet containing 35 thumbnail images on a single page, to a sheet of wallet-size photos (see Figure 19.10) or standard 3.5×5-inch prints.

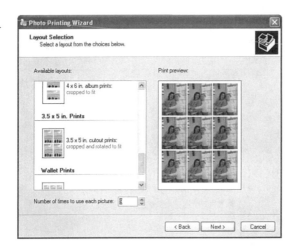

Set as Desktop Background

The Set as Desktop Background option allows you to proudly display any picture you
have in your computer as a background on the desktop. You can activate the feature
in one step by clicking on the Set as Desktop
Background option shown in the Picture Tasks
menu on the left side of the screen, or you can
right-click on the image and select Set as Desktop Background from the pop-up menu (see
Figure 9.11).

Copy to CD

Making the transition from analog to digital
photography requires that you develop a new
routine for saving those old photos—because
there's no way to just toss your digital images
into an old shoe box. One of the best ways to
archive your digital images for posterity—or just
to free up some space on your hard drive—is to
store the pictures on a CD.

When you click on Copy to CD in Picture Tasks,
Windows XP automatically places a temporary
copy in a directory called CD Burning. Files will
be stored there until you are ready to copy, or
"burn" them, to a recordable CD.

tip

After you have opted to set
a picture as your desktop
background, you can also
control the size and placement
of the picture. You can center
the picture on your desktop,
stretch the picture to fill the
entire space, or tile the image
across the desktop. Here's how:

1. Right-click on the desktop
   image, and then select
   Properties.

2. Click on the Desktop tab.

3. Open the drop-down list
   under Position, and choose
   Stretch, Center, or Tile.

FIGURE 19.11

Choosing the Set as Desktop Background option gives you a one-step way to freshen up your XP desktop, and show off a favorite picture.

Burning Your Photos onto a CD

After you've selected photos to burn onto a recordable CD, you can finish the process by using the CD Writing Wizard (see Figure 19.12). You can launch the wizard by inserting a blank disc into your computer, or by clicking on the My Computer link listed on the left under the heading Other Places, and then double-clicking on the icon that is shown for your system's recordable or rewritable CD (CD-R/CD-RW) drive.

When you open the window for your CD-R/CD-RW drive, a menu for CD Writing Tasks will appear in the upper left of the screen. Click on Write These Files to CD to launch the CD Writing Wizard, and follow the onscreen instructions.

After you have burned your images onto a CD, you can delete them from your computer to make more room on your system's hard drive.

note

Remember, to complete this CD writing process, you first need to insert a blank CD-R or CD-RW disc into your computer's CD drive.

FIGURE 19.12

The first screen of the CD Writing Wizard prompts you to enter a name for your new CD. You can use the current date or any name you want.

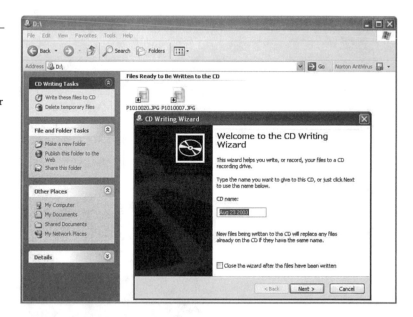

THE ABSOLUTE MINIMUM

Under the smooth, simple-to-operate exterior of Media Center's My Pictures interface beats the heart of a powerful photo enhancement system. Just peel back the cover by selecting a digital image and pressing More Info on your remote control to reveal the Picture Details screen. Remember:

- The Touch Up option tells My Pictures to analyze your image and automatically perform a range of enhancements.

- If the subjects in your photo have glowing red eyes, they're not possessed—your camera's flash just caught them at the wrong angle. Touch Up will fix the problem, called red-eye. Just select Save to accept the change.

- The Contrast feature works in the same way. This Touch Up process automatically optimizes the contrast for better viewing and printing of your image.

- If you didn't find all the photo enhancement or output options you need within the My Pictures interface, exit to the Windows XP desktop and launch My Pictures for more choices.

20

CUSTOMIZING THE MY PICTURES EXPERIENCE WITH MICROSOFT PICTURE IT!

We've covered all the basics for maximizing your enjoyment of digital images using Media Center's My Pictures interface. Now you're ready to move on to the advanced class: how to finely adjust your My Pictures image files using advanced Windows tools, such as the Microsoft Picture It! program.

In mid-2003, Microsoft "soft-launched" a new version of its photo-enhancement software, offering free downloads of Microsoft Picture It! Version 7.0 via the Windows XP Media Center home page. At last check, the company had started charging for the program, although mail-in rebates and other promotions are often available. There is also a

Premium version (sold at `http://shop.microsoft.com` and other retail sites) that adds numerous templates for photo-related projects—from trading cards to wedding albums.

Whether you decide to use the Microsoft product described here, or another of the many fine "third-party" commercial photo-finishing software products, you'll find many of the same basic features and capabilities. All should offer a range of capabilities for enhancing your digital images beyond the rudimentary "fixes" offered within the Media Center My Pictures interface, and the Windows XP operating system itself. However, Microsoft's consistent use of common Windows XP conventions, and the overall programming quality applied to most of its products, makes Picture It! an excellent choice for a photo-enhancement companion product to complement—in fact, to complete—the digital image experience offered by Media Center.

One of the things that makes Microsoft Picture It! a good choice for Absolute Beginners is the extensive use of wizards within the program. The opening screen shows a project selection wizard that lets you jump right into a productive, photo-related activity (see Figure 20.1) .

FIGURE 20.1

This is an example of the many wizard routines found in Picture It!

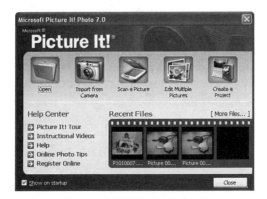

Opening Photos with Picture It!

After you have installed the photo-enhancement software, you have multiple options for getting started. Either of the following methods will get you going:

- Open the Picture It! program from the Windows XP Start menu; then choose from one of the photos displayed under the Recent Files heading, or choose Open and browse to the image file you want to work on.

- Open the My Pictures directory from the Windows XP Start menu, find the image file you want, and right-click on it. Choose Open With, and then select Picture It! 7.0 (see Figure 20.2).

FIGURE 20.2

The right-click method is one of the easiest ways to open a digital image file in Picture It!.

After you have opened an image in this fashion, you'll be viewing a screen with the image you selected displayed on the main screen, and a pane on the left listing several common tasks. Here you'll find the Touchup option, which guides you through some of the most basic yet powerful features contained in the Picture It! program.

Touching Up Photos

Touchup tasks available in Picture It! include the following:

- **Levels Auto Fix**—Much like the Fix Picture features in the Media Center My Pictures interface (see Chapter 19, "Preparing and Sharing Digital Images"), this one-step feature automatically adjusts the visual qualities of your photo. Clicking here allows Picture It! to analyze the shadows, midtones, and highlights of your image, and automatically tweak the levels for the "average" photo. However, this one-size-fits-all approach may not suit your needs for a particular photograph. If so, just move on to one of the manual controls described in the following text.

- **Brightness and Contrast**—This option lets you experiment with and choose your own light and contrast levels, by dragging the slider bars pictured in Figure 20.3. You can also type in numerical values between -100 and 100. Dragging the slider to the right increases the value (brighter, or higher contrast), and dragging to the left decreases the value (darker, or lower contrast). When you move the slider to a new position and release it, Picture It! will show you the visual change in the photo. Click Done (located in the lower left of the screen) to accept the changes, or you can choose Reset or Cancel to continue without changing the photo.

FIGURE 20.3

This detail from Picture It! shows the manual Brightness and Contrast controls.

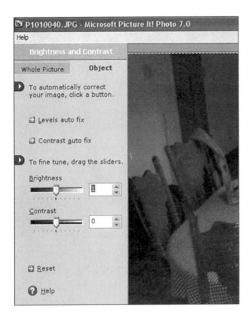

- **Fix Red Eye**—This gives you the same ability to fix red-eye distortion as discussed in Chapter 19, but with greater control. Instead of allowing My Pictures to automatically find and fix the red-eye problem, Picture It! allows you to manually position the red-eye fixing tool (a circular, see-through bullseye cursor) to achieve the best results. Click in the center of the red-eye area. Use the Zoom control (see Figure 20.4) if necessary to see exactly where the problem is. These controls allow you to type in a magnification value, increase or decrease the zoom level using a slider bar, or click Zoom to Entire Page, Zoom to Page Width, or Zoom to Selection. After you have the right magnification and have highlighted the affected area, click on Red-Eye Auto Fix to correct the problem.

FIGURE 20.4

This detail from the lower right of the Picture It! main screen shows the Zoom controls.

- **Sharpen or Blur**—This option is useful for sharpening up an out-of-focus photo, or blur the image slightly to soften the picture. This is done by means of moving a single slider bar. Drag it to the right to increase the sharpness of the picture; drag it to the left to blur the picture.

- **Learn More**—This option appears in many of the menus. Choose it to view detailed instructions and background information on the task you are attempting.

Cropping, Resizing, and Creating Cutouts

The Crop or Rotate menu item in Picture It! offers the following choices:

- **Rotate**—Although this feature provides essentially the same functionality available in the My Pictures interface or in the Windows XP Explorer window for My Pictures (see Chapter 19), it does so with an enhanced, easy-to-use thumbnail view (see Figure 20.5).

caution

As good as the photo-enhancement tools in Picture It! and similar programs are, they can't work miracles on bad photographs. All they have to work with is what the image contains. If the image was shot too dark, too bright, out of focus, and so on, don't expect the program to be able to put in detail that wasn't captured by the lens in the first place. The digital darkroom techniques are pretty impressive, but even they can't turn a rotten photo into a great one.

FIGURE 20.5

From the Rotate menu, Picture It! displays three small thumbnails, offering previews of how the photo will look after it's rotated.

■ **Crop Canvas**—A very useful tool missing from the basic photo-enhancement options covered in Chapter 19, the Crop feature lets you pare away the extraneous portions of your image to emphasize the subject. You can drag a rectangular shape over the photo to indicate how you want it cropped, or choose another shape, such as a heart or a star (see Figure 20.6).

FIGURE 20.6

Simple cropping can emphasize the subject and trim away unwanted portions of your image, or you can crop using one of almost 70 shapes.

■ **Create a Cutout**—Want to get creative? Try using the cutout tool to trim away the background. Then insert a new background photo, or create a shape to place behind your cutout. The only limit now is your imagination!

Adding Text or Shapes to Your Photos

Picture It! enables you to add graphics and text, and so on, to your images via the Add Something menu item. Choices include the following options:

tip

You may want to use the Soft Edges effect (see "Adding Edges, Frames, and Mats") in conjunction with the cutout tool to subtly blur the edges and produce a better blending effect in your final image.

■ **Text**—This full-featured text tool lets you type a caption or greeting directly into your image. Simply click and type. You can reposition the text box by dragging it, in addition to resizing, stretching, or skewing it. Just click and drag any handle to get the desired effect (see Figure 20.7).

FIGURE 20.7

As shown in this example, you can easily tilt the text, change font styles, and even vary text colors to achieve the look you want.

■ **Shaped Text**—This feature allows you to add text to your photo in a geometric shape so that the letters conform to the shape of a triangle, a circle, an arrow, or other shapes. The addition of shaped text, such as the arch-shaped greeting shown in Figure 20.8, can enhance and complement the shape of the image's subject.

■ **Shape or Lines**—Use this feature to add a standard drawing object, such as a line or shape, by choosing it from the Picture It! gallery. Or choose one of the Draw options to create a custom line or shape on your image.

■ **Picture from the Gallery/ My Computer/Scanner/ Digital Camera**—These options allow you to insert another image, which you can blend with the existing image in various ways. Choose the source of your image (the Picture It! Gallery, another folder on your PC, or a scanner or digital camera), and then choose some of the other actions described in this chapter to adjust and blend the images.

> **tip**
>
> When you first insert the new image, Picture It! tends to plaster it on top of your existing image. Your first step will probably be to reorder the objects on your screen by right-clicking on the top image, selecting Move Forward or Backward, and then choosing an option such as Send to Back. This will reveal your original image in front of the new image you just added. Then you can select the object you want to change, and go to work on it.

FIGURE 20.8

In this example, the cutout tool was used to remove the background, which was replaced by a custom shape with a gradient fill.

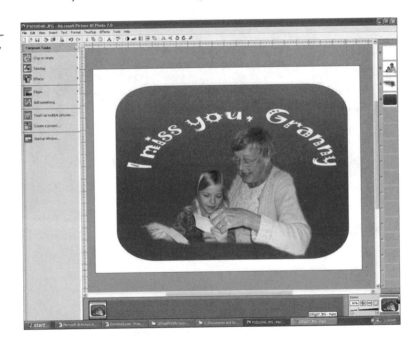

Adding Edges, Frames, and Mats

The Edges menu item gives you access to several options for dressing up your finished photos. Choices include these:

■ **Highlighted Edges**—This option adds a colored border around an object or a picture. You can change the color and width of the highlighted edge to suit you (see Figure 20.9).

FIGURE 20.9

As shown in this detail from the Highlighted Edges screen, you can select one of the effects shown, or choose a custom edge.

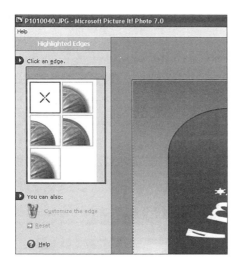

■ **Soft Edges**—Use this option to fade the outside edges of an object or a picture. Picture It! lets you set both the width of the edge you want to soften, and the transparency of the softened edges. As noted previously, this feature can be used in conjunction with the cutout capability to remove the background from an object in a picture and insert the object into a new picture, without creating a jagged line around the inserted object.

■ **Frames and Mats**—This option lets you customize your photo by placing it behind a virtual mat, or into a virtual frame. Picture It! contains dozens of styles to choose from (see Figure 20.10). To add a frame, choose one of the many themes to see the available choices. Click to open the frame you want, and then drag your image from the tray of thumbnails at the bottom of your screen and place it in the frame. To use the Build Your Own feature to create a custom frame or mat, choose the Photo Simple Frame or Photo Simple Mat option. Select from one of the many choices presented (see Figure 20.11), click Next, and then adjust the size of your picture under the frame or mat. Click Done to accept the changes.

FIGURE 20.10

Picture It! lets you choose from about 15 frame categories, or you can create your own custom frame.

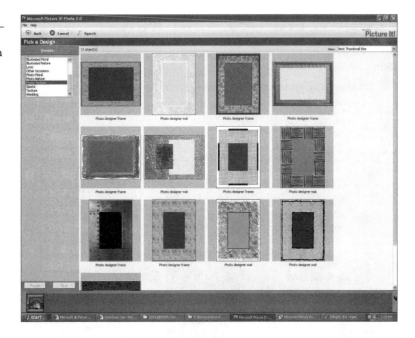

FIGURE 20.11

When you decide to build your own custom frame or mat, Picture It! asks you to select a pattern.

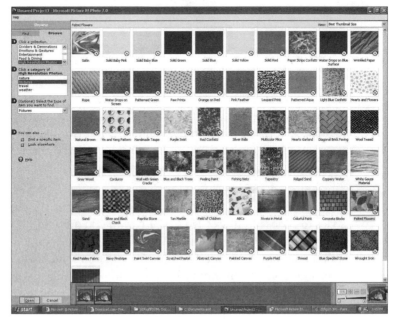

Adding Special Effects

The Effects menu in Picture It! includes the following one-step special-effects options:

- Antique
- Black and White
- Negative

Each of these options provides a simple way to create stunning changes in your pictures. Simply choose the corresponding tab to apply a sepia-toned patina to your photo by using Antique, to change it from a color to a monochrome image by using Black and White, or to completely reverse the colors by choosing Negative. If you like the results, click Done. If not, click Cancel to return to the original image.

Two of the Effects options provide a little more leeway for customization and creativity. Here's how they work:

- **Hue and Saturation**—This feature allows you to fundamentally change the color properties of your image, using an inventive and functional interface (see Figure 20.12). When you move the cursor over your picture, the cursor becomes an eyedropper. Click to select an area of your picture to use as the basis for your color changes. Then click and hold the clear dot in the colored bulls-eye on the left. As you drag the dot around the circle, you'll see the image's color properties change. When you find the spot where the colors suit your taste to a tee, simply click Done to proceed. If you want to start over, click Reset.

FIGURE 20.12

Using Hue and Saturation instead of the Black and White one-step Effects tab produces a more pleasing monochrome image.

■ **Freehand Painting**—This option is designed to bring out the Rembrandt in each of us. To hand-color your image (see Figure 20.13), follow these steps:

1. Choose a paint tool. The options include brush, airbrush, pencil, eraser, marker, and charcoal.

2. Pick a paint color. You can choose from one of the eight colors displayed, or click on the palette icon to explore the full range of color choices.

3. Choose the brush size you want to use. When you move the cursor over your image, you'll be able to see how large the brush you've chosen is in relation to the image.

4. Begin painting by clicking and dragging your brush across the image.

tip

You can't use the Hue and Saturation command on a black and white image, because it is essentially a color correction tool—and that requires the presence of color. However, you can use the controls to create a black and white image. If you find that using the instant Black and White special effects tab creates an image that is either too dark or too washed out, try using the Hue and Saturation controls to create a more customized monochrome effect. This method produced excellent results in the image shown in Figure 20.12.

tip

To get finer detail in your painting, try selecting a smaller brush size and increasing the magnification of the photo using the Zoom control (see Figure 20.4). To avoid mistakes, use shorter brush strokes and pause frequently. This way, if you do make a mistake, you can use the Undo Your Last Stroke command to remove the error, and you won't have to repeat a great deal of your handiwork.

FIGURE 20.13

This image was altered using the Antique effect, and then some of the detail was brought back using the Brightness and Contrast controls.

Additional Options

Two other notable options are afforded by Picture It! 7.0: the capability to apply touch-up procedures to multiple photos at once, and the option to launch into various creative tasks via the Create a Project Wizard.

- **Touch Up Multiple Pictures**—When you select this menu item, Picture It! opens the Mini Lab (see Figure 20.14) interface, which is designed to allow you to quickly apply similar changes to a whole collection of images—just as a professional photo-finishing lab does. This can be a major time-saver when you want to apply the same changes to numerous images. There are four steps to this process:

  1. Load the photos you want to make changes to into the Mini Lab. Mini Lab already contains photos you have recently worked on, but you can click on Open More Files to import additional images.

  2. Select the pictures you want to work on, either by clicking on the Select All Pictures option or by clicking on individual pictures while holding down the Ctrl key. You can also choose a range of shots by holding down the Shift key when you click on the photo at the end of the range.

3. Choose an editing option. All the following procedures are available in the Mini Lab: Levels Auto Fix, Rotate (clockwise or counterclockwise), Crop, Brightness and Contrast, Fix Red Eye, and Adjust Tint.

4. After you have used the Mini Lab to process your pictures, choose Save, Save As, or Print.

FIGURE 20.14

Mini Lab's humdrum appearance belies its power as a major time-saver.

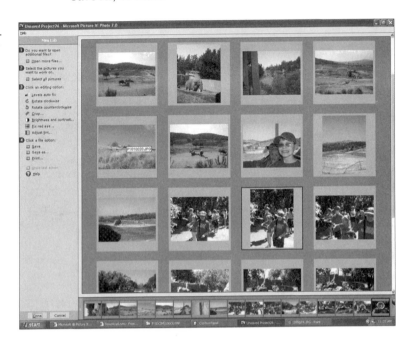

■ **Create a Project**—Clicking on this menu item opens a menu of project wizards (see Figure 20.15) that will guide you through the creation of everything from a photo album to an "online gift." The Online Gift Designs Wizard allows you to create an image to be placed on a gift item—anything from a baby bib to a clock—and then lets you order the custom item from an online vendor.

FIGURE 20.15

This detail from the Create a Project menu shows about a dozen categories of creative projects for outputting and sharing your images.

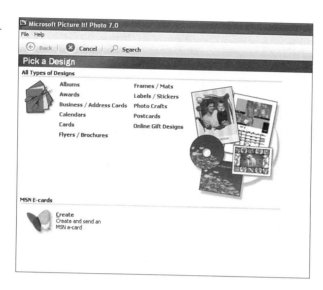

THE ABSOLUTE MINIMUM

Putting the finishing touches on your photos and digital image files often requires going "outside the box" and incorporating additional photo-enhancement software features that aren't found in the standard Windows XP Media Center Edition software. An excellent choice for a photo-enhancement add-on product is Microsoft's own Picture It! 7.0 software, which integrates nicely with your operating system and Media Center capabilities to fulfill all your basic digital imaging needs. Here are a few points to remember:

- If you've tried using the Fix Pictures features in the Media Center My Pictures interface, and you still can't quite get the effect you want, it may be time to try an add-on product such as the Picture It! program.

- Try experimenting with the Picture It! one-step operations when they are available, such as Levels Auto Fix. If you don't get the desired results, try making manual adjustments.

- Despite the advanced features for photo touchup that are included in packages such as Picture It!, remember that no software is a miracle worker when it comes to making a lousy photo into a great one. The old "garbage in, garbage out" axiom applies, so try to get the best shot you can in the first place.

- Try using the Mini Lab feature, accessed via the Touch Up Multiple Pictures option, to speed up your processing time on a collection of images.

ADVANCED MEDIA CENTER SETTINGS AND OPTIONS

21

CUSTOMIZING THE XP MEDIA CENTER INTERFACE

Unlike a typical Windows XP machine, your Media Center PC is more than just a work tool, or even a simple leisure device designed to occasionally blow off some steam. In addition to filling those roles, Media Center is part of your lifestyle, and yes, even part of your decor.

Because of its 10-foot interface, Media Center is not simply a "personal computer," but a social experience that you share with friends and family. Consequently, its appearance says as much about you as any possession in your home, so why not take a few minutes and customize the look and feel—even the sounds—of your Media Center PC to suit your tastes? Celebrate your individuality!

Changing Your Media Center's Appearance and Background

Media Center allows you to change various settings to customize the appearance of onscreen features and menus. For example, you can do the following:

- Change your background colors
- Optimize Media Center for your display device
- Turn systems sounds on or off
- Turn transition animations on or off (see Chapter 4)
- Keep Media Center "always on top"—even when minimized (see Chapter 5)

Changing Background Colors

To change the background color in Media Center, press the Start button on the remote control to display the main Media Center menu. Choose Settings, General, then Appearance (see Figure 21.1).

FIGURE 21.1

The Appearance category tops the list of General Settings.

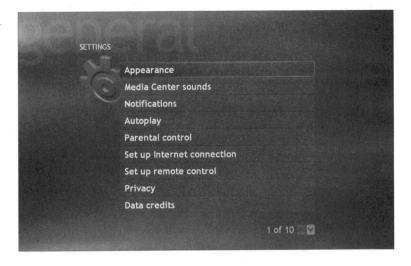

Under the Background Color heading, choose the – or + buttons to change the default value (Black) to one of nine shades of gray, or white (see Figure 21.2). Your choice will dictate the appearance of blank areas of your PC or TV screen. Those areas can be large or small, depending on the program you are watching and the shape of your display screen. For example, if you are watching a letter-box formatted program on a standard TV-sized screen, you're likely to see quite a bit of background color showing through. Try experimenting with your display color settings to select the option you find most appealing.

Adjusting Media Center for Your Display Device

The Appearance Settings menu also lets you choose to format your Media Center interface for display on a computer screen or a TV. Choosing TV changes the resolution to provide the best picture quality on the given device. You'll also notice some subtle changes in the appearance of the Media Center menus (see Figure 21.3).

Adjusting Display Settings with the Display Calibration Wizard

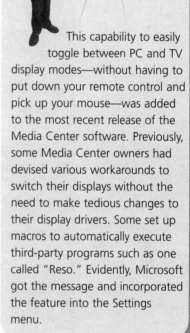

note

This capability to easily toggle between PC and TV display modes—without having to put down your remote control and pick up your mouse—was added to the most recent release of the Media Center software. Previously, some Media Center owners had devised various workarounds to switch their displays without the need to make tedious changes to their display drivers. Some set up macros to automatically execute third-party programs such as one called "Reso." Evidently, Microsoft got the message and incorporated the feature into the Settings menu.

Whether you want to watch video using your PC display, a TV, or both, Media Center has a wizard designed to help you optimize those display qualities. The wizard will make it much easier to optimize your display image, regardless of whether you are viewing on a standard CRT (cathode ray tube) monitor or TV, a flat-panel LCD or Plasma screen, or a rear-projection or front-projection television display.

To launch the Display Calibration Wizard, select Adjust Display Settings from the Appearance Settings menu. The following screen (see Figure 21.4) will offer you a choice of launching the display wizard immediately or watching an instructional video first.

FIGURE 21.2
Although Media Center affords you a choice of 11 background "colors," you are still essentially limited to black, white, or gray.

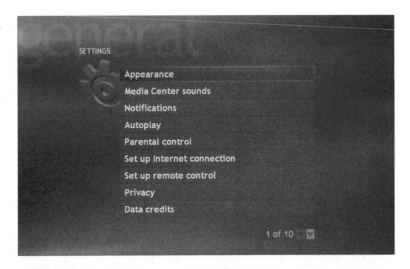

FIGURE 21.3
When the display is formatted for output on a TV, you can see the wider letters and reduced sharpness (compare to Figure 21.1).

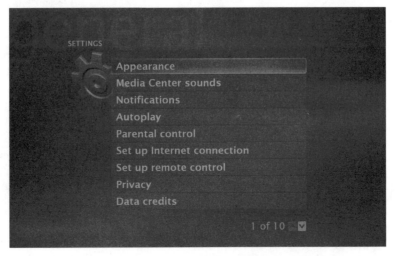

FIGURE 21.4

The Display Calibration Wizard is designed to use a series of calibration tests to help you achieve the best picture for your display device.

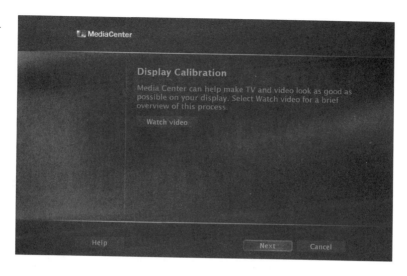

To explain the calibration process and make it less intimidating for consumers, Microsoft has included a video that shows a roomful of happy users, effortlessly illustrating how the wizard allows them to optimize their display for providing bright, colorful, and detailed images (see Figure 21.5).

After you've watched the video, go ahead and launch the wizard. Follow the onscreen directions as they walk you through all the steps involved in optimizing your display for Media Center. The primary steps in the calibration process include the following:

- Choosing your type of display device
- Specifying whether you have a wide-screen display
- Specifying the type of video connection you are using
- Centering and sizing your display
- Adjusting the aspect ratio, or shape of the display
- Adjusting brightness
- Adjusting contrast
- Balancing the color

FIGURE 21.5

The Display
Calibration
Wizard intro-
duction video
takes about 2
minutes to
watch.

When you are finished, select Done to return to the Appearance settings screen.

Turning Caller ID Notifications On or Off

Another personalization feature in Media Center is the capability for your computer
to let you know if you're getting a phone call—even to the extent of telling you
who's calling. You'll need to have a phone line connected to your Media Center PC,
of course, and if you want to know who the caller is, you'll have to subscribe to
Caller ID from your phone service provider. Here's how to activate it:

1. Follow the procedure described previously for accessing the General Settings
   menu (as shown in Figure 21.1).

2. Select Notifications.

3. Choose the Telephone Call Notifications setting you want (see Figure 21.6),
   then highlight Save and press OK on the remote control. If you change the
   settings and then attempt to leave the Notifications display without selecting
   Save or Cancel, Media Center will prompt you to do so before you can continue.

FIGURE 21.6

There are three settings for Telephone Call Notifications: Calls with Caller ID, All Calls, and Disabled.

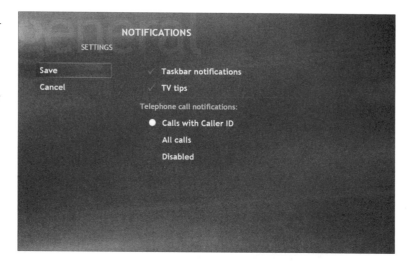

If you have enabled the All Calls option in Telephone Call Notifications, you'll begin seeing pop-up alerts (see Figure 21.7) each time you receive a phone call. If you select the Calls with Caller ID option, only incoming calls that have Caller ID data will result in an onscreen alert message.

FIGURE 21.7

The message "Incoming Phone Call— Your Phone Is Ringing" pops up when you have selected the All Calls telephone notification feature.

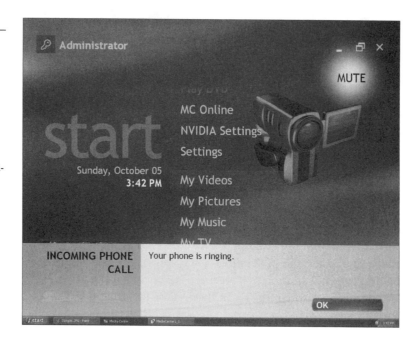

Turning Media Center Sounds On or Off

Another way to personalize your Media Center experience is to decide whether you want to hear the variety of sounds Media Center generates in response to your menu selections and navigation choices. If you find that the sounds intrude on your entertainment experience, just switch them off using the Media Center Sounds Settings screen (see Figure 21.8).

FIGURE 21.8

Media Center's audio acknowledgments simply provide you with a subtle signal that the computer is carrying out your commands.

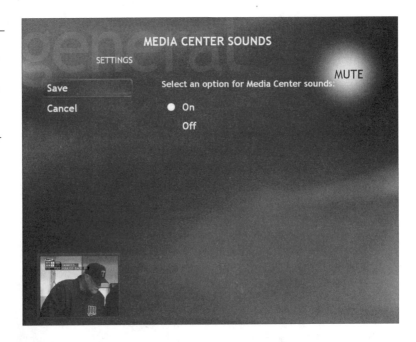

To change your sounds setting, choose Media Center Sounds from the General Settings Menu. On the Media Center Sounds Settings screen, choose On or Off, and then Save your changes.

Setting Media Center's Parental Controls

Media Center not only allows you to choose appearance settings that reflect your individual tastes and preferences, but it can even reflect your values and beliefs. Setting parental control limits lets you manage what the children in your household can and cannot watch on TV. In these video-filled times in which we live, it can be a useful way to let the next generation in your household know exactly what you consider to be appropriate entertainment—even when you're not around.

Here's how to set the parental controls on your Media Center PC:

1. Choose Parental Control from the General Settings menu.

2. At the Create a 4-Digit Code screen (see Figure 21.9), input a four-digit code using your remote control keypad or the keyboard. Remember to use a number sequence you won't easily forget, and/or write it down and put the reminder in a safe place. If you still forget your code, there is a procedure to reset it. For details, see the Tip later in this section.

FIGURE 21.9

Media Center's parental control features rely on this four-digit code.

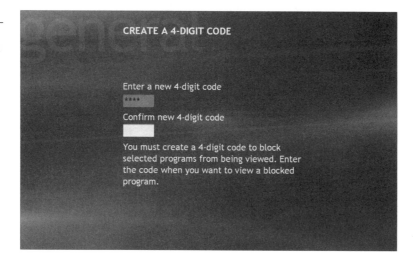

CREATE A 4-DIGIT CODE

Enter a new 4-digit code

****

Confirm new 4-digit code

You must create a 4-digit code to block selected programs from being viewed. Enter the code when you want to view a blocked program.

3. Select the category of parental controls you want to change. You can choose TV Ratings or Movie/DVD Ratings.

4. When you select TV Ratings, you must first place a check mark next to Turn on TV Blocking (see Figure 21.10) to set a TV rating level. You can choose a maximum allowed TV rating by clicking on the – or + symbol until you see the appropriate rating level. Rating levels include TV-MA (for mature audiences only), TV-14 (parents strongly cautioned), TV-PG (parental guidance suggested), TV-G (general audience), TV-Y7 (for older children, ages 7 and above), and TV-Y (for all children). There is even a category for None, in which all rated programs will be blocked.

FIGURE 21.10

To set the maxi-
mum TV rating
allowed, you
must choose
from among the
seven rating cat-
egories.

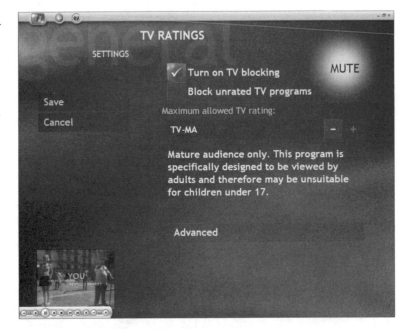

5. To fine-tune your controls even further, select the Advanced tab to access the
Advanced TV Ratings screen (see Figure 21.11). Here you can set levels for the
following categories of video content: Fantasy Violence, Suggestive Dialogue,
Offensive Language, Sexual Content, and Violence.

FIGURE 21.11

The Advanced
TV Ratings
screen lets you
set individual
viewing thresh-
olds for five cat-
egories.

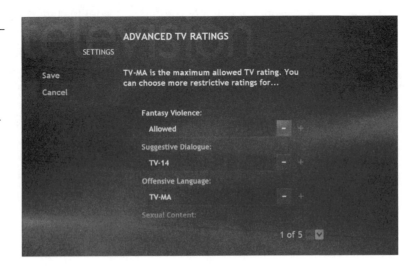

6. Save your choices before proceeding to the Movie/DVD Ratings screen (see Figure 21.12). As with TV ratings, you must first place a check mark next to Turn on Movie Blocking to set the rating level. Viewers will not be able to watch programming that exceeds these limits unless they know your four-digit code.

7. Save your settings to return to Media Center.

Changing Your Four-Digit Code

Should the secrecy of your four-digit code be exposed or compromised by an inadvertent security breach, you can easily change it to preserve the sanctity of your parental rights. Simply return to the main Parental Controls menu and select Change 4-Digit Code. You'll be asked to enter the old code before inputting the new code. Repeat the new code to confirm, and then select OK (see Figure 21.13).

tip

Forgot your four-digit code? Don't worry. Microsoft has made it easy—maybe even too easy—to reset the code and start from scratch. Just follow these steps:

1. Return to the General Settings menu from the main Media Center start page.

2. Highlight the Parental Control tab.

3. Using the keyboard, press and hold down Ctrl+Alt while you select OK on the remote.

4. When prompted, enter a new four-digit code. (This time, write it down!)

FIGURE 21.12

The Movie/DVD Ratings page lets you choose the maximum allowed movie rating—from None to X and everything in between.

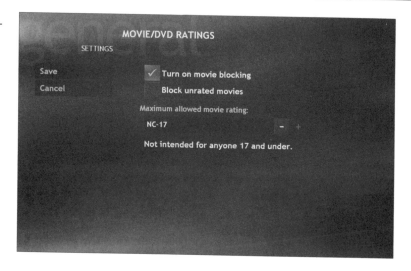

MOVIE/DVD RATINGS
SETTINGS

Save

Cancel

✓ Turn on movie blocking

Block unrated movies

Maximum allowed movie rating:

NC-17   – +

Not intended for anyone 17 and under.

FIGURE 21.13

Media Center will display a confirmation notice to indicate that you have successfully changed your four-digit security code.

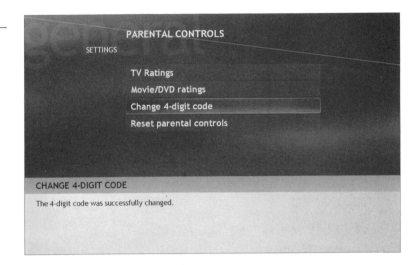

Setting Your Privacy Options

If you're concerned about revealing too much personal information to Microsoft and its commercial partners, Media Center provides you with a set of controls to limit how much data you send across the Internet. You can also tell Microsoft whether to automatically acquire copyright permissions, or to access online media identification databases, for content on your Media Center machine.

The Privacy Settings screen (see Figure 21.14) can be accessed from the General Settings menu. It allows you to configure the following:

caution

Should you check the box to acquire licenses? Microsoft warns that if you don't, you may be prevented from playing "protected files." If you are worried about the ability to play these types of copyrighted media files without interruption, you may want to make sure that Acquire Licenses is checked. Then again, you may want to wait until this actually becomes a problem before changing your selections.

■ **Send Usage Data**—If you uncheck this box, Media Center will not automatically transmit your personal usage data to Microsoft. The company states that by providing this data, you can help Microsoft design software and services that serve you better—but it's your call.

■ **Acquire Licenses**—This tells Media Center to automatically acquire licenses to play specific content, as required by digital rights management (DRM) information encoded within the content.

■ **Work Offline**—Checking this box tells Media Center not to automatically connect to the Internet to retrieve information from online sources. This includes retrieving CD or DVD data from the Internet every time you insert a new disc with commercial content.

If you want the low-down on Microsoft's privacy policy, you can read the Media Center Privacy Statement in its entirety by choosing it from the Privacy Settings menu discussed previously. One of the key points Microsoft stipulates is that when you agree to send usage data, it will be collected *anonymously*. In other words, Microsoft will gather information about your hardware configuration, and how you use its software and services, but it promises not to connect that information back to you personally. Instead, the data is aggregated, or pooled with that of other users, to provide statistics and usage patterns that can help guide future improvements in the design. If you don't mind letting Microsoft use the data in this fashion, and you have confidence that the company will keep its word in regard to respecting your privacy and anonymity, then you should have no objection to checking the box to send usage data.

FIGURE 21.14

If you're not interested in giving Microsoft an intimate view of your viewing habits, you can disable the sharing of usage data.

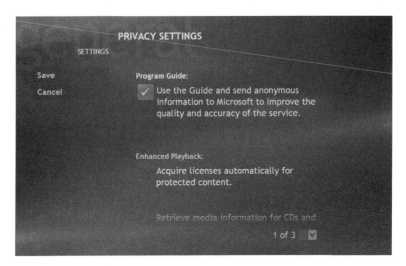

THE ABSOLUTE MINIMUM

Personal computers are, well, personal. Media Center PCs have their personal side—the so-called "2-foot" experience—but they also contain a more public persona. They are deliberately designed to be shared with your friends and family. That's one of the things that makes setting up your Media Center interface so different from setting up your personal desktop: The choices you make directly reflect on who you are and what you like. So when you're placing the final touches on the look and feel of your Media Center display, here are a few things to remember:

- You can customize the background color of your video playback screen, choosing between the default black background and several shades of gray, or a white background.

- It's worthwhile to take the time to optimize Media Center for your display device. Choosing the right output settings and running the Display Calibration Wizard can make an enormous difference in your picture quality.

- Maybe you don't want any distractions when you are entranced by a great TV show or movie, but if you're concerned about missing an important phone call, Media Center 2004 (otherwise known as Harmony) has an integrated Caller ID/phone call notification feature that provides onscreen alerts for incoming calls.

- Another way to customize Media Center is by activating parental controls. Using the Advanced tab lets you micromanage which shows can be displayed on your system.

- Media Center allows you to choose whether to share your usage information with Microsoft. You can also configure Media Center to automatically download licenses for copyrighted content on your system.

22

XP Media Center and Your Home Network

Media Center was primarily designed to offer the best multimedia experience for people living in a space-constrained environment, such as a college dorm room. In such a setting, the idea of combining your personal computer, television, stereo, DVD player, and so on into a single space-saving device—and all sharing a common display screen—makes an enormous amount of sense.

That was the starting point, but only because creators of the system saw those single-room dwellers as the most likely early adopters of Media Center. From the outset, the eyes of Microsoft and its partners have been on a much larger prize: the living rooms of the world. While the initial focus on dorms and one-room apartments moved the development of most network-related features to the proverbial back burner, networks are no longer uncommon even in these small-footprint living spaces. However, to appeal to that larger marketplace, the Media Center still needed a sound network strategy.

Today, Media Center offers complete networking capability from its "2-foot" PC side, by virtue of the underlying Windows XP Professional operating system. That networking allows only limited entertainment-related functionality in Media Center, however. Look for that to change. As Microsoft continues down this development path, new technologies and capabilities will emerge that place Media Center at the hub of a household's entire digital experience. Video and audio data will eventually course throughout your home, just like water, heat, and electricity do today. Turn on the digital tap in any room of the house, and you'll have instant and complete access to your library of images, games, audio, and video entertainment.

The Media Center machine you own today is just the beginning. Adding it to a network in your home may not completely rock your world at the outset, but that connectivity promises to spark a new generation of applications and activities to expand the definitions of both "fun" and "functional," as they pertain to home computers.

Networking Your Media Center PC: What You Can and Can't Do

So let the networking begin! First, it's always a good idea to set your expectations, based on a reality check of what you can and can't expect to do with your networked Media Center.

Here's what you *can* do:

- Share printers and files
- Share Internet access
- Watch TV shows recorded on a Media Center from other Windows XP computers on the network

And here's what you *can't* do:

- Open Media Center applications from a remote computer on the network
- Watch live TV on other (non–Media Center) computers
- Have Media Center automatically record TV shows to a network drive

Types of Network Connections

Now that you know what to expect from your Media Center PC after your network is up and running, let's cover some basics. The first step in getting your PCs connected to each other is to set up your physical network. This means making physical data connections between the computers in your home. There is an ever-expanding list of network architectures to choose from, but the most popular options for home networking today include Ethernet, wireless, phone line, and power line.

Ethernet

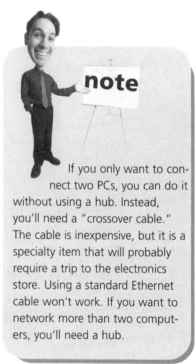

The "old standby" in networking, Ethernet cables are one of the best supported and downright cheapest ways to get the job done. They can also provide much faster network speeds (typically 100Mbps) than the other options listed in this chapter, and they are easier to keep secure than the new-fangled and enormously popular wireless variety. Your Media Center PC comes with a network interface card (NIC) installed, so all you need to do is plug an Ethernet cable into it, then plug the other end into a device such as an Ethernet hub. Follow the same procedure for your other PCs, and you'll soon be in business.

If this is your first networking experience, you might consider buying a preconfigured Ethernet kit, such as the one pictured in Figure 22.1.

note

If you only want to connect two PCs, you can do it without using a hub. Instead, you'll need a "crossover cable." The cable is inexpensive, but it is a specialty item that will probably require a trip to the electronics store. Using a standard Ethernet cable won't work. If you want to network more than two computers, you'll need a hub.

FIGURE 22.1

This inexpensive kit from Linksys contains two NICs, cables, drivers, and a five-port hub.

Wireless

Wireless networking is enjoying great popularity in the home market these days, primarily because of the absence of (you guessed it!) wires.

Maybe your PCs are spread out around the house. Or maybe you have a mobile computer, such as a laptop or tablet PC, that you want to be able to use in different rooms as the mood strikes you. Maybe you just don't want to bother trying to conceal unsightly cables running from room to room. For any of these scenarios, a wireless network may be just the ticket.

Balancing out the flexibility issue are the less-than-stellar speed and security issues. Achieving good signal strength from end to end of a home that is spread out, or that contains building materials that aren't conducive to wireless connections, can also be a challenge.

Newer 802.11G equipment is now becoming widely available, and increasingly affordable. These products offer faster data transmissions than popular 802.11B networks, which reach speeds of only 11Mbps. The 802.11G systems support data transfers at 54Mbps (still only half of 100Mbps Ethernet). Whichever flavor of wireless you settle on, you'll need an "access point" device, which functions more or less like an Ethernet hub without wires, and a wireless network adapter for each PC on the network. For a typical example of a wireless access point, see Figure 22.2.

FIGURE 22.2
The 802.11G equivalent of an Ethernet hub is a wireless access point, such as this WAP54G from Linksys.

Phone Line

A bit of a hybrid, the phone-line networking option offers simplicity, security, and affordability, though not particularly high performance. Instead of laying new network cables around your house, or relying on insecure airwaves to transmit data, you just tap into your existing telephone lines. The technology is called HPNA, after the Home Phoneline Networking Alliance which developed it. Speed for HPNA 2.0 adapters is limited to 10Mbps, which is comparable to 802.11B, the most pervasive form of "Wi-Fi," or wireless networking. All you need is an HPNA adapter (such as the one shown in Figure 22.3) for each PC. These are then connected to standard phone jacks. The result is instant network connectivity without laying new wires, and generally, there is no interference with normal voice use of your phone line.

Power Line

Power-line computing works in a similar fashion to HPNA, except the network data is transmitted through your home's existing electrical wires instead of telephone lines. Typically, you plug the adapter into a standard 110-volt electrical outlet and attach a USB or Ethernet cable from the adapter to your PC. This has a slight edge over HPNA from a convenience standpoint, because most houses probably have fewer than 10 phone jacks, whereas they typically have dozens of electrical outlets. You don't need to give up a lot of speed, either, because power-line networks can operate at 14Mbps. Price can be a bit of a drawback. External USB adapters, such as the Belkin F5D4050 pictured in Figure 22.4, can retail for nearly $100, though street prices are typically much lower.

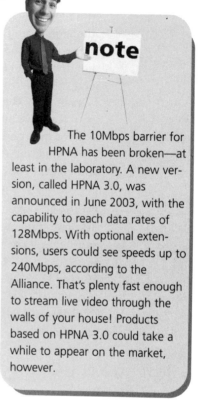

note

The 10Mbps barrier for HPNA has been broken—at least in the laboratory. A new version, called HPNA 3.0, was announced in June 2003, with the capability to reach data rates of 128Mbps. With optional extensions, users could see speeds up to 240Mbps, according to the Alliance. That's plenty fast enough to stream live video through the walls of your house! Products based on HPNA 3.0 could take a while to appear on the market, however.

FIGURE 22.3
This HPNA 2.0 adapter connects to the PC via a USB cable.

FIGURE 22.4
Products such as Belkin's Powerline USB Adapter make network connections about as easy as they can get.

Setting Up Your Network for Media Center

Although setting up your physical network connections can get tricky, it's really on the software side that things tend to get seriously complex. Because most of the network capabilities that Media Center relies on are actually part of the underlying operating system, we'll leave it to excellent books such as Robert Cowart's and Brian Knittel's *Special Edition: Using Windows XP Professional* to sort out all the dos and don'ts involved in setting up and troubleshooting your XP-based network.

For the most part, Media Center will operate independent of the network. However, there is one exception: if your Media Center PC relies on a network to connect to the Internet. That's because Media Center gets its online television guide via the Internet. Without that critical connection to the outside world, Media Center's TV recording features will be seriously crippled.

note

Like their counterparts at the HPNA, the HomePlug Powerline Alliance has also set its sights on the capability to stream video through your home, via the electrical outlets. Called HomePlug AV, the new version is being designed to support up to High Definition television (HDTV) signals. Look for products to appear in late 2004 at the earliest.

Testing Your Connection

Generally, the acid test for determining whether Media Center will be able to connect across your network to receive guide data is to launch Internet Explorer, and see whether you can surf. If you can roam the Internet freely, including gaining access to sites using Secure Sockets Layer (SSL) encryption, you should have no problems getting guide data via your networked Web connection.

Media Center has its own test routine for ensuring that it has Internet connectivity. We'll discuss this whole concept in greater detail in Chapter 23, "XP Media Center and Your Internet Connection," but you may want to run the test to ensure that your home network is functioning properly. The diagnostic utility is part of the Set Up Internet Connection wizard found under Settings, General.

If you experience problems with downloading program guide information, or you just want to check whether your network connection to the Internet is working, choose the Internet Setup tab and follow the onscreen instructions until you see the page titled An Internet Connection Is Set Up (see Figure 22.5). Select the Test button to confirm that your connection is working. If the wizard fails, it will return the ominous message "Test failed: LAN connection not working. Check the connections or reboot." Bottom line: Media Center will not be able to download TV guide data until that LAN connection is restored.

Network Troubleshooting

If you are able to browse the Internet on your Media Center PC via a network connection, but are still unable to download guide data, it could be that your Internet connection is set up correctly for browsing, but not for Media Center. When you set up a networked Internet connection in Internet Explorer (using the settings in Tools, Internet Options, Connections, LAN Settings), you are not necessarily affecting the settings that Media Center uses.

Media Center's guide data download process runs in what Microsoft calls the System context. System is like an all-powerful user identity, making the default Administrator user identity that you probably logged on with appear weak and worthless by comparison.

note

SSL, originally developed by Netscape and later adopted by Microsoft for its Internet Explorer browser, is one of the most common ways for securing Internet transmissions. When you see a Web site whose address begins with `https:` instead of just plain `http:` it's probably using SSL security. As you may have guessed by now, the site where Microsoft stores its TV program guide information relies on SSL security.

FIGURE 22.5

In this example from the Set Up Internet Connection wizard in Media Center, the test was not a success.

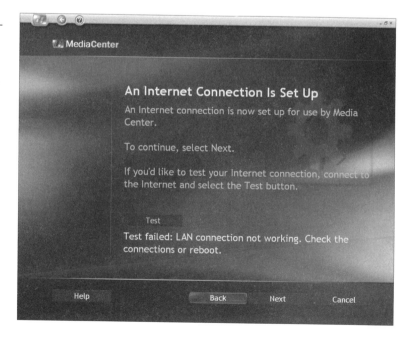

MediaCenter

An Internet Connection Is Set Up

An Internet connection is now set up for use by Media Center.

To continue, select Next.

If you'd like to test your Internet connection, connect to the Internet and select the Test button.

Test

Test failed: LAN connection not working. Check the connections or reboot.

Help   Back   Next   Cancel

Because of its reliance on the System context, Media Center will use whichever default Internet connection settings the SYSTEM user has—and these may be quite different from what you see from the Administrator standpoint.

Checking the Internet settings for the System context is a bit tricky, but if you've already tried everything else, it's often worth a shot. Here's how to do it:

1. From the Windows XP desktop, open the Start menu and choose Run.

2. Type CMD in the window and click OK. This will open up a DOS command window.

3. Next, we're going to schedule a job to automatically open and run Internet Explorer in the System context. First, choose a time (rendered in 24-hour format) that is about 3–5 minutes from the current time. For example, let's say that the current time is 4:49 p.m. Then you would type the following command exactly:

```
at 17:04 /interactive "%ProgramFiles%\Internet Explorer\
IEXPLORE.exe "
```

4. Be sure to note the spaces and quotation marks, as well as where to use forward slashes and back slashes.

> **caution**
>
> In fact, the System context is so powerful that Microsoft doesn't even mention its existence in most support literature, because there's a distinct potential for its misuse, potentially wreaking unintentional havoc with your system. Microsoft may eventually decide to do away with providing access to the System context altogether, because of its security ramifications. If you decide to follow the procedure outlined in the following text, exercise caution. One false step and you could wind up seriously disabling your system.

If you entered the command correctly, you will receive the following confirmation message: "Added a new job with job ID = 1." If so, simply wait until the appointed time, and a new Internet Explorer window will appear. It will look like any other IE window, but its connection properties will reflect the settings for the System context, not the user that is currently logged in.

In the new IE window, select Tools, Internet Options, Connections, LAN Settings, and check to make sure that all proxies and related information are correct.

Finally, try navigating to www.microsoft.com/ from that browser window. If you can reach Microsoft's Web site, Media Center also can.

Adding Network Folders for Storing Recorded TV Files

Although it is possible to configure Media Center to look for recorded TV files in folders other than the default Recorded TV folder on your local hard drive, this isn't exactly a supported feature. In fact, Microsoft technicians warn that this is considered "a power-user technique," requiring knowledge of the Windows registry and familiarity with the use of the registry editor.

Using this technique, the TV recorder in Media Center can be configured to "watch" folders on your network to look for new recorded TV programs. You may want to enable this if, for example, you have multiple Media Center machines on your network, and you want to be able to access shows recorded on any of them, from any Media Center machine.

Here's how to do it:

1. From the Windows XP desktop, open the Start menu and choose Run.

2. Type REGEDIT in the window and click OK. This opens the Registry Editor.

3. Navigate to the following registry key: HKEY_LOCAL_MACHINE\SOFTWARE\ Microsoft\Windows\CurrentVersion\ Media Center\Service\Recording\ WatchedFolders = REG_MULTI_SZ "<path>".

   You accomplish this by clicking on the + symbol next to the entry for HKEY_LOCAL_MACHINE in the left pane of the Registry Editor, then doing the same for SOFTWARE, Microsoft, Windows, and so on, until you reach the final registry key stated previously.

caution

Use care when editing your registry files—once again, you're getting "under the hood" of your operating system, and any mistakes you make could seriously damage the operation of your PC. It is a good idea to always back up your registry before making changes. Here's how:

1. From your Windows XP desktop, select Start, All Programs, Accessories, System Tools, and then select Backup. This will start the Backup Wizard.

2. Click Advanced Mode.

3. Select the Backup Wizard (Advanced).

4. Click Next, and then select the check box Only Back Up the System State Data.

5. In the Backup Destination screen, type the full path and filename where you want to store your backup file, and click Next.

6. Choose Finish. A status window will be displayed while the backup file is created (see Figure 22.6).

7. When the backup is complete, click Close.

FIGURE 22.6

The Backup
Utility displays
the following
progress window
while it is per-
forming a
backup of your
system state.

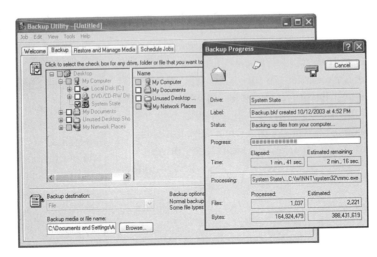

4. When you have located the final registry key in the right pane of Registry
   Editor, right-click on the entry and select Modify.

5. A small window with the title Edit Multi-String (see Figure 22.7) will appear.
   The Value Name is WatchedFolders, indicating that the folders listed in the
   Value Data box will be watched by Media Center to see whether new recorded
   TV programs are stored in those locations. You will see an existing folder
   listed on your local drive (the default location is C:\Documents and
   Settings\All Users\Document\Recorded TV).

FIGURE 22.7

This Edit Multi-
String window
in Registry
Editor allows
you to input
additional fold-
ers where you
want Media
Center to look
for recorded TV
files.

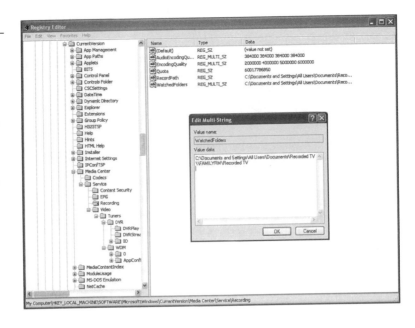

6. On the line below the default folder, enter another folder you want Media Center to watch, such as \\NetworkPC\Recorded TV.

7. Exit the Registry Editor and reboot the PC for your changes to take effect.

Mapping a Network Drive for Recorded Video

If you made the changes as noted previously, and new recorded TV content from the network folder you specified *still* doesn't show up when you open Recorded TV in the Media Center My TV menu, you may need to map the network drive in the System context. If so, open a command window as described previously, except this time, type the following statement:

> **note**
>
> If the registry key previously noted is not present, you may need to add your own local folders registry key to the watched list. Just use the Registry Editor to add the `WatchedFolders` value in the Recording key path as a multi-string value, as shown previously.

```
at 17:04 /interactive cmd
```

As before, substitute a time value that is a few minutes ahead of the current time shown on your PC, and make sure it's in 24-hour format. When the time you specified rolls around, a new command window will pop up, and this time it will be in the System context. The next command you enter in this window will have the following format:

```
NET USE Z:  "\\NetworkPC\Recorded TV"
```

Use any drive letter you want, as long as it isn't already in use. Press Enter, and you will be prompted to enter the user name and password for the network machine (if it's another XP Media Center PC, the default user name will be Administrator, and the password will be blank, unless you made some changes). You'll get a message telling you that the command completed sucessfully. Now try restarting Media Center and navigating to Recorded TV. You should see listings for the recorded TV shows stored on both PCs.

THE ABSOLUTE MINIMUM

Although Windows XP Media Center generally doesn't require a home network to deliver its media management capabilities, adding that network dimension still has its advantages. For example, if you're running out of room for new TV shows on your Media Center, you can conveniently stash them on another networked hard drive. You can also pull pictures and audio files from anywhere on the network into your Media Center applications. Here are a few things you should remember:

- There are several ways to enjoy network connectivity in your home—Ethernet, wireless, phone line, power line, and so on—and each offers a slightly different equation for cost versus performance, and overall ease of use. Do a little research and choose the network technology that's best for you. You can even mix and match multiple network architectures to get the right mix of connectivity and flexibility you're looking for.

- Although Media Center generally doesn't care whether you have a network, there is one exception: if you are sharing your Internet connection from a remote PC on the network. Media Center must have an active Internet connection to access TV guide data, which is an essential ingredient for getting full enjoyment from Media Center's My TV experience.

- Some network troubleshooting and customization features described in this chapter require making changes to your system via the Registry Editor and/or the System context. Exercise great caution when working in these environments, because it's quite possible to severely damage your PC's operations.

23

XP MEDIA CENTER AND YOUR INTERNET CONNECTION

Although it's possible to operate a Media Center PC without an Internet connection, doing so would cripple some of the most interesting and compelling features of the device. These include the interactive program guide, Internet-only radio stations, the ability to look up liner notes and details for audio CDs, and access to a wide range of content, software, and services available through a Media Center feature called Online Spotlight (see Figure 23.1).

The Online
Spotlight pro-
vides access to
music, movies,
news, and
usage tips to
enhance your
Media Center
experience.

So, to ensure that you are getting the most out of your Media Center, you'll need to configure and confirm your Internet connectivity.

Establishing Internet Connectivity with Media Center

If this is your first experience establishing Internet access for your home, check out the choices available to you by reading the section "A Few Words About Your Internet Connection," in Chapter 1, "Preparing for XP Media Center." You'll need to do some basic research to find out which Internet service providers (ISPs) have offerings in your area, and which one makes the most sense for your lifestyle and pocket-book.

After you have signed up and had your service enabled (including any physical equipment installation that may be required in the case of broadband or wireless connections), you're ready to hook up and get online. If you are setting up your Media Center for the first time, just follow the procedure for using the First Run Wizard as outlined in "Setting Up Your Internet Connection," in Chapter 3, "Getting Started and Taking the Tour."

But what if you have already configured your Media Center PC for one ISP, and decide to switch? Or how about if you previously set up your machine to run without Internet service, and now want to add it? The First Run Wizard just mentioned won't come into play in such cases. Instead, you'll want to follow another procedure. To access it, choose Settings from the Media Center Start menu, and then select General, and Set Up Internet Connection (see Figure 23.2).

FIGURE 23.2

The Set Up Internet Connection option in General Settings is the starting point to reconfigure your Web access.

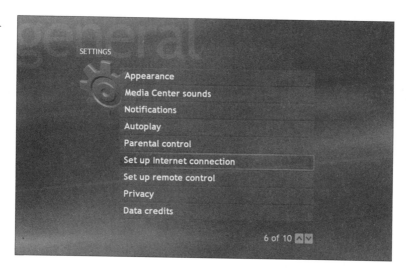

The first screen to be displayed is a confirmation screen (see Figure 23.3). Select Next to continue.

FIGURE 23.3

Selecting the Set Up Internet Connection button leads to this confirmation screen.

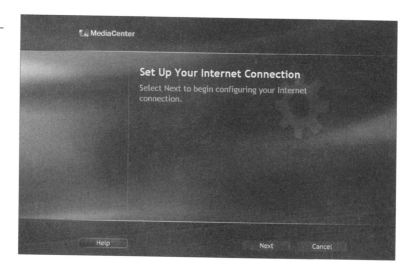

At this point, you are presented with a few choices for downloading program guide information (see Figure 23.4). At this stage, Media Center wants to know whether it should always try to connect automatically, wait until you are already connected to the Internet, or sit tight until you initiate a manual download of guide data.

FIGURE 23.4

This screen allows you to specify your preferred download method.

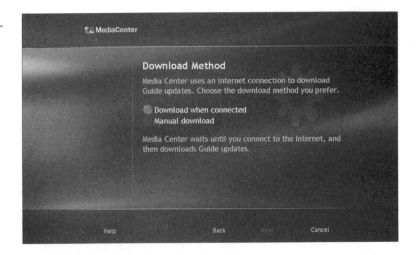

Download When Connected

Selecting the Download When Connected option on the Download Method screen tells Media Center to wait until you establish an Internet connection before automatically pulling down guide information. If you connect to the Web only occasionally, this may be a better choice.

When you select Download When Connected and choose Next, you will proceed directly to the An Internet Connection Is Set Up screen (see Figure 23.5).

FIGURE 23.5

This screen
announces that
your Internet
connection has
been config-
ured, and gives
you an opportu-
nity to test it.

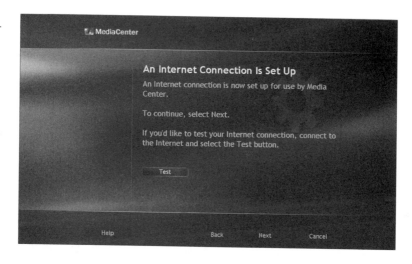

Manual Download

With the Manual Download option, Media Center lets you have complete control over the process of receiving guide data updates. Choose this if you want to initiate the update manually each time. (For instructions on getting guide data manually, see "Downloading Guide Data" in Chapter 7, "Finding Shows to Record.")

When you choose manual download, Media Center will present you with some advice (see Figure 23.6): "For the most up-to-date information, it is recommended that you connect to the Internet and get Guide data at least once per day." If that gives you any second thoughts, you can simply select Back to configure an automatic download instead.

Select Next, then Finish to complete the Internet connection setup process.

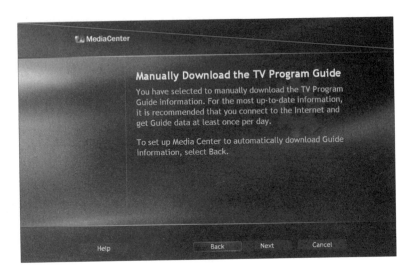

Online Spotlight

Besides the program guide and possibly the ability to look up audio CDs on the Web, the most important reason to have your Media Center PC hooked up to the Internet may be the ability to take advantage of Online Spotlight.

Introduced along with Microsoft's first major refresh of the Media Center software in September 2003, Online Spotlight is a showcase for Microsoft partners to offer content and services using Media Center's 10-foot interface. In general, this means that all the offerings in Online Spotlight are accessible using your remote control, and the screens adhere to the basic Media Center design—from the big, bold typeface for titles and descriptions, to the predominantly blue-and-white color scheme, with green highlights to show you what you've selected (see Figure 23.7).

In the next few pages, we'll take a look at some of the types of services and content available through the Online Spotlight portal. Categories can change as new companies decide to partner with Microsoft, but as of the Online Spotlight launch, they included the following:

- Music
- Movies
- News
- Download
- Tips

FIGURE 23.7

The MSN TV news headlines page from Online Spotlight is designed for Media Center's 10-foot experience.

To access a particular service, select the category name. Online Spotlight will present you with a list of providers in that category. You can then select the service or product you want to try (see Figure 23.8).

Music

The initial Online Spotlight music partners included the resurrected Napster music download service, and streaming audio service Live365.com. Let's take a brief look at each provider.

Napster

The rise and fall—and rise again—of Napster is the stuff of legend in the Dot-Com world. The once high-flying file-swapping service boasted millions of subscribers at one point, nearly all engaged in the ultimately illegal act of trading copyrighted material without paying any royalties

caution

Up to this point, most of the features available from Media Center have been free—with the exception of your Internet service, of course. Now that you're getting ready to venture into the Online Spotlight area, be prepared: Many of the services featured here will not be a free ride. Be on the lookout for subscription and download costs, and have your credit card handy if you plan to sample the merchandise.

to the copyright holders. A highly publicized court case eventually grounded Napster, forcing it into bankruptcy. Roxio, a software company best known for its CD-burning application for PCs, purchased the Napster name and relaunched it in the Fall of 2003 as a pay-to-play download service. As such, it has the full support of the beleaguered record industry.

FIGURE 23.8
Selecting a category title, such as Music, in Online Spotlight gives you access to individual content providers.

Unlike most of the initial Online Spotlight providers, the new Napster requires that Media Center users exit to a Windows-based browser to sign up (see Figure 23.9). After you sign up, the service promises to give you access to a half-million songs, at the affordable price of 99 cents per track, or $9.95 for a full album. The songs come in pristine digital form, and allow unlimited listens from your Media Center PC (some restrictions on use apply, however, if you want to burn the songs onto a recordable CD).

Live365.com

Tired of commercial radio, and its inevitable rehash of tired old Top 40 tunes? Choosing Live365.com (see Figure 23.10) sends you directly to the company's voluminous library of live streaming "radio" stations. If your musical tastes tend to take you off the beaten path, you'll find every imaginable genre here, from alternative rock to zither music. Best of all, it's absolutely free.

FIGURE 23.9

The first time you try to access the Napster service, you'll see a message like this.

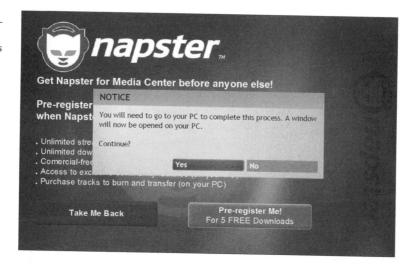

FIGURE 23.10

Choosing Live365.com's streaming audio service launches you directly into a nirvana of free music stations.

From the launch screen of Live365.com, you can select one of the "editor's picks" that are displayed, or choose the Genres tab to zero in on your particular taste in music.

After you find something you like, you can bookmark it by selecting the Add to My Radio button (see Figure 23.11). You'll see a pop-up screen advising you that a file is about to be stored on your computer by the streaming service. Press OK on your remote, and the station will now be available to you when you select Radio from the main Media Center start menu (see Figure 23.12) .

FIGURE 23.11

Selecting the big green + symbol next to the words Add to My Radio will make this warning pop up.

Movies

Two fledgling movie download services were represented at the launch of Media Center 2004's Online Spotlight service: CinemaNow and Movielink. Both represent a relatively new venue for pay-per-view aficionados, allowing you to download a movie to your PC for viewing at your convenience.

FIGURE 23.12

Choosing OK in the Save File window places a shortcut in your Media Center Radio menu.

CinemaNow

The CinemaNow service allows you search for movies, read details, watch the trailer, and, if you choose, download the movie to your PC. To start the download process, choose a movie you want to watch, and select Download Movie (see Figure 23.13).

After you have completed the registration process for the service, which is handled completely within the Media Center interface, you will be shown a list of instructions (see Figure 23.14), which include installing the CinemaNow software. This part of the process requires the use of a mouse.

Download times vary depending on the speed of your Internet connection. Prices also vary, reflecting the popularity of the film you've chosen, its length, and how recently it was released. In any case, you have 48 hours to begin watching the movie, and then 24 hours of unlimited viewing from the time you start watching.

FIGURE 23.13

CinemaNow offers an extensive roster of movies for download. The service offers easy home shopping, right from within Media Center.

FIGURE 23.14

Using CinemaNow requires that you first install some software to handle the transaction.

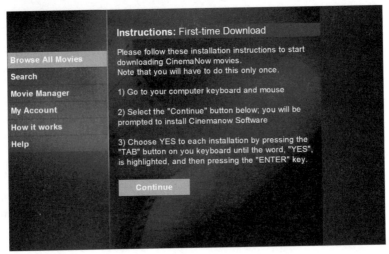

Movielink

Like CinemaNow, Movielink (see Figure 23.15) gives you access to a library of feature and short films. Unlike its competitor, Movielink allows you to download and store a movie for up to a month. After you start the movie, however, you can watch it as many times as you can stand, but within a 24-hour period before your access rights expire.

FIGURE 23.15

With Movielink you can view theatrical trailers, or choose Rent This Movie.

After selecting a movie to download, choose Rent This Movie to proceed to the checkout screen. On the way, you'll be required to give your consent to Movielink's Terms of Use contract (see Figure 23.16).

When it comes to choosing between Movielink and CinemaNow, the other early entry in the Online Spotlight movie-rental business, you may find that Movielink offers slightly more flexible terms. Both services give you 24 hours to enjoy the movie, after you start it. But Movielink gives you up to a month to play the movie for the first time, before it expires. CinemaNow requires you to begin playing the film within two days of downloading it.

FIGURE 23.16

Movielink's rental terms are slightly less rigid than those of CinemaNow.

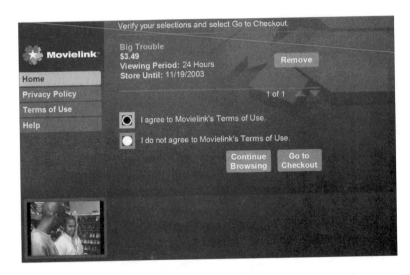

News

Provided by MSN TV, the interactive news channel gives you access to up-to-the-minute information in the following categories:

- Top Stories
- Business
- Technology
- Sports
- Entertainment
- Travel

When you access the MSN TV Today news service home page (see Figure 23.17) in Online Spotlight, you can select Choose Your City to customize the weather report.

The service also provides a small preview of what's possible in the future, as content providers learn to take advantage of Media Center's integrated media-handling capabilities. Choose any news topic and a button appears in the bottom center of the screen (see Figure 23.18). Select the Tune to MSNBC button, and Media Center automatically looks up the listing for the Microsoft/NBC joint venture TV channel in your program guide, and turns to it.

FIGURE 23.17
This image of the MSNBC TV home page takes on a personalized feel when you add your hometown weather report.

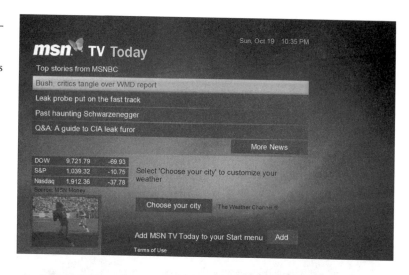

FIGURE 23.18
The unassuming Tune to MSNBC button gives a subtle hint of the kind of powerful TV/Internet integration that Media Center is capable of.

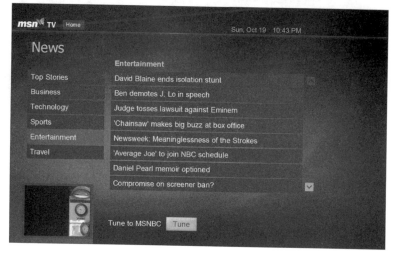

Downloads

The first independent software vendor to show up in Media Center's Online Spotlight Downloads category is Sonic, with its PrimeTime DVD burning application. For a full description of the impressive PrimeTime product, which allows you to burn DVDs directly from Media Center's program guide, see the section on PrimeTime in Chapter 12, "Creating DVDs on an XP Media Center PC."

To buy PrimeTime via the Online Spotlight section of Media Center, select the Sonic Store from the Downloads offerings, and then choose the PrimeTime button. Then you'll need to decide whether you want to purchase the software immediately, or just download a trial version (see Figure 23.19).

FIGURE 23.19

Sonic has included links to its Web-based home page and its eStore site.

Tips

If reading this book has only served to whet your appetite for ways to push the Media Center envelope, check into the Tips category (see Figure 23.20) in Online Spotlight to view detailed directions on topics such as these:

- Turn Off the Automatic Start Setting for TV
- Record TV Shows with One-Touch Recording
- Use the Computer While Recording TV
- Pause, Skip, and Fast-Forward Live TV
- Fix Pictures with the Remote Control
- Avoid Recording Reruns

FIGURE 23.20

Microsoft has prepared a full menu of tips to help you master Media Center.

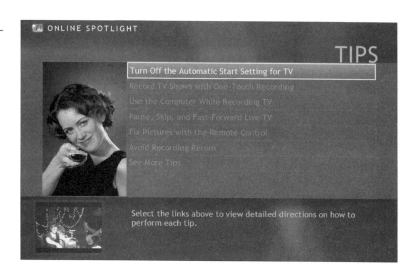

THE ABSOLUTE MINIMUM

As far as Microsoft is concerned, using a Media Center PC without an active Internet connection is practically unthinkable. Here are a few dos and don'ts to keep in mind as you get online:

- Media Center and broadband were born for each other. If you have an "always on" broadband connection, the easiest and most effective way to configure Media Center's program guide acquisition features is to allow the system to connect automatically to the Internet.

- If you don't have broadband—or even if you do, but you're still a bit of a control freak—you can configure Media Center to wait until it senses a Web connection before downloading guide data, or you can tell it to wait until you connect manually.

- Next to the guide data, one of the biggest reasons to connect your Media Center PC to the Internet is to take advantage of integrated content services via the Online Spotlight.

- The idea of Online Spotlight is to let third-party (non-Microsoft) companies offer goods and services to you from within the comfort of your Media Center 10-foot experience. The concept is to make it extremely easy to buy movies, music, and more, with just a few clicks of your remote control—but be careful, your Online Spotlight bill could start to add up in a hurry!

24

DOWNLOADS AND ENHANCEMENTS

Operating systems used to be something that you simply installed and then ignored. In fact, most people bought—and still buy—PCs with an operating system already built in. You might have thought about upgrading to the latest version of Windows when the OS was refreshed every few years, or you might just as likely have decided to forget about it until you upgraded to a new PC, which would again come with the latest and greatest version of the OS already onboard.

Things change. The onslaught of viral computer worms and security hacks targeting the Windows platform have turned the OS into a swiftly moving target. To keep ahead of the hackers and "script kiddies" who cut and paste together new viral variants every day, it has become necessary to regularly update your operating system.

In addition, although your Media Center PC has been configured to work perfectly right out of the box (granted, this sometimes works better in principle than in practice), Microsoft is constantly writing and revising its code to fix bugs and add new features.

As a result of these driving forces in operating-system development—the security, quality control, and continuing innovation—it's necessary to have a strategy for keeping your OS up-to-date.

Making Sure You Have the Latest Version of Media Center

If you bought your Media Center PC before September 30, 2003, it came with the initial version of the Media Center software. That date marked the introduction of the first major upgrade to the Windows XP Media Center Edition operation system. Even if you bought your PC in the months following that introduction, remember that it can take several weeks for PCs built before that time to filter down through the retail sales channels of stores and mail-order distributors, and so on.

If you're not sure whether you have the latest version, called Windows XP Media Center Edition 2004, you can check by following these steps:

1. Launch Media Center, and choose Settings.

2. Select General, and scroll down to the bottom of the list.

3. Choose About Media Center. The following screen (see Figure 24.1) should indicate that you are running the 2004 edition.

How to Upgrade

If you don't have the latest version of Media Center, the best way to get it is by contacting the

caution

If you were one of the thousands involved in testing interim, or "beta," versions of Windows XP Media Center Edition 2004 (aka Harmony)—or somehow obtained a beta version of the OS to run on your PC through unofficial channels—you cannot immediately upgrade to the final RTM (release to manufacturing) version of the operating system. Before you can upgrade, you will need to revert to the previous official RTM version of the software—the original Windows XP Media Center Edition (aka Freestyle)—before you can complete the upgrade successfully.

company that manufactured your Media Center PC and asking them to provide you with an update disc.

FIGURE 24.1

This About Media Center information page provides details on your installed version of Media Center.

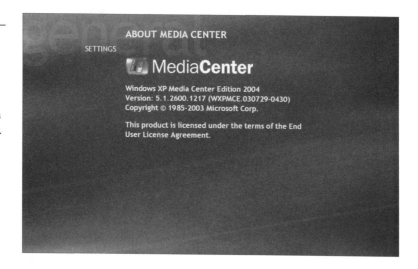

How to Update

In addition to making sure you have the most current version of your operating system, you need to stay on top of updates that seem to be trickling out from Microsoft with increasing frequency. The best and easiest way is to put Windows XP in charge of keeping itself updated by using the Automatic Update features described in the section "Check For and Install Software Updates," in Chapter 3, "Getting Started and Taking the Tour."

If at any time you want to manually update your Microsoft OS software, you can do so by launching Internet Explorer and visiting www.windowsupdate.com. When the page comes up, click on the Scan for Updates button, as shown in the center of Figure 24.2.

FIGURE 24.2

The Windows Update Web site will automatically analyze your system software and recommend upgrades.

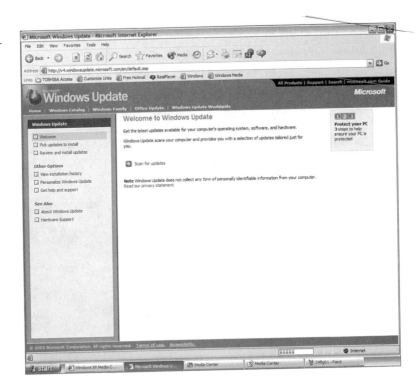

Special Media Center Downloads

Microsoft offers an intriguing array of downloads to enhance and enliven your Media Center desktop. You can generally access these files by logging on to the Media Center Download page at `www.microsoft.com/windowsxp/mediacenter/downloads`, as shown in Figure 24.3.

At the time of writing this chapter, the page included the following types of download files:

- Microsoft PowerToys
- Previous versions
- Skins
- Songs
- Screensavers
- Desktop Images

In the next few pages, we'll describe each of these downloadable options for your Media Center machine in greater detail.

FIGURE 24.3

The Media Center Download page provides numerous add-ons to customize and update your Media Center experience.

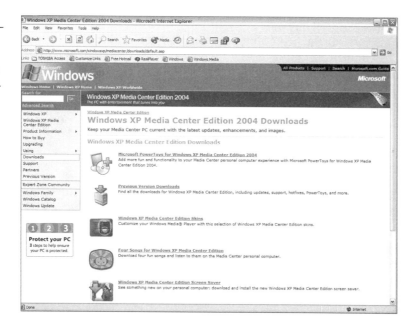

Microsoft PowerToys

Formally called Microsoft PowerToys for Windows XP Media Center Edition 2004, the PowerToys download consists of numerous software elements designed to spruce up and spice up your Media Center experience.

The PowerToys available for download at the time Media Center Edition 2004 was introduced in the fall of 2003 included the following:

■ *Alarm Clock*—Designed to work like an old-fashioned clock radio, the Media Center Alarm Clock PowerToy (shown in Figure 24.4) lets you choose a song and have Media Center wake you up with it at the time you designate. Of course, everything can be configured using your Media Center remote control. The file is only 1.18MB to download.

■ *PlaylistEditor*—The Playlist Editor program (see Figure 24.5) allows you to create and edit music playlists via your Media Center remote control. You can

caution

Although Microsoft maintains that the PowerToys applications are safe and sane add-ons to your Media Center desktop, the company does not actually support the software contained in the PowerToys downloads. If they don't work quite as advertised, be prepared to uninstall them, because Microsoft says it will not answer questions or provide technical assistance with the programs.

sort and add songs by various attributes, such as album, artist, title, or genre. The download file is 1.2MB.

■ *Solitaire*—The quintessential Windows time-waster, Solitaire (see Figure 24.6), has been adapted to run on your Media Center, via remote control. The download file is 2.06MB.

Installing PowerToys

PowerToy programs, along with other third-party applications designed to run in conjunction with Windows XP Media Center Edition 2004, require that you download and install the software from the Windows XP desktop. If you click on the appropriate link on the Media Center Downloads Web page (shown earlier in Figure 24.3) the process is fairly simple:

1. Follow the link to find the file you want to download, and then click on it.

2. A pop-up window will ask whether you want to save the file to disk or open it.

3. Select Open, and follow the onscreen prompts to install the software.

note

Before you can work with audio files and playlists from within Media Center, you need to first load some music files onto your system, and then run Windows Media Player to add the files to your Media Library. You can also copy CDs directly into Media Center using the My Music interface, as described in the section "Ripping a CD from the My Music interface," in Chapter 13, "Preparing Your Music Collection for XP Media Center."

FIGURE 24.4

The Media Center Alarm Clock allows you to configure Media Center to wake you up to your favorite audio selection.

FIGURE 24.5

The Media Center Playlist Editor allows you to sort and choose songs, and then save sets of them as preconfigured playlists.

FIGURE 24.6

Nothing on My TV? This clever adaptation of the classic card game of one-sided one-upmanship can keep you occupied for hours.

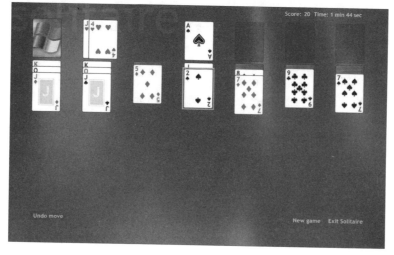

To launch and use the programs after you have installed them, launch Media Center and select More Programs from the main menu. You should see a list of programs that includes the one you just installed (see Figure 24.7) .

Previous Versions

The Previous Version Downloads section of the Web-based Media Center Download pages includes various performance updates, patches, and bug fixes, along with utilities to enhance or expand the capabilities of your Media Center machine. Among other things, you can download software that will provide support for additional set-top boxes, or update the firmware for your remote sensor to correct a bug that causes remote-control commands to get "stuck," or repeat themselves.

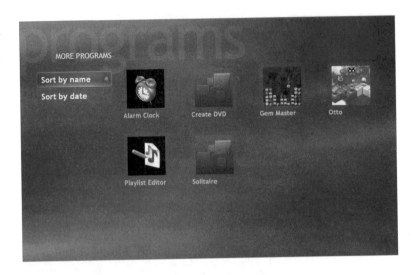

FIGURE 24.7

The More Programs screen contains links to games and other software programs designed to run from within Media Center.

Watching Recorded TV on an XP Machine

You can also download a utility that will allow you to watch Media Center recorded TV programs on another PC that's running a standard version of Windows XP. To do this, you'll need to install a file with the catchy name of Q810243_WXP_SP2_x86_rENU.exe on your Windows XP machine. You will also have to install the Windows XP Service Pack 1, and you'll need Windows Media Player 9 software, or another player that is compatible with Microsoft's DirectShow multimedia architecture.

After you have the software installed on your XP machine, just transfer the show you want from your Media Center machine via a network connection, recordable CD or DVD, and so on. Remember that recorded shows are stored by default in your Media Center's C:\Documents and Settings\All Users\Shared Documents\Recorded TV folder, with the extension .dvr-ms.

caution

Even if you do everything right in installing and transferring the files needed to play recorded TV on a separate Windows XP machine, there is a possibility that some files won't work. This is because broadcasters can use a technology called CGMS-A to protect their content. If this is the case with a particular show, you will be able to watch it only on the Media Center PC that originally recorded the show.

Skins

Skins refer to software that changes the look of your Windows Media Player. Although changing skins won't really affect the look or operations of Media Center itself, Microsoft has created several Media Player skins that are specially designed to complement the look of your Media Center interface (see Figure 24.8). To try on a new skin, click on the download link for the skin you want, and then choose Yes in the dialog box. The new skin will be installed automatically, and you'll see it the next time you use Windows Media Player.

> **tip**
>
> It's easy to toggle between skin mode and the traditional full screen (aka "full mode") in Windows Media Player. If you're in skin mode, press Ctrl+1 on your keyboard to switch to full mode. To switch from full mode back to skin mode, use the keyboard shortcut Ctrl+2.

FIGURE 24.8

These are two of the skins designed to give the Windows Media Player application a look and feel that complements Media Center.

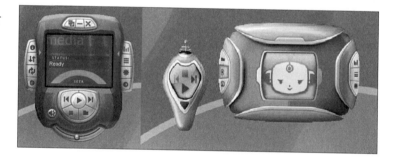

Songs

How about a Media Center theme song? Microsoft has provided a few original tunes to help you get into the Media Center frame of mind. The tunes, available free for download, include "Home of the Future," "Enjoy," "Remote Control," and "Online." The style is appropriately Techno-Pop, and all are performed by Microsoft's own "house band" formed for the occasion, "Press the Green Button."

Screensavers

If you have installed the skins, have downloaded the tunes, and are fully determined to live "La Vida Media Center" in every possible way, then of course you will also need to get the Media Center screensaver (see Figure 24.9).

FIGURE 24.9

This screen-saver shows two Media Center aficionados having a rol-licking good time watching Media Center My TV.

Also available from the Media Center Downloads page, the file mcesaver.exe weighs in at slightly under 2MB. The screensaver is actually larger, but it has been com-pressed, or "zipped." To install it, do this:

1. Click on the file link, and then click on Open in the file download dialog box. After the file is downloaded, the WinZip Self-Extractor will launch.

2. Click Browse in the Self-Extractor window and choose a directory to unzip the file in.

3. Choose Unzip. Then click on OK, and Close.

4. Open My Computer from the XP Start menu, and go to the directory where you unzipped the file.

5. Double-click on the file called Windows XP Media Center Edition Screen Saver to install it. Choose Next, then Finish, and finally OK.

6. The Display Properties dialog box will appear, with the Screen Saver tab already selected. The Media Center screensaver is now set as the default. You can change the timer settings, preview it, and so on. Press OK to complete the process.

Desktop Images

The finishing touch for totally redoing your desktop decor in a Media Center motif is to add some new wallpaper. Microsoft offers a complete selection, from a green start button sized appropriately for the Jolly Green Giant himself, to a Media Center–inspired party scene.

To install one of the Media Center wallpapers, simply click on the image you want. This will open another browser window containing a full-screen version of the graphic. Right-click anywhere on the image, and select Set as Background. Close or minimize all the open windows to admire your handiwork (see Figure 24.10).

FIGURE 24.10

This wallpaper image from the Windows XP Media Center Downloads page shows off the sleek design of the Media Center remote control.

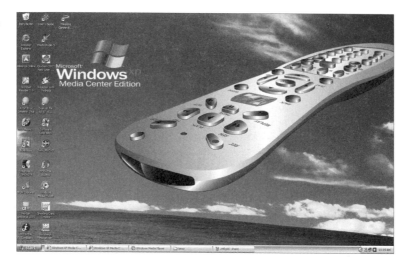

FIGURE 24.10

This wallpaper image from the Windows XP Media Center Downloads page shows off the sleek design of the Media Center remote control.

Third-Party Software Enhancements for Media Center

Many of the third-party (non-Microsoft) software applications available specifically to work with your Media Center Edition PC have already been discussed in previous chapters. As the number of Media Center PCs continues to grow, more and more such programs are likely to be developed. However, there are a few more programs already available that bear mentioning.

My Karaoke

My Karaoke, from Eatsleepmusic Corp. in Canada, is designed as an application that runs from within Media Center, allowing you to subscribe to a service that promises access to more than 20,000 sing-along tunes.

To install the demo version, follow these steps:

1. Go to the Web site www.mykaraokemce.com, and select the link for Download the Demo Now.
2. Click Open in the File Download options box.
3. Accept the folder location (or browse and select a new one) by clicking on Start, and then click OK.
4. Restart your PC for the changes to take effect.

To launch My Karaoke, go to the More Programs menu item in Media Center, and select the My Karaoke icon. My Karaoke will load and then display the Welcome page (see Figure 24.11). From here you can browse existing playlists or create new ones, adjust settings, or get help.

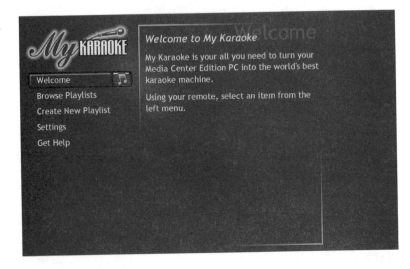

To run My Karaoke through its paces, so that you can decide whether to sign up for a subscription, choose the Browse Playlists button, and select from among the following preconfigured lists:

- Cool Rockin Tunes
- Crooners Delight
- Good Ole Cowboys
- Pop Party Hits
- Rollin New Country
- Sing the Classics

When you choose a playlist, the Play Songs screen will appear (see Figure 24.12). Using the remote control, select the song you want to sing along to, and get ready to rock the house!

As the music plays, the lyrics will appear in the inset screen, turning from yellow to green to keep you in synch with the score. You can select the inset window and press OK to display the lyrics full-screen.

Games

There are two more little jewels of third-party programming tucked away in the More Programs section of the Windows XP Media Center Edition 2004 operating system: Otto and Gem Master. Developed by games house Wild Tangent, these programs were designed to bring console-quality gaming into the Media Center experience. Best of all, they are free with the 2004 version of the OS, and they don't require any additional downloading or installing.

FIGURE 24.12

My Karaoke for Media Center displays lyrics that turn colors to keep you in synch with the music.

Otto

This Media Center version of the Otto's Magic Blocks video game challenges you to rescue Otto—a sort of gumdrop-shaped Pac Man sporting a single star-studded deelie-bopper—as he is chased around by various nefarious creatures with names like King FrixFrax, Fuzzabound, and Hoverbug (see Figure 24.13).

FIGURE 24.13

The unflappable Otto must keep away from the dastardly Fuzzabound in the Media Center game Otto's Magic Blocks.

The game controller is your Media Center remote control. Use the direction buttons to move Otto, and the OK button to jump over obstacles and foes. To complete each level, Otto must land on every square, without falling off or colliding with bad guys.

Gem Master

Wild Tangent's Gem Master: Mystic (see Figure 24.14) is a puzzle game inspired by the arcade favorite Tetris. Instead of colored blocks dropping from the sky, it's raining precious stones, and many are imbued with special properties.

FIGURE 24.14

In Gem Master: Mystic, the object is to arrange the gems by color.

Once again, your remote control wields the power. Use the right and left arrows to move the line of falling gems. The up arrow switches the order of the stones, and the down-arrow button speeds up their descent. Each time you maneuver three like-colored jewels so that they touch each other, they disappear, making room for more stones.

THE ABSOLUTE MINIMUM

As Windows XP Media Center Edition gains momentum in the marketplace, it is attracting a growing number of independent software developers who see the operating system as a viable platform for selling products and services directly into your living room.

As you add software to your Media Center machine, keep the following in mind:

- Media Center is an integrated hardware/software system that is finely tuned to handle the strenuous demands of processing real-time video. Be very careful about installing any software for use with the Media Center applications that doesn't come from a developer who has been "blessed" by Microsoft as an official partner.

- Whether or not the third-party software comes from an official Microsoft partner, if it seems to interfere with the smooth operations of Media Center, you should remove it and contact the developer. That includes new software applications written by Microsoft too!

- Keeping your operating system up-to-date is one of the best ways to protect against hacks and online vulnerabilities. However, you should also be running a good antivirus software program on your system at all times.

- Microsoft can change the contents of its downloads page and PowerToys offerings at any time. Check back every few weeks to see whether anything new and interesting has been added.

25

HARDWARE FEATURES AND OPTIONS FOR MEDIA CENTER PCS

One of the features that makes Microsoft's Windows XP Media Center Edition Software unique is that it's among the very few Microsoft products that can't be purchased by themselves. You must buy the operating system as part of a configured Media Center PC—or you can't have it at all.

There are those who have circumvented this policy, of course, but they are on their own. Microsoft does not support them, and neither does this author. Of course, when Media Center Edition was first made available, hardware systems were running in the high-flying $2,500-and-up range. At those prices, one could hardly blame the poor souls who lusted after the Media Center experience but couldn't quite afford it. Today, however, Media Center machines are available at all the major PC price points, including systems for well under $1,000. Practically everyone who can afford a new PC should be able to find a Media Center system that fits their budget.

Media Center PCs: What's the Difference?

Because all Media Center PCs are running the same operating system software, and all have essentially equivalent hardware features for audio and video capture and playback, one could reasonably ask, "What's the difference?"

In some respects, the differences are subtle, a matter of a few gigahertz of processor speed, megabytes of memory, or gigabytes of hard drive space. These internal differences cannot be seen or felt until the system is up and operating. A good rule of thumb is to buy as much as you can reasonably afford—as much processor, memory, and storage capacity. The more powerful the system, the happier you will ultimately be with its performance. However, as in all things, moderation is also a virtue. Don't spend more than makes sense to you for the application you have in mind, which in this case is probably watching TV while running some routine desktop productivity applications—not splitting the atom or modeling the genome.

Although these internal specifications do make a difference in your system's performance, there are other differences that appear much more obvious, namely, the physical size and form of the system. Lastly, price will always be a major differentiator of PC products, of course.

To define the Media Center hardware species, it's necessary to make some classifications of the various subspecies. As in biology, we'll base our distinctions on the most glaring differences, and classify our systems according to their physical form factor. Currently, Media Center PCs come in four basic shapes and sizes:

- The classic desktop or tower format
- The compact or "shuttle" format
- The laptop
- The "all-in-one"

In the following sections, we'll take a closer look at each of these Media Center hardware classes and highlight some of their pluses and minuses.

Desktops and Towers

The very first Media Center PC to hit the market in the fall of 2002 was a standard tower system from Hewlett-Packard. This style is still the most prevalent on the market, and for good reason. Namely, it's the natural choice for buyers who are looking for a multipurpose Windows XP–based personal computer, but who are also attracted to the media-handling marvels of the Media Center Edition software.

The tower design, along with traditional desktop versions, was also easier to produce, because it did not require a great deal of new hardware engineering and could be assembled from existing off-the-shelf parts—including the system chassis itself. Although the exterior styling of these models tends to be rather conventional (see Figure 25.1), some manufacturers have worked to create exterior designs that set their systems apart (see Figure 25.2).

FIGURE 25.1

Dell's top-of-the-line Dimension 8300 Media is loaded on the inside, but its office-attire exterior won't turn any heads.

Does anybody really care what the outside of their PC looks like? That's a matter of personal taste, of course, but remember that the Media Center is not an ordinary putty-colored PC destined to hide under a desk. It's literally the center of your home media and entertainment system, designed to be placed close to your TV. The television, of course, not only is positioned in plain view, but often occupies one of the most conspicuous locations in your home. Although you are right to devote more time and attention to what's actually *inside* the PC "box," because that's what will determine the actual performance of your Media Center system, sooner or later you may regret buying a PC that you feel is an eyesore.

FIGURE 25.2

The Systemax Double X MCE has windows in the hardware—in the form of stylish see-through panels built into the tower-style case.

Compact Systems

There are instances in life in which less really is more. This may well be the case for Media Center PCs based on the small form factor (SFF) platform popularized by boutique PC makers such as Shuttle, of Taiwan.

About the size of a sturdy shoebox, these compact systems are small enough to fit unobtrusively into your entertainment center, or snuggled up against your TV set (see Figure 25.3).

Another major advantage that SFF systems can claim over their bulkier desktop or tower brethren: They are quieter. Fan noise may not seem like a major problem with your typical desktop or tower PC when you're using it in your office, but you may be surprised at how that little bit of "white noise" can make you see red—especially when that steady hum begins to intrude on your enjoyment of a movie or an audio selection. This attribute alone has long served to make SFF PCs a favorite among do-it-yourselfers building their own versions of a PC-based home theater system.

FIGURE 25.3

This SFF model, the Media Center PC 8200 from ABS Computer Technologies, is based on a "bare-bones" XPC chassis designed by Shuttle.

What will you be giving up if you opt for an SFF system instead of a more traditional design? You may lose a little firepower in terms of CPU, memory, and hard drive size, compared to a desktop or tower machine. And the compact case makes it difficult to fit all the peripherals inside, so you may find that the floppy drive and modem are available only as external units. However, you don't need to give up a lot of extras when it comes to connectivity. For example, the front panel of the SFF-based Media Center PC 8200 from ABS Computer Technologies sports a recordable DVD drive, along with slots to accommodate SmartMedia, Secure Digital/Multimedia, Memory Stick, and CompactFlash/Microdrive cards (see Figure 25.4). Ports for speakers, headphone, microphone, USB, and FireWire are also represented.

The rear view of the ABS/Shuttle Media Center PC (see Figure 25.5) also reveals connectivity that exceeds even some tower and desktop versions of the Media Center hardware.

FIGURE 25.4

This front view of ABS Computer's Media Center PC 8200 offers an impressive array of slots and connector inputs.

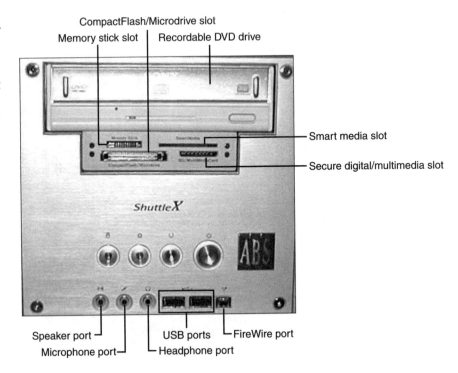

CompactFlash/Microdrive slot

Memory stick slot   Recordable DVD drive

Smart media slot

Secure digital/multimedia slot

Speaker port ┘   USB ports   └ FireWire port

Microphone port ┘   └ Headphone port

If you're interested in a compact Media Center but find the short and squat SFF shape to be a turn-off, Dell also makes a compact case that resembles a pared-down tower design (see Figure 25.6) .

Laptops

The concept of a Portable Media Center PC is an intriguing one, and Toshiba was the first company to step up to the challenge in the summer of 2003. The flagship of the Toshiba line is the P25 (see Figure 25.7), sporting a gargantuan 17-inch screen, and designed to deliver "a true personal theater experience."

Although the size and weight—nearly 10 pounds without the battery, remote control, infrared sensor, AC adapter, and so on—make it a pretty impractical machine to take on the road, the P25 provides a formidable multimedia experience for a so-called "portable" PC. The built-in Harman/Kardon sound system with subwoofer is enough to give every other laptop ever made an inferiority complex, and the NVIDIA GeForce FX Go5200 graphics-powered active matrix display is visually stunning, as is the sleek silver-and-cobalt-blue exterior of the system.

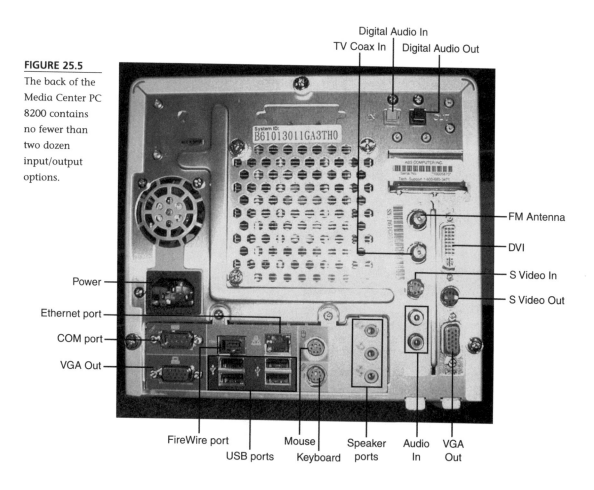

FIGURE 25.5

The back of the Media Center PC 8200 contains no fewer than two dozen input/output options.

The P25 is a masterpiece of PC integration and design in all respects but one: TV reception. The front-loading, removable TV tuner module leaves much to be desired. Toshiba claims to be working to fix the problem, but in the meantime, some users have found that reducing the screen resolution down to about 1024 by 768 (the default setting is a whopping 1440 by 900) can produce a much more acceptable picture for watching TV. Others say reducing the screen size and watching TV in a smaller window improves the experience.

For a truly mobile Media Center solution, Toshiba has also introduced the Satellite P15 model, with a more manageable 15.4-inch screen size (see Figure 25.8).

FIGURE 25.6

On the right, the Dell Dimension 4600C with Windows XP Media Center Edition is attractive for fans of its compact 12-inch-tall design.

FIGURE 25.7

The Toshiba P25 combines Media Center software, a 17-inch XGA active matrix display, and integrated Harman/Kardon speakers.

All-in-Ones

And now for something truly revolutionary: a Media Center system designed with the same flair as the P25, but built to stay put. Introduced in conjunction with the launch of Windows XP Media Center Edition 2004 on September 30, 2003, Gateway's eye-popping all-in-one 610 Media Center design (see Figure 25.9) nearly stole the show.

FIGURE 25.8

FIGURE 25.8

Although it doesn't evince the same "wow factor" as its bigger sibling, the P25, the P15 lets you truly order your Media Center "to go."

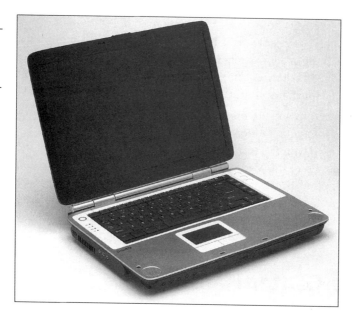

FIGURE 25.9

Like the P25, the Gateway 610 Media Center sports a 17-inch, wide-screen, LCD display.

Although the 610 does have a handle, it's quite a handful at 30 pounds—about as portable as the typical TV it hopes to replace. Chances are that after you've set it up, it's going to stay put. With its Pentium 4–based PC parts tucked neatly behind the 17-inch flat panel display, this is one Media Center system you won't be tempted to hide behind a potted plant.

Built-in PC speakers have never been synonymous with great acoustics, but the 610 sounds as good as it looks. This is owing to its twin front-mounted speakers and rear-facing built-in subwoofer. Your integrated FM tuner won't go unused with this combination. And like its compact and portable Media Center counterparts, the system is rigged for silent running with a minimum of fan noise.

Gateway has also gone to great pains to see that no strings are attached. Aside from plugging it into your TV signal source and AC power, the machine is completely wireless. Along with the infrared keyboard and mouse, Gateway may be the first PC maker to get rid of the Media Center's IR receiver "dongle." The remote control uses the same built-in IR receiver as the other wireless input devices. This provides for a clean, uncluttered, and easy-to-install solution rather than the usual rat's nest of wires that accompanies most Media Center systems. Built-in wireless networking and a recordable DVD drive are also included in the high-end 610XL model.

Other Media Center Hardware

Media Center PCs are self-contained units, for the most part. There are a few exceptions, in the form of optional, additional items you may need in order to configure and connect your machine to your existing TV signal and home entertainment equipment (see Chapter 2's section "What You May Need to Supply for Yourself"). However, the Media Center hardware was designed to provide pretty much everything you need, right out of the box.

Although Microsoft has at least 15 independent hardware vendors (IHVs) signed up to make various parts and pieces of Media Center systems, most of these items are not made available directly to consumers. Instead, the parts—mostly internal tuner cards, infrared receivers, and remote controls—are sold directly to original equipment manufacturers (OEMs), who build the PC systems that we buy.

However, there are a few interesting add-on items, which could be used to create a Media Center PC out of an ordinary Windows XP machine—if Microsoft ever decided to make a version of Windows XP Media Center Edition available as a software-only upgrade. (It's important to note that to date, Microsoft has never confirmed that it has any plans along those lines.)

External Tuners

Along with the September 2003 launch of the 2004 edition of Media Center software were a number of announcements from Microsoft IHVs, concerning new external hardware that could theoretically turn just about any PC into a Media Center–capable machine.

AVerMedia

Milpitas, California–based AVerMedia's external tuner (which the company also refers to as a "notebook tuner," if that gives you any ideas) connects to the Media Center PC using USB 2.0. Shown in Figure 25.10, the small silver-and-black unit provides for IR, S-Video, composite video, and RCA audio inputs. This external AVerMedia device provides a very different tuner solution for a Media Center notebook than Toshiba's current design. The latter allows TV video input only via a lower resolution coax cable.

FIGURE 25.10

The AVerMedia external TV tuner and input device joins the company's full line of internal TV tuner cards for Media Center PCs.

Emuzed

Another maker of internal tuner cards, Emuzed, has an external input and tuner device called the Bali-II USB PVR Beanbag (see Figure 25.11). Beanbag is the code-name Philips used for its IR receiver/transmitter unit for Media Center, and the term has become somewhat synonymous with external dongle devices that perform these functions. By combining the IR receiver/emitter "beanbag" circuitry with a TV tuner in one convenient package, Emuzed and others say they hope to simplify the design and setup of Media Center systems.

FIGURE 25.11

The Emuzed Bali-II USB PVR Beanbag is similar to the company's Bali USB PVR external TV tuner and input device unit, shown here.

Pixela

Pixela was the third company to join in the Media Center 2004 launch festivities with an external TV tuner/beanbag device. The PIX-MPTV/U4W (see Figure 25.12) offers both S-Video and composite video input, and provides its encoded MPEG-2 video output to the Media Center PC via USB 2.0.

FIGURE 25.12

Pixela's external TV tuner device is an attractive unit that can be laid flat or placed vertically to save space.

With the rampant availability of these external tuner/beanbag devices just around the corner, it's likely that a new crop of Media Center portables is about to hit the market. In addition to making it easy for laptop makers to add Media Center hardware capability to their existing products, external tuners have other advantages.

When the tuner is placed outside the rather inhospitable confines of the PC enclosure, the electronics no longer have to contend with heat and signal interference. As a result, they can often provide better performance than internal units.

Instead of crawling on your hands and knees trying to plug in and twist on your various A/V inputs and outputs, these external devices can offer easier setup and configuration of your video and audio I/O. Just attach everything to the tuner/beanbag device, and then connect that to your PC with a USB cable.

THE ABSOLUTE MINIMUM

Although all Windows XP Media Center computers have the same basic features, don't assume that all are created equal. Remember:

- Processor speed, hard drive size, and the amount of onboard system and video memory will probably have the biggest impact on how your Media Center PC actually performs. The general rule is "the more, the better," whether you're talking about gigahertz or gigabytes.

- When it comes to Media Center PCs, appearances matter. Unlike typical workaday computers that hide under desks or lie buried under paperwork, Media Center systems are designed to attract attention. It makes sense to select a system based on form as well as function.

- If you want to literally take the show on the road, Toshiba's notebook Media Center systems make it possible. Note that the P25, with its huge 17-inch screen, may not lend itself to use by "road warriors" riding in the coach sections of commercial aircraft.

- Gateway's sexy "all-in-one" Media Center is worth doing a double-take. Although most Media Centers are essentially a PC with the TV built in, the Gateway 610 Media Center reverses the equation.

- Look for an even wider array of Media Center-capable systems—particularly portables—in the near future as external "beanbag" devices offer to take over the media-centric duties of handling video and IR input/output.

Index

How can we make this index more useful? Email us at indexes@quepublishing.com

How can we make this index more useful? Email us at indexes@quepublishing.com

How can we make this index more useful? Email us at indexes@quepublishing.com

Q-R

How can we make this index more useful? Email us at indexes@quepublishing.com

How can we make this index more useful? Email us at indexes@quepublishing.com

How can we make this index more useful? Email us at indexes@quepublishing.com

How can we make this index more useful? Email us at indexes@quepublishing.com

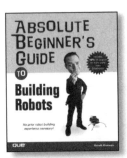